Translation Issues in Language and Law

Translation Issues in Language and Law

Edited by

Frances Olsen
University of California

Alexander Lorz
Düsseldorf University

and

Dieter Stein
Düsseldorf University

palgrave
macmillan

First published 2009 by
PALGRAVE MACMILLAN

Palgrave Macmillan in the UK is an imprint of Macmillan Publishers Limited, registered in England, company number 785998, of Houndmills, Basingstoke, Hampshire RG21 6XS.

Palgrave Macmillan in the US is a division of St Martin's Press LLC, 175 Fifth Avenue, New York, NY 10010.

Palgrave Macmillan is the global academic imprint of the above companies and has companies and representatives throughout the world.

Palgrave® and Macmillan® are registered trademarks in the United States, the United Kingdom, Europe and other countries.

ISBN-13: 978-0-230-20350-1 hardback
ISBN-10: 0-230-20350-7 hardback

This book is printed on paper suitable for recycling and made from fully managed and sustained forest sources. Logging, pulping and manufacturing processes are expected to conform to the environmental regulations of the country of origin.

A catalogue record for this book is available from the British Library.

Library of Congress Cataloging-in-Publication Data

Translation issues in language and law / edited by Frances Olsen, Alexander Lorz, and Dieter Stein.
p. cm.
"This volume represents a selection of papers from the International Conference on Language and Law at Heinrich–Heine–University Dusseldorf, Germany, in May 2006, jointly organized by the University of California at Los Angeles Law School, Heinrich-Heine-University University Law School and the Department of English Language and Linguistics"—Preface [?]
Includes bibliographical references and index.
ISBN 978–0–230–20350–1 (alk. paper)
1. Law – Language – Congresses. 2. Law – Translating – Congresses. I. Olsen, Frances E. II. Lorz, Alexander. III. Stein, Dieter, 1946–

K213,T734 2009
340'.14—dc22 2008030453

10 9 8 7 6 5 4 3 2 1
18 17 16 15 14 13 12 11 10 09

Printed and bound in Great Britain by
CPI Antony Rowe, Chippenham and Eastbourne

Contents

List of Figures

List of Tables

Acknowledgement

This volume would not exist had it not been for the indefatigable and painstaking work by Alexander Tokar, Research Assistant and PhD candidate working with Dieter Stein at the chair for English Language and Linguistics at Heinrich-Heine-University, Düsseldorf. Alexander Tokar has overseen the origination of the volume from the first call for papers for a reviewed volume to seeing the paperwork through in the final stages of administering the volume and overseeing the indexing and proofreading.

Notes on the Contributors

Enrique Alcaraz Varó[†] was Professor of English Language at the University of Alicante.

Louis Beaudoin is Lecturer of Legislative Drafting at the University of Laval (Quebec City).

Jean-Baptist Bigirimana is a PhD researcher at the Catholic University of Leuven.

Oliver Brand is Assistant Professor of Law at the University of Münster.

Agnieszka Doczekalska is a PhD student at the European University Institute, Florence.

Maurizio Gotti is Professor of English Linguistics at the University of Bergamo.

Uwe Kischel is Professor of Law at the University of Greifswald.

José Lambert is Professor of General Literature at the Catholic University of Leuven.

Alexander Lorz is Professor of Law at the University of Düsseldorf.

Karen McAuliffe is Lecturer at the School of Law at the University of Exeter.

Frances Olsen is Professor of Law at the University of California at Los Angeles.

Lawrence M. Solan is Professor of Law at the Brooklyn Law School.

Dieter Stein is Professor of English Language and Linguistics at the University of Düsseldorf.

Volker Triebel is a Partner at Lovells in Düsseldorf.

Introduction: Forensic Translation – Practical Issues and their Theoretical Underpinnings

Dieter Stein

This volume addresses a topic that assumes an increasing significance in contact situations between legal cultures in everyday practice of law as reflected in practical problems of translation, as well as a theoretical problem of clash and convergence of legal cultures, again reflected in linguistic issues. While the issues in the circumference of contact between legal systems have traditionally been discussed in comparative law, extensively represented in this volume, these issues acquire a new significance through the fact that legal systems are no longer static, a priori given systems, but are themselves subject to change, to issues of mutual influence, to issues of convergence and divergence. The volume hopes to achieve a balance between practical issues and theoretical underpinnings of these issues that may provide a rationale for practical solutions.

The volume is organized in three parts which are centred on different sides of the issue. Part I ('Language and Different Law Cultures') addresses the issue of cultural contact as the basis of the linguistic and translational problems.

Uwe Kischel ('Legal Cultures – Legal Languages') makes the point that linguistic differences are really epiphenomena of deeper differences in legal cultures on many levels, ranging from different techniques of legal reasoning (e.g. the technique of subsumption in German legal culture) to different styles of arguing and what counts as an argument in, for example, German and American legal cultures. He makes, among other arguments, the interesting point that borrowing a shared word form may well act as a Trojan horse to import a legal concept that did not previously exist in the borrowing culture, a point also addressed in the chapter by Oliver Brand ('Language as a Barrier to Comparative Law'). He demonstrates how linguistic and conceptual differences inhibit the progress of a whole standard field of legal inquiry, comparative law.

Not looking at the outside conditioning forces determining law, at the 'actors', and engaging in 'textism' bars access to more fundamental differences in legal cultures. In an intriguing turn of argument, Brand argues that language analysis has been instrumentalized by a 'functional approach', i.e. the mere technical functioning of legal systems, to mask deeper differences between the legal systems. He goes on to suggest a conceptual meta-instrument that contains all the possible kinds of conceptualizations of legal institutions as a set of universal choices from which individual legal cultures make their specific decisions – a procedure reminiscent of a translation theory that is based on a universal interlingua, into which meanings are translated and out of which meanings are formulated in language-specific terms. It is also isomorphic to the approach in modern linguistic typology, which establishes a universally possible set of linguistic structures, from which individual languages make individual sets of choices.

The chapter by Lawrence Solan ('Statutory Interpretation in the EU: the Augustinian Approach') presents a very different take on the role of different languages. The different conceptualizations of a reality in different languages (and even different speakers) which are the subject of discussion in the majority of chapters in the volume, are amenable to an approach based on comparing equivalent texts in different languages. What is normally considered a problem, several languages, is here seen as an advantage. Given a basically teleological approach to interpreting statutes, the multiplicity of versions in different languages provides a welcome range of constraints on how to interpret a text, and a welcome corrective to 'what is in the text': the 'text' is really 'several texts'. Their ensemble not only precludes American-style textism, but is also seen as a fortunate condition for a multiple perspective on textual meaning.

Maurizio Gotti ('Globalizing Trends in Legal Discourse') discusses a development that countervails the differences caused by culturally different conceptualizations. He contextualizes differences in legal culture from the point of view of a more general effect of globalization: communicants tend to accommodate to the needs of the presumed audience not only in the economy, but also in law. Beyond the much discussed – including in this volume – issue of English taking the place of Latin and French as a lingua franca of law, Gotti's data from arbitration processes show evidence, for all culturally based divergence and the formulation processes taking account of these differences, of legal formulation – again – repeating processes that are well known from linguistic contact situations: incipient hybridization as the result of accommodating negotiation of formulation and concepts.

Part I closes with what is arguably the most political chapter in the volume and, at the same time, a befitting closing chapter for this more theoretically and fundamentally oriented first part. José Lambert ('The Status and Position of Legal Translation: a Chapter in the Discursive Construction of Societies') stresses the fact, adumbrated in the chapter by Brand, that translation is an epiphenomenon of the fact that law is always linguistically constituted in discourses and that all constitutions and normative texts, signally including the Code Napoléon, always have multicultural and multilingual ancestry, even if a reductionist tendency of constitutions towards an illusion of a pure and single legal culture and language, inherent in lawyers' discourses on languages, misguidedly seems to suggest the contrary. If all legal discourse, like all languages, has multiple ancestry, the central role of translation becomes apparent, as well as the requirement of a research agenda into the role of language in law that is based on an enlightened, and culture-based, theory of translation. Thus, the chapter echoes, for the area of translation theory, Brand's suggestion to base translation theory on a broader and more general theoretical basis.

Part II ('Handling Legal Discourse in the Modern World') deals with organization of language mediation activities in practical institutional settings. How do organizations pragmatically cope with the challenges of having to translate and interpret? Karen McAuliffe ('Translation at the Court of Justice of the European Communities'), based on an empirical study at the front line of translation in the European Union, gives us a glimpse behind the everyday practice and the language and translation policies and politics that are involved in adding new member states to the EU. It also discusses the effect of the specific type of language contact involved in translation in the EU and its effect in the shape of 'hybridization', such that expressions have specific EU meanings that are not present in any single EU language, thus instantiating a point similarly made by Gotti, that there is a development in the direction of an international legal English, or an *Ausgleichssprache*.

Discussing another practical context of translation, Agnieszka Doczekalska ('Drafting or Translation – Production of Multilingual Legal Texts') discusses a solution, successfully practised by several political bodies, to the notorious problem of the primacy of a source text from which the target texts are translated. Co-drafting is the solution for bijural and bilingual systems, the effect amounting to a dissolving of 'the text' and its authority into several texts with shared authority, much in the vein of the Augustinian approach described by Solan.

Finally, Louis Beaudoin ('Legal Translation in Canada: the Genius of Legal Language(s)') offers a case study in very concrete terms of the way nearly all problems and solutions that have bedevilled a bijural and bilingual country in the historical development of its linguo-legal culture, up to the present point of co-drafting, with an extensive history of legal–linguistic takeover of the French by the English culture. Like Lambert, he makes the point that given that law is made up of language, proper linguistic training is paramount for the legal profession, and in particular for jurilinguists.

Part III ('Concrete Problems in Legal Translation') takes the bull by the horns and discusses individual issues of translational equivalence and strategies in trying to achieve as much equivalence as possible.

Volker Triebel's contribution ('Pitfalls of English as a Contract Language') sets the tone with a very rich and detailed compendium of cases, gleaned from a rich practical everyday experience, of examples where the German and English law culture concepts are both treacherously close, but conceptually miles apart, and therefore offer dangerous traps for the not properly trained to fall into. The rich discussion, from and for the civil lawyer's practice, ranges from a historical account of the divergencies to the potentially dismal effects of seemingly small points of grammar.

In a similar 'contrastive' vein, Enrique Alcaraz Varó ('Isomorphism and Anisomorphism in the Translation of Legal Texts') looks at differences and pitfalls in Spanish–English translation in terms of isomorphism and its counterpart, a concept denoting structural parallelism or its absence as a basically aesthetic concept, with isomorphy functioning more like a facilitator and anisomorphy more like a pitfall for legal translation.

Part III closes with a contribution by Jean-Baptist Bigirimana ('Translation as a Dynamic Model in the Development of the Burundi Constitution(s)') that discusses the very complex, but typical situation a developing country finds itself in when trying to formulate a constitution. The many practical problems faced by developing countries include issues, repeatedly mentioned in previous contributions, of the contact between indigenous vs colonial legal systems and are aggravated by the issues of different languages in which they are couched, and to what extent translation of the resultant into the indigenous language can and should be done to enhance acceptance. Based on a discussion of the linguistic situation, the author sketches in a detailed analysis the tug of war between the different forces shaping the content and linguistic form of the Burundi constitution.

Part I

Language and Different Law Cultures

1
Legal Cultures – Legal Languages

Uwe Kischel

Language is important. In 1944, allied intelligence in Italy intercepted a German message to an abbey, asking whether the abbot was still there. The answer was in the affirmative. The service, however, falsely took the German word *Abt* for abbot to be the standard abbreviation for *Abteilung* (division). The information that a military division was still in the abbey led to the bombing and utter destruction of this abbey of Montecassino, one of the centres of medieval culture (cf. Rotondo 2004). Admittedly, problems with legal language will hardly be so dangerous, but rather intellectually stimulating. Comparative lawyers regularly find themselves confronted with questions of language and culture. Let me give you an overview of some typical experiences.

1.1 The myth of translation

1.1.1 Translation and the problems of comparative law

One of the first, and maybe most astonishing insights a comparative lawyer will get, is that the translation of legal texts remains a myth, a sublime aim never to be truly achieved. This is closely connected to some of the typical problems in comparative law: linguistically equivalent legal notions will frequently have different contents in different jurisdictions. The legal significance of notions can differ vastly in their direction and extent. Also, the interconnections within each legal system as well as the legal culture in general influence the meaning and practical impact of legal concepts (cf. in detail Kischel 2005: 17ff.). As a result, the question in legal translation is not which translation is right, but, much more modestly, which one is less wrong.

Let me mention a few examples. The Japanese notion of *jôri* is often translated as reason, or the nature of things, or common sense. *Jôri* is taken to mean a generally accepted reading of facts. In the context of private international law, however, *jôri* can also be translated as *ordre public*. But *jôri* is also a source of law besides statutes and customary law (on the meaning of *jôri,* cf. Marutschke 1999: 16 with further references). All of these meanings do not seem to be diverse concepts accidentally joined by the same word, but seem to form a whole in the minds of Japanese lawyers. In Western languages, there simply is no word that could convey the complex meanings of *jôri*. Legal culture comes even more into play when we look at the usual translation of 'law' in Chinese, *fa* or *falü*. These words do not, however, have the connotation of right and justice, but are rather a source of fear for the average Chinese (cf. von Senger 1994: 26f.). To grasp this typical reaction, it has been suggested to translate *fa* as 'criminal law' (Großfeld and Wang 1995: 301). This, however, is not in conformity with the wider definition of law accepted in the People's Republic of China (cf. on the definition von Senger 1994: 176 [general notion for all behavioural norms incorporating the will of the ruling class, and promulgated or accepted by the state, abidance being guaranteed by the coercive power of the state]). The existence or lack of a legal and terminological equivalent is not, however, a question of yes or no but rather one of degree. Thus, *jôri* can hardly be translated at all, while institutional structures will often find a possible translation, but seldom a good one: Conseil d'État as constitutional council, Supreme Court as Oberster Gerichtshof, *Verwaltungsrichter* as administrative law judge – all that is workable, but does not convey the true meaning. Landgericht or Oberlandesgericht as court of appeals – which is better? Finally, concepts like 'marriage' or 'rape' might find their clear equivalents in German *Ehe* and *Vergewaltigung* – until one thinks of the common law marriage, which exists when a man and a woman simply decide to live together as husband and wife and then do so (cf. e.g. *In re Benjamin*, 34 N.Y.2d 27, 30 [1974]), or statutory rape, i.e. sexual intercourse with a minor even with that minor's full consent.

Sometimes, a legal problem might even be created by a specific choice of words. Take 'comparative law'. A course in comparative law may well start with the observation that comparative law does not exist (cf. Banakas 1994: 113; Watson 1993: 1). This is not only amusing, but even true, since there is no body of legal rules applicable in certain situations that can be called 'comparative' in the same sense as criminal law or tax law. Unfortunately, I could never use this pun to start a German lecture, since the German notion of *Rechtsvergleichung*, literally 'comparing of laws' (but it sounds much better), does not step into the same trap as the English expression.

1.1.2 The question of legal sublanguages

An English lawyer once told me that the worst thing about American lawyers flying in was that they believed they basically understood English law (on the differences cf. e.g. Atiyah and Summers 2002). Indeed, the problems of comparative law are connected with the differences between legal systems, legal families, legal styles. They reflect and are reflected in language and translation, but they appear with similar force when two jurisdictions share the same language. Germans and Austrians, for instance, not only lead emotionally charged debates about the correct word for potato and tomato. There are also many differences in legal concepts and terminology. The Austrian word *Verwaltungsakt* (administrative act), for instance, designates administrative activities in a broad sense, while the same notion in Germany is much more narrow and would, in Austria, be called *Bescheid* (cf. Lohaus 2000: 175f.). One need not look at the famous example of the French *acte administratif* to find a false friend (on the *acte administratif,* cf. e.g. Rivero and Waline 2000: 95, 100; on the comparison with Germany, cf. e.g. Hübner and Constantinesco 2001: 92), here. As a consequence, one is forced, in the legal context, to differentiate on a further level. There is not one German legal language, but several, especially those of Germany, Austria, Switzerland, Belgium and Italy. The list would be even longer for English, of course. When translating, one must always choose between these sublanguages (cf. de Groot 2002: 225ff.). There is a difference between a legal translation from English English to Austrian German or from American English to German German.

1.1.3 Translation as an eye-opener

So far, one might get the impression that translation is an almost impossible, strenuous process, which inevitably leads to major problems; in short, something to avoid, if possible. This is not untrue, and it is also the reason why teaching German law students a course in a foreign language, as some regulations in Germany now require, is in many cases superfluous and futile. Trying to explain the difference between *Ermessen* and *Beurteilungsspielraum* to German students in English, a language that knows only one word – *discretion* – for the two phenomena, would border on the ridiculous. But translation, like much of comparative law, can also be an eye-opener, a new point of reference. It can suddenly make one see the sometimes overly complicated, nearly self-serving nature of concepts which seemed so normal and necessary. I have recently tried to translate a summary of one of my own papers. It dealt with the question whether the legislature is allowed to ignore the German Constitutional Court by simply re-enacting a statute that has just been declared void. Among others, I was invoking the *Letztverbindlichkeit* of constitutional judgments and the necessity to safeguard *verfassungsgerichtliche Autorität* through *faktische Präjudizwirkung*. My first translation of these three terms made me highly uneasy, since I invoked the *authority* of constitutional judgments and the necessity to safeguard the constitutional court's *authority* through the factual *authority* of their decisions. I assure you that I felt compelled to closely review my arguments to see whether it was really necessary to draw distinctions that were so fine that my first impulse was to translate all three with the same word. In this particular case, I upheld the differentiation, but gained a much better understanding of my own thoughts (for the entire argument, including the final translation, cf. Kischel 2006: 227f., 254).

1.2 Legal sources in different languages

Translation turns into a strictly legal problem once there are authoritative versions of a norm in several languages. Such multilingual norms pose problems in two interconnected areas: interpretation when they are applied, and translation when they are drafted.

1.2.1 Interpreting different languages

The problem of interpretation is well known for instance in international law, where multilateral treaties written in several authoritative languages are common. In one case, a provision of the English version of the Treaty of Versailles called for due regard to 'legal or equitable interests'. This phrase referred to well-established legal concepts in England and the United States. The French version spoke of 'droit et intérêts légitimes', which corresponded to no definite legal idea. The arbitral tribunal, therefore, decided that everything pointed to the conclusion that the French phrase was 'merely the translation of the English' and, therefore, applied this English version (cf. *U.S.* v. *Reparation Commission* [1926] 2 R.I.A.A. 777 [792], cited in Harris 2004: 844). Today, Art. 33 of the Vienna Convention on the Law of Treaties codifies the underlying rule. When a possible difference of meaning cannot be removed by ordinary means of interpretation, 'the meaning which best reconciles the texts, having regard to the object and purpose of the treaty, shall be adopted' (Art. 33 para. 4 VCLT; on a possible recourse to the original language, cf. Bernhardt 1995: 1422). The problem of multilingual sources of law is particularly relevant in European law, which in essence follows the same rules as international law (cf. e.g. Schweitzer 1999: Art. 314 EGV marginal note 5ff.; Weber 2004: Art. 314 EG marginal note 13ff.). Thus, the European Court of Justice (ECJ) had no major problem interpreting a norm which in Dutch clearly addressed only the wife as also including the husband (ECJ, case 9–79 – Koschniske/Raad van Arbeid – records 1979, p. 2717; cf. on this case Braselmann 1992: 61f.). From a practical point of view, however, we are forced to admit that this equality of all authoritative languages is frequently ignored in favour of one, mostly the jurist's maternal language. This language is often exclusively used, even if is not authoritative (e.g. all treaties entering into force in Germany are published in the official journal [BGBl II] with a German translation; this translation might even have a certain legal value in German national law, cf. Ipsen: 1999: 124).

1.2.2 Translating into an authoritative language

The quality of translation has found much attention concerning the preamble of the European Charter of Fundamental Rights. Here, the English and French versions invoked the 'spiritual heritage' or *patrimoine spirituel* in Europe, while the German version invoked the *geistig-religiöses Erbe*, thus drawing religion into the picture which is not mentioned by name in any of the other languages. Is the German version a more precise translation or an (intentional) mistake (cf. Meyer 2003: Präambel, marginal note 32 with further references)? On the one hand we are told that the French *spirituel* means not only *geistig*, but also *religiös*, while the German *geistig* alone would have no religious connotation (cf. Burr and Mann 2003: 43). If this was true, it would, indeed, make the explicit reference to religion in the German version correct. Not only, however, have some members of the convention insisted that the French *spirituel* could *not* be interpreted to include religious aspects (cf. Meyer 2003: Präambel, marginal note 25). What is more, the German word *spirituell* could have served as a nice equivalent (some insist that *spirituell* does not sufficiently encompass religious aspects, cf. Burr and Mann 2003: 43; *spirituell* however means *geistig* and *geistlich*, cf. *Duden* 2003: 1269, *geistlich* meaning *kirchlich* [pertaining to the church], *Duden* 2004: 419; it should also be noted that the reference to 'héritage [...] réligieux' in a prior version had been explicitly deleted, cf. Meyer 2003: Präambel, marginal note 24f., 32).

1.3 Borrowing legal terminology

The legal interaction between different countries on all levels has led to the phenomenon of borrowing legal terminology from a different legal system and culture. This is by no means new, as a quick look at the influence of Roman law all over Europe across borders and across time proves.

1.3.1 Borrowing of concepts with terminology

Often, a new legal concept or institution is imported together with the word. *Ombudsman, factoring, franchising* are probably the best-known German examples. A commonplace observation in comparative law teaches, however, that such imports quickly tend to adapt and change once they come into contact with a different legal system. Thus, after a short while, the same word no longer signifies identical objects. It is quite doubtful, for instance, whether the rather generalized meaning of 'Ombudsman' in German discussions still has a lot to do with the formal legal institution of ombudsman in Scandinavia (cf. Simonnæs 1999: 142).

1.3.2 Showing off – the problem of anglicisms

To use foreign words when talking about a concept that stems from the respective foreign country is quite acceptable and unproblematic. It would not be necessary, and might sometimes even seem laughable, to look for a German linguistic equivalent at all costs. Quite another topic, however, is the unnecessary use of foreign words where a German equivalent is well established. Sometimes simple terms of art are suddenly exchanged, the new language in nearly all cases being English. So the *Verschmelzung* of two companies is called 'merger', a legal paper or application written in German looks for 'issues' instead of *Themen*, or a German *Behörde* is suddenly called *Agentur*, a word that has several meanings (cf. *Duden* 2003: 55), but none that equals that of the American 'agency'. One major input, here, seems to come from social science, where anglicisms like *Dezision* or *Performanz* abound. There are probably two reasons for such anglicisms. One is the constant use of English as a working language by some professionals, which makes the switch back to German difficult and sometimes awkward. Most people who have spent some time abroad will to some degree be familiar with this phenomenon. The other reason seems to be the plain desire to sound important – a simple case of showing off. In certain social environments, 'venture capital' sounds more important than *Wagniskapital*, 'public finance' more than *Finanzwissenschaft*, and 'practice group intellectual property' more than *Arbeitsgruppe geistiges Eigentum*. The showing-off aspect is underlined by the experience that frequently persons with a really good knowledge of the English language are least prone to try and impress their audience this way.

1.3.3 Seeming anglicisms

One should, however, be careful, since a seemingly unnecessary anglicism might in reality be an unknown term of art. A majority of jurists in Germany will for example take the word *Emergenz*, sometimes used in legal debates, as a totally unnecessary anglicism that could easily be substituted by *Erscheinen* or *Auftauchen*, the usual translations of the English word 'emergence'. However, *Emergenz* seems to be used as a term of art, especially by systems theory, describing the phenomenon that not all traits of a system can be explained through its single elements, in other words the old insight that the whole may be more than the parts (cf. Stephan 1999: 303). I must admit that I was impressed when I first learned about this word, but I now have new doubts, since it seems that in the English language, the very same term of art is simply 'emergence' (cf. Casti 2001), i.e. a simple, everyday word. It is difficult to understand the need to create a new word in German when a common word is sufficient in English.

1.4 Legal style of writing

Language is more than single words and sentences. Language, especially legal language, also has a certain style which is a result of, as well as a reason for, a certain legal culture.

1.4.1 Personal vs impersonal

One notable difference is the personal or impersonal style used in legal presentations. You might have noted that I use the word 'I' in this essay, which is quite an aberration from German standards, but seems much more usual in the United States. The use of 'I' is even more unusual, close to socially forbidden, in German law review articles. This has been criticized as a futile effort to claim an objective nature of the statements made and to ignore the real influences (cf. Haltern 1998: 73ff.). The criticism itself, however, reveals the intimate connection between German legal style and German legal culture, where legal realism has never arrived.

1.4.2 Style of judgments

The style of judgments is also markedly different. A typical German judgment is written in an impersonal style, highly structured, and developing the solution of the case and the relevant issues not unlike a law review article. Scholarly statements and case law are abundantly cited, at least in decisions of higher courts. The French judgment, however, consists grammatically of a single sentence, in which facts and merits are listed in shorter points that are introduced by phrases like *attendu que* (considering that). Quotes of any kind, even of the court's own jurisprudence, are very uncommon. As a result, it is often hardly possible to understand the case and the solution by simply reading the judgment. The necessary information is often provided by scholarly comments, which are added to the decision when it is reprinted in a law review. Such comments might even stem from one of the judges. All in all, the pretence of total objectivity, of simply applying the law, is even more pronounced here than in Germany. The very opposite can be experienced in English judgments. They are written in a most personal style, using 'I', and clearly rendering the personal opinion of the judge, who tries to make clear, through his judgment, how he arrived at the result. Phrases like 'this is a difficult case', are not considered unusual. Lord Denning once started a judgment about a traffic accident with the sentence 'It was bluebell time in Kent (...)' (*Hinz* v. *Berry* [1970] 2 Q.B. 40, 42). He became famous for a very clear, concise and laconic style that is better heard than explained. Here is buying a parking ticket à la Lord Denning: 'The customer pays his money and gets a ticket. He cannot refuse it. He cannot get his money back. He may protest at the machine, even swear at it; but it will remain unmoved. He is committed beyond recall. He was committed at the very moment when he put his money into the machine. The contract was concluded at that time' (*Thornton* v. *Shoe Lane Parking Ltd.* [1971] 2 Q.B. 163, 169). The law in a given country reflects the style of its judgments, and this style reflects the law.

1.4.3 Subsumtion

The decisive influence that the style of writing may have on the legal culture is particularly evident in the German *Subsumtion*, which itself is only roughly approximated by the English word 'subsumption', combined with the style of an expert opinion (*Gutachtenstil*). Both are techniques to answer legal questions by starting from the words of a relevant norm, defining each of these words, sometimes with subdefinitions, and then arguing whether or not the facts match – or are subsumed under – these definitions. The *Subsumtion* starts with the statement of a possibility – e.g. X might have stolen the book – and ends with the result – X has/has not stolen the book (cf. Busse 2008). This specific style and the method of analysis that goes with it have been trained into all German law students for decades, all core exams necessarily being written in that style. Later, the style is often replaced by what is called the judgment style. The main difference, however, is simply that the judgment style proceeds in the inverse order, starting with the result instead of ending with it. The basic way of thinking remains the same. I believe that many specific features of German law can be attributed to this specific training. It, for instance, largely immunizes the lawyer against the allure of legal realism or critical legal studies. It might also explain the adherence of most practising German jurists to the old-fashioned but very effective catalogue of interpretative methods founded by Savigny (on the classical canon of interpretation and subsumption, cf. Kischel 2003: 6, 15 with further references). It is unlikely that anybody could understand the functioning of German law and German legal culture properly without understanding the technique of *Subsumtion*.

1.4.4 Structuring

The structuring of legal texts differs from country to country. French legal articles and books, for instance, strive for a certain balance and rhythm in their structure. Thus, parts are followed by titles, followed by chapters, followed by sections. The respective numbers of titles, chapters and sections are often evenly spread out, with a marked preference for two or three, at most four of each. If chapter one has two sections, so should chapters two and three, and so forth. Especially law students are trained to adhere to a very rigid version of this structure. When a French student, for instance, writes a paper in Germany, it is an important and often difficult task to explain to the student that the topic might require seven chapters, the first two of which have no sections, while the third has five. I once asked a French lawyer how they could manage to press everything into a rigid structure and what they would do, if, for example, a certain action had six requirements with highly different sets of subrequirements. The French lawyer smiled and mildly explained that after decades of thinking about the law in an evenly structured way, the law simply *is* evenly structured.

1.5 Sounding stupid

Talking (or writing) about law in a foreign language is difficult and often awkward, more so if one is talking about one's own legal system, less so if one is talking about a foreign system. The best and most important reason for avoiding the use of a foreign language in legal discussions, however, is not the difficulty of translating, speaking and writing, it is the simple danger, or even certainty, that one will sound stupid, or at least more stupid than one really is.

1.5.1 Lack of polishing

The first possible reason is known to some Germans as BSE, which, here, is not, as usual, the abbreviation for mad cow disease, but stands for 'bad simple English'. A subtle thought, a fine differentiation between two concepts, an artfully constructed theory is difficult to express with a limited vocabulary and grammar. This might be less of a problem in, say, physics or biology. But it is a major obstacle for a subject that lives of and through language alone, like law (cf. e.g. Isensee, part I [language as precondition for the possibility of law]). Many lawyers are, due to their training, particularly attuned to the finer points of language, and one need not go back to Goethe to find an astonishing number of literary authors among German lawyers. What is more, it is very difficult to make a good joke in a foreign language, let alone expressing subtle humour or an ironic remark. The typical speech by a non-native speaker will be rather dry, and therefore less appealing.

1.5.2 Untypical language

Additionally, each legal culture has a specific mode of talking. Even if two lawyers share the same common language, they will know if the other comes from a different jurisdiction. When an Englishman talks about costs, lawyer's fees are included, this is not so for an American. When an American lawyer talks about an opinion, an Englishman would talk about a judgment (cf. Atiyah and Summers 2002: xiiif.). Whenever German and Austrian lawyers come together, the respective other group sounds a bit different, slightly off key, and that always implies slightly less competent, even if we consciously know this reaction to be unfounded.

Forcing lawyers to speak and interact in a foreign language can lead to interesting results. I once visited the European Court of Justice, where the working language is French, with a group of jurists and asked a rather large group of judges in essence why the judgments of the ECJ never went into more detail, never explained and argued more expansively. The answer given by one judge, whose native language was not French, was most revealing. He simply asked me to imagine sitting there with a group of lawyers and having to write a judgment in *Latin*. 'How long', he asked, 'do you think your judgment is going to be?'

1.5.3 Lack of conceptual background in the audience

The problem of sounding stupid also arises because the audience will often lack the implicit conceptual background which lawyers from one's own country automatically share. If in a German audience of constitutional lawyers one mentions 'state and society', most will automatically think of an old and high-level debate in German constitutional theory. This is not likely to be the case for French or Swedish lawyers. It is even quite possible that some Germans will not quickly grasp the import of the words if they hear them in English or any other translation. Similarly, if I were to talk about the question whether state warnings about religious sects are an infringement of the freedom of religion, German lawyers will automatically start thinking in the framework of 'area of protection, infringement, limits' and view my remarks against a backdrop of this generally known concept of German constitutional law. Lawyers from other countries might believe they are hearing empty talk.

1.5.4 Different concepts of proper (scientific) approach

Finally, the relative cultural conceptions of a proper approach to legal questions vary vastly. In Germany, most lawyers would call for a scientifically and dogmatically sound approach. In the United States, however, the very notion of a science of law – quite natural in Germany – sounds rather ludicrous, and 'dogmatic' only makes one think of answers that may not be questioned. This is not only a mere choice of words, either. While the US lawyer would look for the facts of the case and would try to draw all aspects – political, economic, etc. – into the picture, the German lawyer would rely on norms and legal concepts, their interpretation and application, while arguments that are not directly connected with the legal prerequisites as prescribed by the norms are considered irrelevant (on the question of formalism, cf. Kischel 1994: 249 with further references; on fact-based and norm-based approaches, cf. Damaška 1968: 1367ff., 1374f.). This difference in approach becomes much more noticeable when one of the two translates his approach into the language of the other, thus entering the other's linguistic territory. In the end, the German lawyer is likely to take the US approach to be quite funny and charming, but a bit too shallow and too removed from the norm and the law as it is. The US lawyer, by contrast, is likely to consider the German quite intellectual, but far too removed from legal practice and the real world, and maybe a bit stuffy.

When a German lawyer speaks in English about problems of language, the real problem is that the audience is likely to apply all his conclusions to his very speech. In this sense I hope you have considered my remarks *neither* too stuffy *nor* too shallow. They were born out of experience and are very open to discussion.

2
Language as a Barrier to Comparative Law

Oliver Brand

2.1 Introduction

Comparative law appears to be in a lamentable condition. Recently, it has been described as a 'boggy field' (Brand 2007a: 407–8), where 'peril' lurks 'under every footstep' of the comparatist. Ernst Rabel (1951) adds to the gloomy picture, when he warns us of 'poisonous darts' that are 'threatening the unwary explorer in the jungle of comparative law'. The environment for comparative lawyers becomes so hostile, because he is subject to the constant threat of fundamentally misconceiving foreign law and thus thwarting a meaningful comparison. Language, as we will see, proves to be one of the main obstacles. Nevertheless, interest in language and law has been kindling slowly among comparatists. First steps in the late 1970s remained largely inconsequential (Großfeld 1985; Hiller 1978; Marasinghe 1977). DeGroot was among the few who kept the topic alive during the 1980s and early 1990s.[1] A lively debate was only sparked in the mid 1990s. Unsurprisingly, a scholar from a bilingual legal system leads the field. Pierre Legrand (1997: 123; 1999: 31) has attempted to redefine comparative law as a hermeneutic exercise (*démarche herméneutique*),[2] an aim to penetrate the façade of language that encapsulates law. In this chapter, I endeavour to sketch which 'façades of language' have become barriers to meaningful comparisons in law and what needs to be done to surmount those barriers.

My argument is split into five parts. I will begin with some general remarks on comparative law and its relation to language (2.2). Subsequently, this chapter will focus on linguistic aspects of the objects comparative lawyers work with (2.3). After that, translation as the fundamental operation of the comparatist will be examined (2.4). The fourth part deals with linguistic pitfalls under circumstances where no translation from one language to another takes place (2.5). Finally (2.6), I will try to explain the difficulties that comparative lawyers have with language by the methodology they apply. A proposal for a fresh start concludes this study (2.6.2 and 2.7).

2.2 Comparative law and language

'Comparative law' is conventionally defined as the scholarly search for interrelations between different legal systems (Brand 2003: 1083). Its object and purpose[3] are subject to a lively debate. More optimistic scholars want to support legislators (Drobnig/Dopffel 1982; Großfeld 1984: 296–7; Kamba 1974; Mansel 1991) and judicial bodies (Drobnig and van Erp 1999; Aubin 1970; Kötz 2000; Koopmans 1996) in discovering the best applicable rule in a given socio-economic context; furthermore, they see comparative law's function in the coordination between national and supranational law in a globalizing world (Buxbaum 1996: 212; Kötz 2002: 261–2; Remien 1996: 12ff.), and finally in the unification, integration and harmonization of laws (Neumayer 1988; cf. Sturm 1975: 235). Other scholars are more cautious: they see comparative law only as a contrastive tool that allows societies to be appreciated in their uniqueness and in their complex social and political context (see also Balkin 1996: 368–9), or as an instrument to reveal the political dimension of law (Frankenberg 1985: 434; 1997: 261–3; see also Olsen 1997: 278; on the reciprocal nature of the relationship between language and law see Bergmans 1987: 93–6).

Wherever the individual comparatist may see the uses of his discipline, he needs to deal with language. The vast majority of legal notions in a modern society exist within the realm of language.[4] Law is 'read' as a bill in parliament, it gets published as a text in the official records or as a court decision. Contracts are concluded verbally or in writing. Accordingly, language becomes the comparative lawyer's most important instrument in choosing, describing and analysing the objects of his comparison. Language, however, is not only a tool in the hand of the comparatist. A particular language can also have a coining influence on the legal terms it expresses. Pitfalls of terminology, therefore, haunt the comparatist not only in his novitiate (see Gutteridge 1938), but throughout his life (Markesinis 1997: 199). Much more urgently than his colleagues from other comparative disciplines, he needs to develop safeguards to make sure that he grasps the ideas and concepts behind the words in which law is presented to him. Roscoe Pound (1954) accordingly labelled the comparative study of the law a *Wortwissenschaft*, a science of words.

2.3 Objects

Let us begin our observations with a look at the role language plays in determining the objects of a comparative study. Three issues demand particular attention.

2.3.1 Monolingualism

The first one is monolingualism. To make his comparison meaningful, the comparatist needs to describe foreign law in 'its particular coordinate system, (...) according to the original sources, with its own instruments, spirit, and perspective' (Brand 2003: 1087; Constantinesco 1972: 151). This demands command of the respective legal system's language. However, the will and ability of the comparative community to deal with other languages than the common lingua franca, English, seem to be in decline (Markesinis 2003). A leading South African comparatist (Chaskalson 1993) frankly admits at the beginning of a study on the constitutional protection of property: 'The selection of countries is based on my inability to read any other (...) language than English.' Non-English legal systems, rules, judgments and scholarly comments increasingly remain unnoticed. Accordingly, the influence of concepts on other legal systems withers when their proponents do not take part in the international discourse, which is dominated by English (Mattei 1994: 206–7). Such a fate has befallen Germany in the case of the export of her concepts on fundamental rights. Today, the respective provisions of the South African constitution of 1994, which are modelled on those of the German Basic Law (*Grundgesetz*), are rather interpreted with regard to comparative material from Anglo-Saxon legal systems than with regard to linguistically less accessible expertise from Germany (see Blaau 1990; de Wet 1995). This is not a singular event. Recent studies on mixed legal systems,[5] like South Africa, suggest that English, the language of the common law, generally tends to overpower the language of civilian elements in a mixed system, and that subsequently common law elements gradually replace their civilian counterparts – first in public law, later in private law, too (Palmer 2001: 8–9, 57; Loubser 2003; Fassberg 2003: 153). The tendency towards monolingualism subjects comparative legal studies to the jeopardy of all monocultures: sterility.

2.3.2 Textism

The objects of comparative law are also affected negatively, because in law written language has sidelined oral expression (Großfeld 2003: 162–4; see also Busse 1992). At conferences we present 'papers', our students attend 'lectures' and learn their law in libraries.[6] Comparative law is no exception. Originally, it almost completely turned around written texts.[7] Only in the mid 1980s did comparatists become uneasy with this 'textism' (Eskridge 1990), and slowly turned their eyes towards 'law in action', i.e. the law in its practical application (Frankenberg 1985: 438; Friedman 1990; Legrand 1996: 235). They began to understand that a textual approach to law regularly gives a false impression of precision and security. There is always a dichotomy between 'black letter law' and 'law in action'.[8]

Often, the law in the books differs from the law under which people live, because they are unable or unwilling to invoke the protection of the formal legal rule (Reitz 1998: 630). Attachment to traditional lifestyles is a good example. In 1926, Turkey imported the Swiss civil code and accordingly the concept of civil marriage. In rural Turkey, people nonetheless continued to marry under the rules of Islamic law. As a result, all children from these 'marriages' were illegitimate (Lipstein 1957: 72; Jonas 1987; more generally Agostini 1988: 243ff.). In Brazil, the gap between the law in action and the law in the statute book has become so wide that the term *jeito* has been coined to describe it.[9] Comparative lawyers need to be aware of such gaps between black letter law and living law in order to precisely describe the objects of their comparison and to choose their sources wisely.

2.3.3 Interpretation of texts

Textism leads me to my third point, the interpretation of texts. The notable focus of comparative lawyers on written language has made them sensitive to the existence of different kinds of texts. It is widely accepted today that a court judgment needs different ways of interpretation than an Act of Parliament. Less well disseminated is knowledge about the need to assess different styles in writing and the need to adapt one's hermeneutics to style. The fact that different writing styles require different hermeneutics (Großfeld 2003: 166) becomes obvious, when we compare Western European legal texts with legal texts in Arabic. The Arabic alphabet – like Hebrew – contains only consonants and no vowels. It therefore affords impressive leeway for interpretation (see Souaiaia 2005: 127–34). The aim of the interpreter is not to find a unique meaning of a text, but to find evermore possible meanings and flexible answers to a concrete situation. Things are different under the Latin alphabet. Vowels are ubiquitous and a change of meaning by a mere change of vowels is not possible. A text is more likely to have a singular meaning and it is more difficult to adapt it to other requirements than those in its original context. Accordingly, legal texts in Europe and those in the Near and Middle East have to be read differently.

The coining influence of a particular language on the legal terms it expresses can also be discovered within the Western European legal sphere (Großfeld 1985: 800). A characteristic of the German legal language, for example, is that the past participle stands at the end of a sentence, as does the verb in subordinate sentences. These features require advance planning; good sentences are constructed in a way that the listener is able to discover early the meaning of words in the latter part of the sentence. German language is a constant training in linguistic construction. Small wonder, then, that German law is more abstract, constructed and technical than English or American law.

2.4 Translation

This brings us to the centre of the problems language holds for comparative lawyers. In the mid nineteenth century, Feuerbach (1966 [1833]) famously complained: 'why is it that the anatomist has his comparative method, but the legal scholar has not?' One answer to this question lies in the need of the comparatist to translate. In order to identify that which we are comparing, we regularly need to find an equivalent word for it in another language. A word can be validly translated into another, if both of them describe the same concept or idea (deGroot 2006: 424; Sacco 2001: 39). The anatomist will have few difficulties in finding a term for 'spinal column' in a foreign language that precisely describes the body part he means. The jurist is in a less comfortable position. Each national legal system uses terminology that does not necessarily correspond with the legal languages of other countries. Therefore, a literal translation of a given legal term into another language may not exactly express the same concept. This might have doctrinal reasons. Possession, for example, in some jurisdictions[10] requires a will to possess (*animus domandi*), in others not.[11] Similarly, the concepts of proprietary titles, of mortgages or the concepts of impossibility (see Wallow 2006: 8–11) vary to such an extent in different legal systems that a literal translation is misleading at best.

The historical or cultural 'web' that law is embedded in often has a similar impact. A 'judge' at an American lower court, for instance, is not the same as a German *Richter*. Out of its colonial experience, the American legal system tends to mistrust professional judges and accordingly limits their role at first instance to instructing the juries and to overruling their verdicts in cases where these are 'grossly excessive' or 'shock the court's conscience' (see Großfeld 1975: 20–2). The German legal system, on the other hand, champions the professional judge. Here, lay persons have a supportive role at best. Misleading homonyms, 'false friends' (*faux amis*), are permanent and irksome fellow travellers of the comparatist (Sarcevic 1997; Watson 1993; Bartels 1982: 92; Kahn-Freund 1966: 52–3; Bergmans 1987: 96–7; for examples see Ainsworth 1996: 20–1).

2.4.1 Untranslatables

As translators, comparatists neglected for too long that their medium, language, considerably conditions the message it carries. The Italian proverb 'traduttori, traditori' – translators are traitors[12] – hints at that. The potential for treason becomes considerable, where language builds a framework of contingent ways of legal reasoning (Legrand 1996: 234, 240; 1999: 123). Comparative lawyers often neglect that they encounter at times foreign legal institutions, which remain better untranslated (Curran 2006: 680).

Words resist a meaningful translation for various reasons. First, there are 'moving targets', words whose meaning constantly changes, depending upon the context. The above-mentioned term *jeito* is an example of that (Nadorff 2001: 606). *Jeito* can mean: a way around, a loophole, a solution, or a favour received (out of compassion, friendship or corruption). Pierre Pescatore, formerly a judge at the ECJ, has assembled a whole list of terms which are frequently used by the court (e.g. *Il y a lieu de, ayant*), but can acquire such different meanings in different contexts that they are a notable threat to meaningful translation (see Colneric 2006; Chatillon 2002: 707–8). Other terms may be barely translatable, because they express a unique legal concept. At times, the comparatist may resort to the methodological instruments of substitution and transposition that conflict of laws offers him in order to find 'equivalents' for untranslatables in his own legal terminology (deGroot 2006: 425–6; Jayme 2000: 131). This will regularly be the case where single legal instruments like the Italian mortgage on cars (Brünjes and Janssen 1995) or the Spanish *salarios de tramitación* (for problems with this term in a comparative perspective see Colneric 2006: 15, 18) – workers' compensation for the time of unjustified dismissals – are concerned. The situation of comparatists becomes more desperate, however, if core terms of a foreign legal system resist translation. The British comparatist Sir Basil Markesinis (1997: 198) insists that 'common law' and 'equity' – key terms to understanding English law – cannot be translated into German or French. Regarding 'equity' there are similar terms in German and French (*Billigkeit* and *équité*). These are frequently offered as valid translations – even by the best specialized dictionaries. In fact, they have a much narrower meaning and less impact on the respective systems than English 'equity', which is not only a doctrine in the law of obligations but a source of law at the same time.

Problems of untranslatables may lead to utter despair if the comparatist is confronted with sources which are based upon another alphabet or on pictograms. Here preserving the original term and circumscribing it to the audience is not even an option.

2.4.2 Non-translation

A reverse image of the problem of 'untranslatables' is the 'non-translation' dilemma. Legal transplants, i.e. the borrowing of legal institutions from other legal systems, have brought this phenomenon upon us. Most legal cultures have grown from absorbing foreign ideas and borrowing from foreign experiences.[13] Currently, the American legal system is arguably the most influential legal system in the world (Langer 2004; Keleman and Sibbitt 2002; Kiener and Lanz 2000; Wiegand 1991, 1996). It exports jurisprudential approaches to law (e.g. legal realism, law and economics, law and literature), reshapes particular areas of foreign legal systems (e.g. antitrust law (Buxbaum 2005; Sullivan and Fikentscher 1998), securities law (Tung 2002), corporate law (von Nessen 1999), international commercial arbitration (Dezalay and Garth 1996: 51–7; Drahozal 2000: 96; cf. Karamanian 2003) or at least lends specific legal doctrines or legal tools (e.g. the antitrust rule of reason (Ackermann 1997; Calvani 2001; Manzini 2002), class actions (Burckhardt 2005; Hodges 2001: 205–302; Gidi 2003; Heß 2000; Roman 1988; Rowe 2001)); legal education (e.g. credits system, evaluation, law school rankings) and profession (e.g. the rise of law firms, see Suzuki 2003) are also subject to Americanization. Detecting, evaluating and accommodating or as the case may be neutralizing such transplants is becoming more and more *the* key concern for comparative lawyers.[14] The phenomenon of non-translation seriously affects their success in doing so. Often, transplants retain the name of the original, as for example the 'essential facilities doctrine', the 'efficiency defence' or the 'rule of reason', which have found their way from American antitrust law into European competition law. The importation of doctrines and tools by name has lulled many comparatists into a false sense of familiarity. Time and again they do not distinguish properly between the transplant and the original in the donating system. This might lead to a misinterpretation of the doctrinal construction, the consequences, and the significance of a transplant. Borrowed legal institutions that remain untranslated are chiefly transplants of signs including a latent context. Separated from their original cultural roots, the signs persist but they might acquire a different meaning due to their new systematic context[15] or because they are transferred on some conceptual levels but not others. (For an example from the field of constitutional review see Langer 2004: 30–1.) The degree of change a transplant is likely to suffer depends on the extent of the difference between the donating and the receiving system. A certain gap will always yawn as the dynamics of the two systems differ.

2.4.3 Hidden implications

The latent context of legal transplants brings us to the problem of hidden implications in legal texts. Such implications cause 'losses in translation', because they are more readily discovered by one comparatist than by another.

Four phenomena have to be distinguished. Let us begin with preconceptions. According to Gadamer (1975: 252), each comparatist is bound by his preconceptions and his own cultural disposition; he will always remain 'one of his [own] people'.[16] As he needs to explain foreign rules in terms that are familiar to himself and his audience, he often superimposes the implications of these terms to seemingly corresponding terms of foreign law, which in fact have entirely different implications. Many Europeans doing business with China, for example, have experienced the complexity of the differing implications the term 'contract' has. Western legal systems regard contracts as binding. In theory, this is also true in China after the adoption of the Uniform Contract Law[17] in 1999. In practice, however, a contract is rarely considered binding per se.[18] The "yes" of a Chinese you enter into contract with might merely signal the beginning of a business relationship and the start for real contract negotiations (McConnaughay 2001; Pattison and Herron 2003: 460). Even worse, it might also have been only a gesture of politeness and not a real acceptance in the European sense. Traditionally, kin and friendship are the binding factors in China, not the conclusion of a contract as such.

Hidden implications might also hamper a meaningful comparison, because regularly, native speakers interpret a text more deeply, filling it with more associations while, in contrast, the foreign interpreter struggles to understand even the main theme (Curran 2006: 701; Horiba 2000).[19] Accordingly, comparatists will regularly miss hidden implications and the valuable hints they give on the 'social function' of legal institutions. The greater the geographic, ethnic and cultural distance between the *comparanda* and the comparatist's own legal culture, and the fewer historical contacts and common models that exist, the more readily hidden implications will be missed. Esteem and disdain, especially, often avert the comparatist's attention. The relevance of a court decision, for example, not only depends on the fact whether a legal system regards court decisions as a source of law or not, but also on the prestige of the judge or panel involved in the decision. Another factor that has been largely ignored in the comparative work on courts is that their significance depends on the attitude of a legal system towards litigation. Citizens may regard involvement in a lawsuit as something quotidian, even as a duty in the obligatory 'struggle for law' (von Jhering 1872)[20] as is the case in the United States. However, they may also see exposure to litigation as something objectionable and active litigation as tasteless, as the 'shame cultures' of Eastern Asia traditionally do.

So far we have looked at two deficits within the person of the comparatist. Hidden implications, however, are also inherent in the objects he works with. This is in particular the case if international agreements are among the *comparanda*. Whenever these texts borrow their terminology from national legal systems, they import connotations as well. The Berne Convention on the Protection of Literary and Artistic Works, for example, uses in its only authentic version, the French text (see Art. 37 (1) (a) of the Berne Convention 1967), the term *droit d'auteur*, in order to summarize the rights that are conferred on the author. This term, borrowed from the national French law on authors' rights, has a wider meaning than the English 'equivalent' *copyright* (Cinni 1992), a fact that has been largely ignored by English-speaking commentators on the Berne Convention. This problem of diverging interpretation has been enlarged since certain provisions of the Berne Convention have been adapted by the 1995 WTO-TRIPs Agreement, which is authentic in English as well in French (Brand 2007b).

Finally, the comparatist needs to be aware of the fact that the implications of terms might change over time. Areas of the law which are strongly influenced by politics or moral value judgments are particularly susceptible to such a change. Often, a change in the connotations of a legally relevant law precedes the change of the respective legal rules, as we can see particularly well in the more lenient approach that many legal systems have recently adopted towards same-sex marriages (McReynolds 2006).

2.4.4 Perspective

The problem of hidden implications leads us to the question of perspective. Seemingly corresponding terms in different legal systems often stand for different legal concepts, because the latter are seen from a different perspective. This is particularly true for areas of law that are subject to strong political, religious or economic influence, as for example the rules governing interest and usury. The German and the English terms for interest only match on first sight.

The English 'interest' can be understood literally as the creditor's interest in returns. Northern Italian merchants brought this term (*interesse*) with them in the early fifteenth century, when they advanced to yard bankers (Brand 2002: 13–14; Gillomen 1990: 280–4). Jeremy Bentham later described the attitude of his country towards interest in the words: 'we must grind the tooth of usury, that it bite (Bentham 1837)[21] not too much, but we must allow interest to attract foreign merchantmen to exercise their business in England'. Interest is seen not as much as a burden for the individual debtor, but instead as a chance for the whole economy to attract investment. Accordingly, England up until today approaches the phenomenon of interest from the viewpoint of the creditor and is therefore comparatively liberal (Brand 2002: 28–100). The German term for interest *Zins* derives from Latin *census*, the headcount for taxation (Brand 2002: 7; Königer 1997: 23). Based on the teachings and the linguistic customs of Luther, we see interest here as a burden from the perspective of the debtor. Germany's traditional approach to interest and usury is therefore more restrictive than its English counterpart. Only now, under the influence of EC legislation (see EC directive 2000/35/EC, OJ L 200, 8 August 2000, 35), are the two approaches slowly converging.

We see that etymology is a valuable instrument in order to detect the impact perspective can have on the meaning of foreign legal terms. Comparative lawyers have left this tool unused for too long. It was a mathematician, Hans Seckelmann (1992: 17), who taught us that 'law follows the path of language'.[22]

2.4.5 Actors

If that is so, it is tragic that jurists, Germans in particular,[23] have been misled to believe that law can be understood independently of the people who have created it. Accordingly, comparative law is weak in actor analysis, which other comparative social sciences use with reward. Actor analysis is of interest for comparatists on two different levels. First, on the level of creation of law: law-creating actors (government officials, judicial bodies, pressure groups) coin the language of law. Their preconceptions become the connotations of the law they produce, or as Karl Llewellyn has put it: 'The meaning of a text varies with the identity of the author and the audience and the circumstances surrounding their encounter through the text.' In this context three aspects demand further consideration. The first is the occurrence of 'pre-eminent lawgivers' (*überragende Nomostheten*). A pre-eminent lawgiver is a person who coins institutional actions (court decisions, enactments) to such an extent that these actions appear as his own rather than actions of the institution he is embedded in. Influential actors like this not only appeared in antiquity (Solon, Drakon, Numa), but also in modern democratic and seemingly fully institutionalized societies. The comparatist needs to watch out for pre-eminent politicians (e.g. Madison's influence on the framing of certain articles of the US constitution (Warren 1928: 625–6, 702; Fenning 1929: 109–17)) or judges that dominate their courts (e.g. Lord Denning (Jowell 1986; Kutzner 2001) and – earlier – Lord Mansfield (Holdsworth 1937; see also Blok 1965) in the UK, or justices Learned Hand (Van Doren 1998) and Rehnquist (Thompson 2006) in the United States). Occasionally, even academics rise to become pre-eminent lawgivers – driving and directing 'the weak machines' of entire interstate conferences as in the case of Eugen Ulmer and the 1967 Revision conference on the Berne Convention on the Protection of Literary and Artistic Works (Reimer 1967). Their language and the meaning they have attributed to it provide the framework for interpretation of the legal acts they have brought into being.

A second instance where the comparatist needs to survey law-creating actors is when a fundamental change in their institutional structure occurs. In particular, changes in the political attitude of a legal system towards race (apartheid), gender (affirmative action) and political philosophy (communism – liberalism), or an entire regime change (Eastern Europe), might hoist a new class or group of people into positions of prominence, where they apply and interpret rules that have been created by another group of people with a different education, mindset or cultural background. Decolonization is a good example. The 'common law' of the former British possessions in Africa underwent radical changes in interpretation when they were no longer applied by British/British-educated judges (see Marasinghe 1977: 507ff.). The same is tragically true for the property rules of the Roman–Dutch law in contemporary Zimbabwe (McClung Nading 2002).

An important question for the comparatist is, furthermore, how much thought law-creating actors have put into the wording of a provision or a *ratio decidendi*. Grammatical interpretation of hasty enactments (e.g. the American Sherman Act of 1890, see Peritz 1996: 13–26) does make less sense than that of an elaborately designed piece of legislation as the German Civil Code. Concerning the interpretation of decisions of public authorities and judicial bodies, it increasingly matters whether the actors involved in decision making have used their mother tongue. In the era of supranational (e.g. ECJ, CFI in the European Union) and international courts (e.g. ICJ) and authorities (e.g. the EU Commission), which all have their 'working language' (e.g. French in the case of the ECJ), more and more judges and civil servants have to express concepts or doctrines, borrowed from their domestic legal experience, in a language that does not necessarily provide the vocabulary for precisely expressing or even circumscribing these concepts. Particularly highly specialized panels, such as those of the European Patent Court or the Office for Harmonization in the Internal Market, have experienced difficulties in this respect.

When we turn to the level of the recipients of law, actors decide about the normative force of the legal provisions under comparison. What, for example, is the normative force of a provision that is not understood by the people required to apply it? Two examples spring to mind. First, the growing number of people that do not speak the official language of a legal system (Jayme 1981; 2000; Schlechtriem 1980), as a substantial and growing part of the Hispanic population in the United States does not (Bender 1996). Furthermore, all Western societies are suffering from a growing number of 'functional illiterates', generally literate people that cannot grasp the meaning of normative texts. About 15 per cent of the German population and 30 per cent in Italy and the United States are affected (Smith 1995: 733–9; Großfeld and Hülper 1999). The existence and the level of functional illiteracy as well as the awareness of a legal system of this problem affect liability standards (e.g. failure-to-warn law (Jacobs 1992) and the reasonable person test (Gilles 2001; DiMatteo 1997) in negligence cases) as well as the level of consumer protection that is afforded.[24]

On the level of the recipients of law, the comparatist also has to take into consideration the will and inventiveness of the local population to evade and circumvent the law. Remember the Brazilian *jeito* or think of the sale and resale practices that replace forbidden forms of interest and compound interest in the Arab world.[25] Often, however, these 'escape devices' are hard to discover, because 'old boy networks' or *guanxi* relations (Chen 2001: 45–9; Seligman et al. 1999; Peng 2001; Großfeld 2003: 184; Pattison and Herron 2003: 484–5; von Senger 2006: 49–54) play a vital role in them and such relations are virtually impenetrable by foreign comparatists.

2.5 Intra-language traps

Finally, language might prove to be a barrier to comparative law, even where there is no apparent translation involved. George Bernard Shaw reminds us of that, when he observes that England and the United States are 'two countries separated by a common language'.[26] Many problematic cases of communication within the same language, like different meanings of words and phrases in different dialects, do have a massive impact on the practice of law (Hovland 1993).[27] They are, however, of secondary concern for the comparatist, because they do not directly affect legal language which is highly technical and largely unaffected by dialects. Here, I would like to concentrate on the phenomenon which has the biggest potential to become a 'legal irritant'[28] for comparatists.

Inconsistent usage of legal terms is a source of great confusion within the comparative community. A particular legal system may use a particular term with differing meanings, sometimes even within the same piece of legislation. The German penal code, for example, uses the term *Absicht* for two distinct forms of *mens rea*. Similarly, French law knows two different significations of 'contract' in Art. 1108 and 1101 of the Code Civil. Such inconsistencies mostly derive from legislation that was drafted too quickly or from later additions to the codes that follow different usages of language than the original text.

In the law of contract we also see that the unification of law is another field where the comparatist encounters inconsistent usage of terminology. Common lawyers have in mind contract in a narrower signification when they speak of their own legal systems, but need to be aware that contract has a broadened meaning in the text of many uniform laws, such as the UNIDROIT or Lando Principles on Contract law. These texts are also authentic in English but draw the concepts behind their terminology from a civil law background (Zimmermann 2005: 265ff.). We have to admit that the connotation problem we have already seen from another perspective, under the heading of hidden implications, can also appear in contexts where no translation is involved.

2.6 Reasons for the neglect of language

Now the community of comparative lawyers has not been completely ignorant of the pitfalls of language. In theory, it is generally accepted that comparatists should study 'law in action' rather than 'law in books' (David 1950: 17–25; Schnitzer 1961: 31–2; Drobnig 1971: 498; Ewald 1998: 383). Comparatists strive for 'legal translations' (Constantinesco 1972: 79–81;

Wallow 2006: 11; Sacco 1994) rather than literal translations, i.e. for a deep historical and contextual analysis of legal terms in order to catch the meaning of the concepts and institutions behind them properly. They also vow not to rely in their terminology on the idiosyncrasies of any particular jurisdiction, in order to escape bias and their own preconceptions as far as possible.

However, in the practice of comparative law, acknowledgement of the importance of language declines into being mere lip service. Textism is particularly omnipresent. The extent of practical disregard for linguistic aspects is in fact so huge that it seems to be firmly linked with the methodology that comparative lawyers conventionally apply.

2.6.1 Functionalism

Comparative law is still dominated by the so-called 'functional method' which other comparative social sciences abandoned some time ago. The functional method is basically a 'problem-solution approach' that disregards differences in doctrinal construction and legal concept. Instead, it directs its attention almost exclusively to the practical consequences of norms, and particularly to the remedy provided in a specified factual situation (Hyland: 1999: 188; see also Zweigert and Kötz 1998: 44; De Cruz 1999: 232–5; Husa 2003: 425). In order to avoid large-scale empirical investigations, functionalists presuppose that different legal systems face essentially the same problems (*praesumptio similitudinis*).[29] They are out for the similarities of legal systems, not for differences in detail (Hyland 1999: 190).

This reductionist approach explains why language has been sidelined by mainstream comparative law. As we have seen, a closer inspection of linguistic aspects unmasks as superficial many of the similarities that functionalists endeavour to establish. Indeed, it is hard to believe that many legal problems are the same in two societies except on a technical level. The underlying political, moral and social values simply vary too much. A proper approach to language in comparative law therefore necessitates a change in methodology. This does not seem too bold a suggestion, because the trust in functionalism within the community is withering anyway.

2.6.2 Alternatives to functionalism

However, alternatives that have been brought forward so far, do not allow for a better appreciation of linguistic aspects. Law and economics enjoys an 'Indian summer' in its comparative variant. In its search for the 'efficient solution of a given problem' though, it is merely a narrowed and specified version of functionalism (Ewald 1998: 383; Peters and Schwenke 2000: 808). It 'radicalizes' (Frankenberg 1985: 263) this method by focusing on one particular function only, the rule's or institution's efficiency. This leaves even less room for linguistic considerations than original functionalism does. Even those comparatists who have sparked the current discourse on language in comparative law have little to offer for the consideration of language in actual research practice. Critical legal comparatists, culturalists and followers of the linguistic-philosophical school of deconstruction are still working on a 'proto-methodological' level (Brand 2007a: 432, 434–5) and have limited their efforts so far to elucidating shortcomings of functionalist studies in paying due respect to the sociocultural context of law.

2.7 Conclusion

A third way is yet to be found. The first steps in that direction have been taken recently under the heading of 'conceptual comparisons' (Brand 2007a; see also the thoughts on alternative approaches to comparative legal methodology by Husa 2006: 1110ff.). This approach acknowledges that many linguistic pitfalls of doing comparative law derive from the fact that, conventionally, two or more different legal systems are directly compared with each other. By contrast, conceptual comparisons try to mitigate the linguistic conflicts involved in direct comparison by devising neutral *tertia comparationis* in the form of theoretical, abstract and unambiguous models (comparative concepts) that represent characteristic properties of a group of legal rules, principles or institutions from different legal systems. In a second step (systematic comparison), real-world institutions and rules can be matched and assessed against these concepts. Using abstract models which dwell 'in between' the existing legal systems as *tertia comparationis* has the advantage of providing the comparatist with tools that are meta-legal, notions and concepts that can be freely defined and applied, without regard to linguistic or dogmatic customs of particular legal systems and therefore without a (legal) history that needs to be accounted for.

However, until conceptual comparisons or a more promising approach has cured the methodological malaise of comparative law, it is up to the individual comparatist to make sure that he pays due regard to the pitfalls that language puts between him and a meaningful comparison. He is well advised to overcome the lawyer's traditional reluctance to work in an interdisciplinary fashion and seek a linguist's advice at times;

team efforts are the future of comparative law. For those who ignore this advice, comparative legal studies will remain an unpleasant 'jump and run' adventure full of 'muddy pools' and 'poisonous darts'.

Notes

1. See the references at deGroot (2006: 422).
2. See also J. Husa (2003: 439), Sarcevic (1997) and earlier remarks by H. Capitant (1930: 7) ; only recently, the subject has found a wide audience (deGroot 2006; Curran 2006).
3. At first, the object and purpose of comparative law have also been found in supporting the development of a universal legal history, and even on the establishment of a *droit commun*.
4. However, remnants of 'mute law' remain; customary law, for example, expresses itself in situations, not in words (Sacco 1995; Jayme 2000: 130); furthermore, the impact of symbols on the law (courthouse architecture, judicial wigs and gowns, etc.) should not be neglected; see Arnold (1935) and the comment by Fenster (2003: 1073–95), Gridel (1979), Großfeld (2003: 158), Posner (1998) and Chatillon (2002: 688).
5. I regard this term as a misnomer. In the wake of legal transplants and reciprocal influences every legal system has become a mixed legal system.
6. But cf. expressions indicating oral tradition as German *Richterspruch, Rechtsprechung, Anspruch* (see Henry (1997: 47); opinions of the House of Lords are still called 'speeches'.
7. The first society dedicated to the comparative study of the law was the French Société de Législation Comparée.
8. To a certain degree this is necessitated by writing as the preferred form of expression of lawyers. Writing is always more abstract than spoken language and therefore leaves a wider gap in understanding (see Großfeld 2003: 164).
9. *Jeito* owes its existence to the necessity of finding ways around the incredibly formalistic legal system that the former colonial power Portugal imposed on its transatlantic subjects (see Rosenn 1971, 1984, 1998; Esquirol 2003: 82).
10. For example, Germany and Switzerland (see Sacco 2001: 42).
11. For example, Austria (see Lohaus 2000: 101).
12. The English translation verifies the proverb by failing to communicate in English its subtlety in Italian, the exchange of one vowel sound for another.
13. The theory of legal transplants is conventionally attributed to Watson (1993, 1995); however, there are earlier studies on the subject including Lenhoff (1951, 1964); an insightful overview is provided by Miller (2003).
14. This is particularly true for transfroming societies (Ajani 1995: 105–10).
15. Langer (2004: 5, 29) speaks of 'legal translation' in order to account for the transformation process a legal transplant might undergo. See also Legrand (1997) and Watson (2000).
16. The term *Vorverständnis* is indebted to Heidegger's notion of fore-conception (*Vorgriff*); see also Großfeld (2000) and Kohler (1901).
17. See Art. 13 UCL; Zhonghua Renmin Gongheguo Fagui Huibian [Contract Law of the People's Republic of China], adopted and promulgated by the Second

Session of the Ninth National People's Congress [NPC], 15 March 1999, translated and compiled by John Jiang and Henry Liu at http://www.cclaw.net/download/contractlawPRC.asp (last visited 12 October 2007); particularly on the formation of contracts: Jianhua and Guanghua (1999: 11–15).

18. 'Non observance of these laws is quite universal' (Orts 2001: 61); a good framework for analysis is provided by von Senger (2006: 45–7).
19. Foreign lawyers, however, are more likely to detect, from their outside perspective, hidden assumptions of legal systems which are difficult to detect by lawyers within a particular system (Kitamura 1995; Sacco 1991).
20. This has been (successfully) challenged by Kohler (1902: 44).
21. Interestingly, the literal translation of the Hebrew term for interest, *nasheh*, means 'it that bites'.
22. I personally believe, however, that law follows trade and that language serves as an intermediary between the two of them (Großfeld and Brand 1999: 811).
23. In nineteenth-century Germany, legal positivism ruled. Its adepts (Puchta, Windscheid) believed that they could explain law exclusively from 'within', relying entirely on grammatical, systematic and doctrinal reasoning. Will and values of law-creating actors were regarded as secondary if not irrelevant. This train of thought continues to affect German legal thought (see Wieacker 1967: 431).
24. For a comparison of different concepts of the 'consumer' in Europe, see Helm (2003) and Weatherill (1996).
25. *Mudaraba* and *murabaha* (see Brand 2002: 139; D. Klein 1995: 539 ff.).
26. Attributed in this and other forms, but not found in Shaw's published writings.
27. For similar effects in criminal law, see Shulman (1993: 176) and Garland (1981).
28. On this term, see Teubner (1998).
29. On the *praesumptio*, with critical remarks see Michaels (2006: 369–72).

3

Statutory Interpretation in the EU: the Augustinian Approach

*Lawrence M. Solan**

EU legislation is written in all of the EU's official languages. Each version is authoritative, and no version is privileged as 'the original', at least not as an official matter. The practice derives from the very first Regulation of the Council of the European Economic Community in 1958, which declared Dutch, French, German and Italian as the official languages.[1] As countries enter the EU, the Regulation has been amended many times to expand the number of official languages to match the official languages of the member states. Moreover, as accession treaties are signed, the treaties themselves contain provisions that show respect for the linguistic diversity of the EU. For example, the 1997 Treaty of Amsterdam says:

> This Treaty, drawn up in a single original in the Danish, Dutch, English, French, German, Greek, Irish, Italian, Portuguese and Spanish languages, the texts in each of these languages being equally authentic, shall be deposited in the archives of the government of the Italian Republic, which will transmit a certified copy to each of the governments of the other signatory States.
>
> Pursuant to the Accession Treaty of 1994, the Finnish and Swedish versions of this Treaty shall also be authentic.[2]

Since then, others have joined the EU, which now has 27 members and 22 official languages.

The existence of a regime of multilingual legislation appears to create a daunting task for a court that must resolve disputes over a statute's applicability in a particular situation. The opportunity for inconsistencies among the various language versions is so profound that it would not be surprising if the entire system collapsed under its own weight.

But that has not happened. Whatever problems face Europe and the EU, statutory interpretation is not high on the list. On the contrary, the European Court of Justice resolves disputes among member states in what appears to be a routine manner. In this chapter, I argue that the proliferation of languages actually *assists* the interpretation of statutes by the ECJ. To the extent that the goal of the court is to construe statutes to effectuate the intent of the legislature and to further the goals of the enacted directive or regulation, the existence of so many versions of the law makes this task easier. In other words, my argument is that the Babel of Europe facilitates communication.

Ideally, the linguistic practices of a supranational legal regime should meet three goals. The first, which is the value promoted most aggressively by the EU, is respect for the equality and sovereignty of the individual member states. By treating each version of an EU law as an authoritative original, EU members are treated equally. Although the EU has three working languages – English, French and German – the final forms of all laws are not limited to these three.

The second goal concerning statutory interpretation in a supranational regime is that the laws should be construed in a manner that is faithful, in some meaningful way, to the intent of the drafters. Although fidelity to the legislative purpose is not the only goal of statutory interpretation (see Eskridge 1989), it is the principal goal in any legal regime. Yet it would appear to be more difficult to accomplish when laws are written in many languages, with each version, at least to some extent, reflecting the nuances of many legal cultures. If the laws mean very different things to the various members, whether because of legal, cultural or linguistic differences among them, the project cannot succeed, since there will be no rule of law for the members to follow.

The third goal is that of efficiency. If the burden of maintaining a supranational legal order exceeds its benefits, it will lose influence over time, and devolve into an obscure, costly burden on its members. A recent report discloses that the Directorate-General for Translation of the European Commission employs some 2200 people at an annual cost of €541 million. Each time a new member joins the EU, tens of thousands of pages of documents must be translated into the language of the new member. To take a recent example, prior to their recent accession, teams of 16 Bulgarian and 20 Romanian translators arrived in Brussels to prepare for the addition of those languages to the group of official languages.[3]

These three goals – equality, fidelity and efficiency – are in tension with one another. It would surely be more efficient to legislate in a single language, or a small group of official languages, perhaps those that are now the working languages of the EU. Such a move, however, would reduce the degree to which the system respects the equality and sovereignty of the individual members, since those whose languages are not represented as official languages would play a somewhat diminished role in the legal process.

The concern of this chapter is with the second goal: fidelity. The question explored is how faithful to the will of the legislative body can decision makers be in a system that produces legislation in many languages and gives equal status to each version. The question would seem difficult to answer in the abstract because there is no particular measure of fidelity. However, it is certainly possible to investigate the extent to which the proliferation of languages affects the ability to render decisions faithful to the legislature in comparison to other regimes, such as ones in which decision makers operate in a monolingual legal order. It is also possible to hypothesize an intermediate legal order limited to a few languages and compare the work of the ECJ with what might happen in such a system. An 'intermediate system' might contain, for example, three official languages in which legislation is written. Disputes could be resolved with reference to:

(a) The three official versions; and
(b) The versions of the parties to the dispute if they differ from the official versions.

If, say, a dispute arises between Finland and Sweden, the ECJ would look to the three official versions (likely, English, French and German), plus the Swedish and Finnish versions in rendering a decision. The three legal orders and their effects on the three goals discussed earlier are set out in Table 3.1.

Table 3.1 The legal orders and their effects on the three goals

	Official languages	*Official languages +*	*All languages*
Equality	–	+/–	+
Fidelity	?	?	?
Efficiency	+	+/–	–

No doubt, the current legal order, reflected in the rightmost column, is both respectful of the sovereignty of the members, and quite costly, in terms of time and personnel. The open question is whether this multilingual legal order makes it easier or harder for a judicial body to remain faithful to the will of the enacting legislative body.

The rest of this chapter explores that issue. Section 3.1 briefly develops the notion of fidelity more generally. Section 3.2 introduces the concept of Augustinian interpretation, the use of multiple versions of the same law as an advantage in discovering its intended meaning. The term reflects the similarity between this approach to interpreting statutes and the same method, developed by St Augustine in the fourth century, for interpreting scripture. Section 3.3 explores the use of Augustinian interpretation in the ECJ, including some recurrent situations in which it falls short. Section 3.4 is a brief conclusion.

3.1 Fidelity to legislative purpose in the EU

Almost as a mantra, the ECJ looks to the legislative purpose in interpreting statutes (see e.g. McLeod 2004 for description). Sometimes called the *teleological approach* or *purposive approach* to statutory interpretation,[4] the method is familiar to those engaged in statutory interpretation in individual states. The court investigates the motivation for the legislation, including founding documents that set forth overarching legal goals, and resolves disputes in a manner that will further those goals. Thus, the court has said in a recent case, *Schulte* v. *Deutsche Bausparkasse Bardenia AG*, 'Where it is difficult to interpret legislation from its wording alone, an interpretation based on purpose becomes fundamental. That is the case where the provision in dispute is ambiguous.'[5] Such references to legislative purpose are easy to find.[6] Barak (2005) has noted that purposive legislation typically 'reflects, at various levels of abstraction, but particularly at the highest levels of abstraction, the intention of the text's creator(s)'.

Just as easy to find are references to legislative intent, which is similar to legislative purpose, but focuses on somewhat narrower goals. In fact, sometimes the ECJ uses both terms in the same case. For example, *Chacon Navas* v. *Eurest Colectividades SA*[7] dealt with whether the dismissal of an employee for reasons of illness violated the EC Framework Employment Directive 2000/78, which makes it illegal to dismiss an employee because of a disability. In holding that the directive does not encompass ordinary illness, the court held that in construing the directive, account must be taken 'of the context of the provision and the purpose of the legislation in question' (¶ 64). But it also gives credence to the argument that it is important to enforce the protection 'intended by the legislature', by not giving employers carte blanche to ignore the disabling effects of certain illnesses (Judgment, ¶ 23). Thus, whether by following a law's language, purpose or intent, the court's obligation is to be faithful, and to give primacy, to the legislative body that enacted the law.

Sometimes, these approaches are contrasted with the goal of ascertaining the intent of the legislature by reference to the language alone, as American textualists would prescribe (see McLeod 2005). However, this distinction can be overstated. In its effort to be faithful to the will of the legislature, the ECJ is perfectly comfortable relying on language as an important clue. Thus, in *Simutenkov* v. *Ministerio de Educacion y Cultura*,[8] decided in 2005, the court noted: 'The starting point for assessing art 23 of the Agreement in isolation must be its wording' (¶ 14).

Because each EU directive is written in all 20 languages, this task is not a straightforward one, as the court noted:

> In so doing it must be borne in mind that Community legislation is drafted in various languages and that the different language versions are all equally authentic. An interpretation of a provision of Community law thus involves a comparison of the different language versions. (¶ 14)

Much of this chapter argues that this additional step adds value to the linguistic analysis that takes place in the interpretation of monolingual legislation. Here, my point is that the ECJ does not ignore language in favour of ascertaining the legislative purpose. Rather, language provides a somewhat unique kind of evidence of purpose, and the court regards language differently for that reason.

Articulating the goal of fidelity, however, is easier than determining exactly when a judicial body is faithful in any particular case. In monolingual settings, the following questions recur: What does the statute say (generally, the best evidence of legislative intent is the language used in the law itself)? Does applying the plain meaning of the statute appear to undermine the intent of the legislature? If the statute is vague or ambiguous, are procedures available for resolving the ambiguity in order to reach a decision? If so, should courts risk compromising the rule of law as reflected in applying the statute as written in order to further the legislative purpose?

These questions are not always easy to answer. To take an example from American law, the Food, Drug and Cosmetics Act permits the federal Food and Drug Administration (FDA) to regulate drugs and 'devices' used for the delivery of drugs. At the time the law was enacted, it was clear that the legislature did not intend to permit the FDA to regulate tobacco or tobacco products. Since then, various efforts have been made to amend the statute to include tobacco, but those efforts did not succeed. Nonetheless, during the Clinton administration, the FDA promulgated regulations that set limits on the distribution of tobacco products. One of the major tobacco companies, Brown & Williamson, sued, claiming that the federal agency had no right to do so.[9] In response, the agency argued that cigarettes can reasonably be seen as devices for the delivery of nicotine, and therefore come within the scope of the FDA's regulatory authority. A principle of American law requires courts to defer to the interpretation of an agency to whom regulatory authority has been delegated if any reasonable understanding of the statute would support the agency's interpretation.[10]

In a 5–4 decision, the United States Supreme Court agreed with the tobacco company, and held the regulation to be invalid. At stake was whether the purpose of the statute should prevail over language – the word 'device' – that seems to permit the agency to have taken the action it did. In this case, the court held that the independent contextual evidence that the legislature did not intend to permit the regulation of tobacco should trump both the language of the statute and the principle calling for deference to administrative agencies.

On many other occasions, however, the Supreme Court has held that 'the language of the statutes that Congress enacts provides "the most reliable evidence of its intent"'.[11] This creates a dilemma for courts that wish to be loyal to the instructions of the legislature, but sensible in drawing inferences about what the enacting legislature intended. To make matters more difficult, in many cases the legislature had no discernible intent at all with respect to situations that arise before courts. Strange things happen in this world, and legislatures cannot possibly predict each one of them. Dan Simon (2004) has argued that when faced with this problem, courts typically speak of purpose and intent, but really use arguments based on coherence to reach a conclusion about how the enacting legislature would have wanted the law to handle a particular situation.

European courts have traditionally been more comfortable than have American ones to put the purpose of a statute ahead of the language in the service of effectuating the legislature's will. But evidence is evidence, whether it is put before an American or a European court, and it is undeniable that the language of a statute provides privileged evidence of what the legislature intended. To take a classic example from the philosophical literature, when a law says 'no vehicles in the park',[12] one can argue about the law's applicability to a child riding a tricycle, but no sane person would think the law sets a minimum age for buying tobacco products, or regulates the dumping of toxins in the sea. That is, language, while often not constraining the range of possible interpretations to one, surely is the principal vehicle through which legislative will is expressed, and that expression is largely successful.

When it comes to the multilingual legislation of the EU, the options for achieving fidelity are both broader and narrower than they are for the monolingual legislation of most individual states. Of course, individual states with legislation written in more than one language must make their own rules to deal with the status of the various legislative versions, as is the case in Belgium, Canada and to some extent Spain.[13] But in the typical situation in which a state's laws are written in a single, authoritative version, courts may use the statute's language as a fulcrum, deciding how much weight to give it in a particular dispute.

In contrast, when a dispute is over which of two fully authentic versions of a law should prevail, the status of the statutory language is itself contested. Courts may still endeavour to find the purpose of a law, but they must do so without the luxury of resort to a single, authoritative text.[14] Thus, the option of being an American-style 'textualist' is simply not available to interpreters of EU law. Also unavailable, but potentially useful, is the translation history of a law. It would be perfectly sensible, for example, for a court to begin with, say, the French version, if that was the one with which the European Commission began during the drafting process. Then, the court could determine whether other versions reflect an error in translation. The ECJ, however, typically does not engage in this method, although there are some early cases reflecting it, shortly after the Treaty of Rome, when there were six countries and four languages involved in EU legislation.[15]

Stauder v. *City of Ulm*[16] provides an important illustration of this early method. An EU regulation empowers members to subsidize the sale of butter to certain consumer groups in need of assistance as a means of assisting the dairy industry. A consumer from the city of Ulm complained when a retailer asked him to reveal his name and address in order to qualify for the benefit, asserting that it violated his constitutional right to dignity. The German and Dutch versions authorized the butter benefit to be given to consumers who had a coupon issued in their name.

The French and Italian versions required only that the consumer present an individualized coupon. Who was right? The court noted that the European Commission, which had to approve the measure, had agreed to a draft written in French. The court thus concluded, '[t]he deviations in the German and Dutch versions must therefore be held to be merely translation errors, which must have arisen in the preparation of the text for adoption by the Commission in the written proceedings' (p. 116).

More recently, however, that method has not been used for the same reason that the EU has not established an official language or given additional status to the three working languages. Reference to the translation history is the functional equivalent of selecting an official language. Doing so offends basic notions of sovereignty and equality among the members.

Yet translation is surely relevant to the interpretation of EU law. The American legal scholar, Lawrence Lessig (1993), proposed that a useful way of characterizing the quest for fidelity to legislative purpose is to liken the judicial role to that of a translator. As Lessig (1993: 1173) puts it:

> The translator's task is always to determine how to change one text into another text, while preserving the original text's meaning. And by thinking of the problem faced by the originalist as a problem of translation, translation may teach something about what a practice of interpretive fidelity might be.

Lessig, whose goal it was to explain statutory and especially constitutional analysis within the American legal system, spoke of translation as a way of expressing the thought that one can be faithful to a text without being entirely literal. Translators routinely must decide how to balance the target text's choice of words against the likelihood that readers will understand the translation as conveying the same information as the original, which may require straying from a literal translation (see e.g. Nord 1997).

Translation cannot paint a complete picture of statutory interpretation in the monolingual context, however. As Levinson (1997) has pointed out, the analogy between translation and monolingual legal interpretation is imperfect. Whereas translators bridge a knowledge gap between two groups of people separated by culture and language, the individual interpreting a monolingual statute is separated from the text only by time. How similar these gaps are is an empirical question.

When it comes to multilingual legal regimes like the EU, however, translation is more than a metaphor – it is a basic fact about the entire structure of the law. While translation history may not be used as extrinsic evidence of a law's meaning or purpose, a comparison of the various versions of the law provides an important tool for the ECJ. It is of crucial importance to determine how effective this tool is, since it must replace both analysis of the plain language of a single statute and do the work of the translation history to which statutory interpreters may not refer. To the extent that reference to different language versions provides useful evidence of statutory purpose, it leads to a remarkable inference: the proliferation of languages in EU legislation actually aids interpreters in their quest for fidelity. In other words, Babel is not punishment, it is a gift.

3.2 Augustinian interpretation in the EU

Among the methods of statutory interpretation that the ECJ employs is a comparison of various versions of the statute in question in different languages.[17] The court looks not only at the versions written in the languages of the parties to the particular dispute before the court, but also at other versions. The goals of this inquiry are to determine consensus among the members as to the intended scope of the statute, and to discover whether a particular interpretation allowed (or not allowed) in the language of one of the members is a matter of linguistic happenstance rather than legislative deliberation. I call this multilingual approach to statutory interpretation *the Augustinian approach.*

In *On Christian Doctrine* (Augustinus 1997), begun in the year 396, Augustine concerned himself with the question of how we can be sure that we understand, and therefore obey, the scriptures. He hypothesized: 'There are two reasons why things written are not understood: they are obscured either by unknown or by ambiguous signs' (Book 2, ch. X). The solution, Augustine opined, was to look at the scriptures in both the original Hebrew and Greek, and in the various Latin translations:

> Against unknown literal signs the sovereign remedy is a knowledge of languages. And Latin-speaking men, whom we have here undertaken to instruct, need two others for a knowledge of the Divine Scriptures, Hebrew and Greek, so that they may turn back to earlier exemplars if the infinite variety of Latin translations gives rise to any doubts. (Book 2, ch. XI)

Ambiguity in text may remain unnoticed, especially if it results from bad translation. Even worse, incorrect translation can lead to mistakes as to the actual content of the divine scripture, which can lead even the faithful to err. The surest way to discover such problems is to place competing versions (both in Latin and in predecessor languages,

Hebrew and Greek) side by side and look for differences. Examining the translation history can root out obvious errors in the Latin versions. Residual ambiguity should be resolved in favour of promoting core religious values, such as charity.[18]

What about those who do not know Hebrew or Greek? A comparison of Latin translations can also be helpful:

> For either a word or an idiom, of which the reader is ignorant, brings him to a stop. Now if these belong to foreign tongues, we must either make inquiry about them from men who speak those tongues, or if we have leisure we must learn the tongues ourselves, *or we must consult and compare several translators*. (Book 2, ch. XXI)

Again, comparing the Latin to the originals in Hebrew or Greek, whether directly or with the help of others who are learned in those languages, is Augustine's first solution. As for comparing various Latin translations with each other, what at first appears to be a third-best method for those not able to consult the originals, has its own advantages. Studying the various translations can be an improvement over relying upon a single translation: 'And yet to those who read with knowledge, a great truth is to be found in each. For it is difficult for interpreters to differ so widely as not to touch at some point.' Furthermore, even when translation is straightforward, some of the Latin vocabulary may be unfamiliar, making it necessary to infer meaning from the surrounding linguistic context. Augustine noted, 'In this matter too, the great number of the translators proves a very great assistance, if they are examined and discussed with a careful comparison of their texts' (Book 2, ch. XXI).

Augustine's reliance on a comparison of Latin translations was also a matter of necessity, we now know. While he embraced whatever learning could be gleaned from studying the translation history of biblical text, he himself was not fluent in Greek and had even less control of Hebrew, at least early in his life. Van Fleteren (2001: 13) notes:

> Unlike contemporary exegetes, Augustine exegizes the Latin text, not the original Greek or Hebrew text; perhaps Augustine was thinking of priest-students in Carthage or Milan, or even his parishioners in Hippo. However, knowledge of foreign languages is necessary for the interpretation of unknown or ambiguous signs – sadly Augustine was not an example of his own principles.

Others make similar observations.[19]

Of Augustine's two methods – comparing translations to the original and comparing translations to each other – only the latter is available to the ECJ. The former method, as noted above, is disapproved as a violation of the principle of equality. Conceptually, it is easy to see how resort to an original text can yield insight into the intent of the drafter of that document. In the absence of being able to draw such an inference, however, it is worth exploring just what makes the comparison of translations a worthwhile activity at all. Augustine provides some insight into this question as well. Not all translations are created equal. Again, in *On Christian,* he complained: 'For in the early days of the faith every man who happened to get his hands upon a Greek manuscript, and who thought he had any knowledge, were it ever so little, of the two languages, ventured upon the work of translation' (Book 2, ch. XVI). It is only by placing a bad translation next to a good one that brings forth the point, through a chain of inferences, that the essence of the passage becomes clear. Sometimes a particular translation has captured it, but at other times, reading the various translations suggests a common theme, expressed in different words by each translator.

Capturing this essence of a scriptural passage is the goal of the biblical scholar (Book 2, ch. XVII), and capturing the essence of EU legislation is the goal of the ECJ. Like Augustine, the ECJ may rely upon consensus among the different versions to uncover outliers that probably have simply got the point wrong, or it may attempt to find various threads running through the different versions which, taken together, suggest an underlying purpose behind the legislation.

Thus, both Augustine and the ECJ are essentialists. It is only if there exists in the first place some deeper, underlying understanding that one can justify an enterprise whose task it is to uncover such an essence. In both cases, language provides strong evidence of that essence, but the essence cannot be reduced to any single version of the text. As discussed below, there is an imperfect relationship between thought (conceptualization) and language (words). When evidence of thought becomes frozen in a single linguistic act, whatever imperfections exist become permanent. The ability to compare different versions and then to triangulate, however, brings out nuances that can help the investigator to gain additional insight into the thoughts of the original drafter. For this reason, one would predict that the proliferation of languages in the EU actually aids in the task of statutory interpretation, making it more likely that the court will come upon the intended goals of the legislation before issuing a ruling.

But biblical studies have one big advantage over the project of discovering the purpose behind EU law. There really *is* an original. For our purposes, statutory interpretation in the EU is statutory interpretation without a single, authoritative text (see Dollerup 2004). Moreover, biblical translation, at least in the time of Augustine, involved only one target language: Latin. Whether the European endeavour will succeed, in contrast, must depend upon a variable not relevant to Augustine: how well Augustinian interpretation will succeed in the multilingual statutory context is a function of what it is that makes languages similar to each other and what it is that makes languages different from each other.

In some respects, it seems likely that the proliferation of languages will help the statutory interpreter. To the extent that one language contains a syntactic ambiguity that allows multiple interpretations of a law, whereas other languages do not, the Augustinian approach will quickly unmask the outlier and make clear that the legislative body intended the meaning in common to the other language versions. Far more difficult are the problems that arise from subtle differences from language to language in the meanings of words. The more people are designed to form similar concepts given similar experiences, the less it should matter which language they speak and the better a multilingual legal order should work. Divergence from one language version to another might be expected to the extent that:

> People in different cultures speaking different languages have different experiences reflected in words that appear to be translations of each other be really aren't (consideration/consideración, cause/causa).[20]
>
> Languages express concepts differently from each other in small ways; there is some truth to the Whorfian hypothesis, suggesting that the concepts one's language makes available influences thought (Whorf 1956); and
>
> People conceptualize idiosyncratically even when they share both experiences and cultural norms. For example, people vary as to whether they would say that a person who has deceived another person into believing something false has lied if the deception does not literally involve a false statement.[21]

If these sorts of conceptual issues did not arise, there would be no particular reason to engage in the Augustinian project because there would be no difference between one language and another. This is not to say that languages are internally crisp. But it does mean that looking at different languages to ascertain the purpose behind a law will only work if the different language versions are not exactly the same as one another, in both the intentional and extensional senses. Yet the languages must be close enough to each other to permit only a small set of possible interpretations. Otherwise, the amount of discretion available to a court would be so broad as to challenge the very notion of a supranational order governed by the rule of law.

The solution to this problem lies in the nature of conceptualization. The concepts of people who speak different languages and live in different cultures will be most alike if people are designed to form the same or similar concepts from the same or similar experiences; and the experiences of people from the various member states of the EU are similar enough. Using somewhat different vocabulary, Engberg (2004) lays out this problem nicely. Thus, the likelihood of identical concepts has both an innate component (our cognitive design) and a cultural one (how culture structures experience and represents it in that culture's language).

As for the innate component, there has been a great deal of study during the past three decades of how people form concepts and categories, with considerable progress. Many now believe that our concepts are complex entities consisting in part of prototypes based on experience, and in part of definitional conditions, whether necessary or sufficient.[22] Peter Tiersma and I (Solan and Tiersma 2005) have used the dictionary definition of the word *chair* to illustrate this point. *Webster's Third New International Dictionary*, one of the leading dictionaries of American English, defines the word as follows:

> A usu[ally] movable seat that is designed to accommodate one person and typically has four legs and a back and often has arms.

The only necessary (i.e. definitional) component is that a thing must be a seat designed for one person. All of the other features are prototypical in nature, expressed in the definition with the words, *usually, typically* and *often*. Psychologists now believe that we conceptualize by forming mental models that contain both kinds of information, and perhaps even more complex elements, such as theories of how a concept interacts causally with the world. No doubt people who speak different languages do not have precisely the same concepts. The fact that our concepts are in part comprised of experientially based mental models would make such uniformity impossible. Moreover, work by the linguist Anna Wierzbicka (1992) shows that very few concepts are universally expressed in the languages of the world.

What is necessary for the success of the Augustinian method, then, is not the universality of concepts, but rather the universality of how our minds are designed. Similar experiences cause us to produce more or less the same concepts, whether considered individually or culturally. As the philosopher Jerry Fodor (1998) puts it, we conceptualize a *doorknob* as 'the property that our kinds of minds lock to from experience with good examples of doorknobs', 'by virtue of the properties that they have as typical doorknobs'. If German and French doorknobs differ from each other, then we may find some differences in the mental models of doorknobs that French and German people form in their minds. But given exposure to the same types of doorknobs, including a sense of what a prototypical doorknob looks like, people of all cultures will make more or less the same thing of their experience. This suggests that not only must we be Whorfians to explain the success of Augustinian interpretation, but we must also be Chomskyans in the sense that an explanation of our innate endowment is a prerequisite to justifying the approach.

3.3 Multilingual interpretation in practice

Augustinian interpretation does not always succeed – but it often does. Before we get to what can go wrong, let us look at a few examples of what may go right. Sometimes, the absence of a linguistic issue is construed as evidence that the linguistic consensus has captured the essence of the legislation. Much of the time consensus among the various language versions is used as a means to confirm the court's sense of the law's purpose, which had already been determined on other grounds. For example, *Pretura unificata di Torino* v. *X*[23] involved a regulation permitting local authorities to exceed concentrations of foreign particles in the water supply under certain emergency circumstances. Criminal proceedings had been brought against an official of Turin for violating Italian law by permitting excessive amounts of a contaminant to enter the water supply. He defended by relying upon the EU regulation. Looking at various versions of the regulation, the court concluded that 'it appears from the different language versions of Article 10(1) that the term "emergencies" must be construed as meaning urgent situations in which the competent authorities are required to cope suddenly with difficulties in the supply of water indented for human consumption' (¶ 14). Since that was not the case, the EU regulation would not provide a defence to the domestic environmental crime prosecution.

At other times, as Augustine noted, the various language versions can be used to find and discard outliers. Sometimes, the issue concerns simple errors in translation. Recall that the court avoids referring to any particular translation history because of the principle of equality. A broad comparison among language versions, however, makes a historical account unnecessary, as long as there is relative consensus. Many of these cases involve word choice. Consider *Lubella* v. *Hauptzollamt Cottbus*.[24] A regulation adopted protective measures with respect to the import of certain cherries into the EU. Just about all of the versions of the regulation used the word for *sour cherries*. But the German version, for some reason, had used the word for sweet cherries (*Suesskirschen*). This fact made the scope of the challenged regulation entirely beyond controversy.

Lubella provides an excellent vehicle for comparing the Augustinian approach to discovering a statute's purpose with a textualist approach to statutory interpretation. The latter approach risks ossifying drafting errors that result from legislation written in clear, but erroneous language. The study and comparison of various versions, in contrast, permit inferences to be drawn based upon consensus and outlying language. Most interestingly, this Augustinian approach does not require courts to stray from official textual material to extrinsic evidence that is subject to manipulation. On the contrary, the absence of a single text and the presence of many texts together provide a great deal of information within the official, authoritative documents that are absent from monolingual legislation. Thus, Augustinian interpretation gives maximum evidentiary weight to documents that actually have official status, reducing the likelihood that judges will substitute their values for those of the legislative body by straying too far from the legislative process in their analyses.

Other cases involve grammatical nuances. For example, in *Peterson* v. *Weddel & Co., Ltd.*,[25] the issue before the court was a criminal prosecution within the UK for violation of a regulation setting certain limitations on the operations of trucks. An EU regulation, however, allows members to exempt from this regulation 'transport of animal carcases or waste not intended for human consumption' (¶ 5). The UK had availed itself of this exemption, so if the shipper's conduct was covered by the exemption, then no crime was committed.

While it is clear that the exemption applies to waste not intended for human consumption, the question was whether it applies only to those carcases not intended for human consumption, or to all carcases. The shipper being prosecuted was shipping, among other things, sides of beef intended for human consumption.

The court looked at a number of versions of the regulation, finding most of them ambiguous. In the Dutch version, however, 'the qualifying words "not intended for human consumption" precede the term "carcases" and consequently can apply only to both waste and carcases' (¶ 11). The non-equivocal version was given a privileged status in this context, and was used to reinforce arguments based upon the purpose of the regulation.

To those versed in American law, the problem resembles cases that consider the proper application of the last antecedent rule, which says that 'a limiting clause or phrase ... should ordinarily be read as modifying only the noun or phrase that it immediately follows'.[26] The problem with that rule, however, is that in situations like the one before the ECJ, it is not possible to determine in advance whether the last antecedent is the entire disjoined phrase, or the last of the disjuncts. Augustinian methodology provides evidence that may help in resolving that question in particular cases.

In contrast, the Augustinian method does not always bear fruit. Jan Engberg (2004) writes about *Commission of the EU* v. *United Kingdom of Great Britain and Northern Ireland*,[27] a case involving how we conceptualize fishing. British trawlers were engaged in joint fishing expeditions in the Baltic Sea with Polish trawlers. The British vessels would cast the nets; the Polish vessels would then trawl for fish; the Polish vessels would then turn the nets over to British vessels, which would bring the fish on board. If these fish were deemed to have been caught by the Poles, then a tariff would be due. If caught by the British, there would be no tax.

The English version of the regulation in question says first that 'goods wholly obtained or produced in one country shall be considered as originating in that country'; and second that 'the expression "goods wholly obtained or produced in one country" means: ... products of sea-fishing and other products taken from the sea by vessels registered or recorded in that country and flying its flag' (¶ 7). The Commission claimed that the Poles had 'obtained' the fish since they were the ones that separated the fish from their natural habitat. The British claimed that 'taken from the sea' should be construed literally, and that the fish did not leave the sea until the British trawler lifted the nets containing the fish that were caught by the Poles.

To resolve the dispute, the court looked at a number of different language versions, but learned nothing from them. The French *extraits de la mer* was subject to both interpretations: taken out of the sea and separated from the sea. Other versions, including the Greek, Italian and Dutch, were just as ambiguous. The German word *gefangen*, meaning caught, was more helpful to the Commission's position. The court conceded: 'Accordingly, a comparative examination of the various language versions of the Regulation does not enable a conclusion to be reached in favour of any of the arguments put forward and so no legal consequences can be based on the terminology used' (¶¶ 15–16). Anthony Arnull (1999) observed that this is the typical approach of the court in such situations. In this case, the court determined, without the assistance of a comparative analysis of the various language versions, that holding the British vessel liable for the tariff was more consistent with the purpose of the regulation. The opposite result would have permitted members to 'game' the regulation by doing with impunity just what the regulation sought to prohibit: importing fish caught by non-members into the EU without the imposition of a market penalty. Thus, the court relied on arguments based on coherence as a surrogate for legislative purpose.

What went wrong? Recall that multilingual statutory interpretation is essentialist in nature. Since there is no single text, there must be some message that the array of texts, taken as a body, has attempted to convey. The significant overlap in meaning implies that to a large extent, the communication is likely to have been successful. When I, as a native speaker of English, refer to fishing, however, I really do not know whether the essential element is pulling the fish out of the water, or catching the fish on the line. It has never really mattered much to me. Perhaps they are both part of the essence, or perhaps they are alternatively part of the essence. If what is true for me is true for many people in my culture and for many people in very similar cultures where Germanic and Romance languages are spoken, then it should not be surprising to find confusion across the board, with only a few languages taking a position on the matter, perhaps as a matter of happenstance, perhaps for more interesting cultural and historical reasons.

What we can conclude from this case is that Augustinian reasoning does not work to clarify a concept when the dispute requires us to take a position on a subtle aspect of the concept that has been neither culturally nor individually resolved. If the essence of fishing is not a universal, and if our common experience permits us to focus on both aspects of the activity with more or less equal attention, then the comparison of different language versions will have taught us only that a particular version's clear statement in one direction or the other is likely to be accidental, and should be ignored. Thus, Augustinian methodology, even when it does not work to give us a single answer, may warn us to be wary of drawing strong conclusions from the clarity of any particular version.

3.4 Conclusion

Let us return to the three values discussed at the beginning of this chapter: sovereignty, fidelity and efficiency. In Table 3.1, the question of fidelity was an open issue. At this point, we can fill in some of the question marks as follows in Table 3.2.

That is, the proliferation of language versions appears to add to the likelihood that the court will get a case right, where getting it right means issuing a judgment that is more likely to further the purpose behind the law, and which is consistent with the intent of the enacting legislature. This is true when the method appears to succeed, and it is even true when the method appears to fail, in that the knowledge that the members' versions lack consensus gives the court due warning that it should not pay too much attention to any particular version that appears intuitively clear as an initial matter.

The conclusion that Babel actually serves to clarify communication is a surprising one, especially for an American academic who is accustomed both to an environment in which at most two languages are spoken, and who comes from a culture in which textual analysis reigns, both in statutory interpretation and the law of contracts. Nonetheless, my happy conclusion is precisely that: Augustine had it right when he concluded that the careful study of different translations of the same text is likely to lead to a deeper understanding of the text's essential meaning.

Table 3.2 The legal orders and their effects on the three goals

	Official languages	*Official languages +*	*All languages*
Equality	–	+/–	+
Fidelity	–	?	+
Efficiency	+	+/–	–

Notes

* Much of this research was conducted while I was a visiting professor of law at Yale Law School during the spring of 2006. My thanks go to Sean Young of Yale Law School and Kimberly Finneran of Brooklyn Law School for their important contributions to this project as research assistants. I benefited greatly from discussion with Jan Engberg, and from comments received at presentations at Aston University in Birmingham, at a meeting of DAJV in Berlin, and at the May 2006 conference on Language and the Law in Düsseldorf. This project was further supported by the Dean's Summer Research Stipend program of Brooklyn Law School.

1. EEC Regulation No. 1, 1958–04-15.
2. Treaty of Amsterdam, Art. 53.
3. See 'Translation in the Commission: Where do we Stand Two Years after Enlargement?', available at http://europa.eu/rapid/pressReleasesAction.do?reference=MEMO/06/173&format=HTML&aged=0&language=EN&guiLanguage=en (last retrieval on 19.02.2008)
4. See e.g. Fennelly (1997) (observing the appropriateness of this kind of approach in a multilingual setting) and Lord (1996) (observing that teleological method is used to bring about harmonization of local laws to comply with EU directives).
5. [2006] All ER 420 (2005) at ¶ 87.
6. See e.g. *Epikouriko Kefalaio* v. *Ipourgos Anaptixis*, [2006] All ER 112 (2004) at ¶ 22.
7. Case C-13/05, [2006] IRLR 706 (2006).
8. [2006] All ER (EC) 42 (2005).
9. *FDA* v. *Brown & Williamson Tobacco Co.*, 529 U.S. 120 (2000).
10. See *Chevron U.S.A., Inc.* v. *Natural Resources Defense Council, Inc.*, 467 U.S. 837 (1984).
11. *Holloway* v. *United States*, 526 U.S. 1, 6 (1999) (quoting *United States* v. *Turkette*, 452 U.S. 576 593 (1981)).
12. The example is widely discussed in the literature. For discussion from a linguistic perspective, see Winter (2001).
13. For an excellent discussion of the bilingual and bi-jural regime in Canada, see Sullivan (2004).
14. For my views on some of the shortcomings of reliance on the literal meaning of the text in monolingual environments, see Solan (2005).
15. Treaty Establishing the European Community, Rome, 25 March 1957.
16. [1969] Case 29/69.
17. For a description and examples of cases using some of these comparative methods, see Van Calster (1998).
18. I only touch on Augustine's philosophy here. For a much fuller and richer discussion see Pelikan (1986).
19. See Bastiansen (2001: 33–4) ('His command of Greek was a limited one, not sufficient for an easy assimilation of the contents of theological treatises.'); Evans (2001: 145–6) (comparing Augustine and Jerome as textual critics, and referring to Augustine as an 'amateur' in comparison because Jerome was conscious of the Hebrew and Greek, whereas Augustine 'was dealing with an Old Latin text which was locally variable').

20. See Alcaraz Varó (2002) for discussion of this classic problem in the translation between Spanish and English.
21. For discussion, see Solan and Tiersma (2005), especially Chapter 11. For a more general discussion of variation in the conceptualization of non-paradigmatic cases, see Schroeder (2007).
22. For some contrasting views, see Fodor (1998) and Murphy (2002).
23. [1988] ECR 5099.
24. [1996] ECR I-5105.
25. [1984] ECR 1567.
26. See *United States* v. *Kerley*, 416 F. 3d 176, 180 (2 [ext] nd Cir. 2005). I discuss this principle in Solan (1993).
27. [1985] ECR 1169.

4
Globalizing Trends in Legal Discourse

Maurizio Gotti

4.1 Globalization in the legal field

In recent years, the dismantling of cultural, disciplinary and national barriers, especially in the context of cooperation and collaboration in international trade, has accelerated moves towards the globalization of sociocultural, business and communication issues. This process of globalization offers a topical illustration of the interaction between linguistic and cultural factors in the construction of discourse, both within specialized domains and in wider contexts. In spite of the fact that specialized discourse has traditionally been considered objective and impersonal, in recent years linguistic research has shown both the existence of overt and covert strategies that modulate the author's control of the recipient's response, and the presence of discoursal realizations aiming at presenting facts and concepts from a non-neutral perspective. This is a confirmation of the fact that language is generally marked both in its cultural content and in the range of available linguistic variants (cf. Kuper 1999), and that people involved in cross-cultural communication clearly construct discourse to suit the communicative needs of an international audience, adapting their native identities to a common plan which implies a new framework of values and shared behaviours.

The globalizing trend has also affected the legal field, where an international perspective is becoming more and more widespread. Legal discourse is thus another significant area where intercultural factors may be investigated. Although legal discourse is often thought to be less likely, in respect to other professional genres, to display strong cross-cultural variations, since law texts are commonly aimed at practitioners closely linked to national legal contexts, cultural aspects do represent an important conditioning factor in its construction and interpretation. Indeed, legal discourse – which used to be employed in narrow professional and local milieus and thus more closely geared to specific cultural values and identity systems – is now more and more frequently involved in globalization processes, which have relevant consequences on the discourse produced by both native and non-native practitioners working in intercultural and cross-cultural settings. Nowadays many of the texts in use at a local level are the result of a process of translation or adaptation of more general documents formulated at an international level. This is the consequence of the fact that in the context of cooperation and collaboration in international trade, law too is fast assuming an international perspective rather than remaining a purely domestic concern. The increasing need at an international level for accurate and authoritative translation of legal texts and documents across languages relies on the need for them to convey appropriately in both languages the pragmatic and functional intentions and implications of the original text.

An excellent example of this trend is the need for a common European legal framework; this task is much more complex than simply translating common normative documents into all the languages of the European Union, because this newly created framework is meant to be interpreted within the contexts of a diversity of individual legal systems and tongues. Significant differentiations may arise in the various member countries of Western Europe, especially when one needs to interpret such issues as human rights, international agreements and contracts, freedom of speech, freedom of trade, protection of intellectual property, all of which have very strong sociopolitical and cultural constraints. Although all legal documents in all languages address these issues, they do so in distinctive and also in overlapping ways, because of the different languages in which they are constructed and the cultural differences of the societies in question and of their legal systems. Indeed, legal terminology is so culture-bound (the reasons being at the same time historical, sociological, political and jurisprudential) that a satisfactory translation of all the legal terms of one text from one context to another is at times impossible.[1] David (1980: 39) underlines this difficulty with a few examples:

> To translate into English technical words used by lawyers in France, in Spain, or in Germany is in many cases an impossible task, and conversely there are no words in the languages of the continent to express the most elementary notions of English law. The words *common law* and *equity* are the best examples thereof; we have to keep

> the English words [...] because no words in French or in any other language are adequate to convey the meaning of these words, clearly linked as they are to the specific history of English law alone.

The adoption of a particular term instead of another may give rise to ambiguity and misinterpretation. Several examples of this are given by Fletcher (1999), who examines the translation into various languages of the English text of the European Convention on Human Rights. For instance, the translation provided for the expression *fair and regular trial* into *juicio justo y imparcial* (Spanish) and *procès juste et équitable* (French) is not satisfactory, as the use of the non-equivalent adjectives *regular* (English)/*imparcial* (Spanish)/*équitable* (French) can easily show. The same could be said for the rendering of the concept of *reasonableness*, basic in common law systems, where expressions such as *reasonable steps, reasonable measures, reasonable person* and *proof beyond a reasonable doubt* frequently occur. This concept, instead, when translated into languages spoken in countries adopting a civil law system, is considered too vague and its rendering as *ragionevole, raisonnable* or *vernünftig* often gives rise to criticism and dissatisfaction.

Other excellent examples of translation discrepancies can easily be found in texts relating to the process of building a common European legal framework. For example, translators into English find it difficult to express such culturally specific French collocations as *acteurs sociaux, acteurs économiques, acteurs institutionnels, acteurs publics, acteurs politiques,* which have no direct equivalent in the target language (Salmasi 2003: 117), and they sometimes transliterate terms or create calques from one language into another, relying on the false premise of a very close relationship between similar lexemes in different languages (see the examples of *transmettre/transmit* and *prévoir/foresee* in Seymour 2002). Indeed, in Europe the legal drafting issue has become extremely important with the elaboration of a multilingual legislation concerning the European Union. This depends on the fact that the official languages of the EU are those of its member states, and as new countries join the Union, their languages are added to the number. This is part of a precise policy aiming to build a community of peoples respecting and safeguarding at the same time the existing variety of customs and cultural identities, a principle based on the conviction that the languages of Europe are part of its immense and diverse cultural heritage, and therefore it is considered the duty of the Union to guarantee their preservation.

As EU legislation must be published in all member states' official languages in order to be valid also at a national level, in the elaboration of European legislation and its introduction into the various national contexts a fundamental role is played by legal drafting and translation. As regards the former, the elaboration of the texts is carried out in a parallel fashion by the various teams, making use of a common multilingual terminological database and relying on shared Community concepts and institutions. This procedure, however, encounters problems mainly due to the presence of different legal systems in the various countries and the existence of a specific tradition of the legal register in each member state. Indeed, closer cooperation between the various legal systems of the EU members has not been achieved through creation of a new legislative framework to replace the existing one. Such systems are still in use and only in very few cases have the more evident discrepancies been eliminated.

The European authorities are aware of these problems and greater and greater emphasis is being laid on the quality of legislation drafting at supranational level. An example of this is the 'Declaration on the Quality of the Drafting of Community Legislation' which is an important part of the Treaty of Amsterdam (1998); this document explicitly states that 'the quality of the drafting of Community legislation is crucial if it is to be properly implemented by the competent national authorities and better understood by the public and in business circles'. This has led to much greater uniformity in the translation of European directives into the various languages of the Union and to more marked homogeneity and interdependence of the resulting texts. Translators work in single-language units of approximately 20 people and translate, almost without exception, into their mother tongue. Their command of foreign languages is expected to be backed up by a good general knowledge and some competence in at least one specialized area such as law, technology, economics, etc. Translators are also assumed to possess word processing and other computer skills such as database interrogation, as they frequently rely on terminology and documentation available in electronic versions.

This new approach to the translation of European directives has also served a harmonizing function, in the sense that from the adoption of the texts of the EU greater uniformity has derived in the use of terminology as well as a higher degree of conceptual homogeneity, which is then transferred into local legal practices. A typical example of this influence of European legislation on the local legal language is the frequent adoption of equivalent definitions of legal concepts deriving directly from European regulations and directives. However, these efforts and initiatives in better drafting procedures have not solved all discrepancy problems, as the final texts are also conditioned by the different rhetorical traditions pertaining to the cultural systems involved, thus often leading to diverging constructions and therefore to conflictual interpretations, with the risk of raising legal controversies. Moreover, in the translation process there is often an addition to and/or alteration of the semantic value of the original, due to the fact that the interpreter brings his/her own experience, knowledge and attitude to the text he/she is translating into another language. For this reason it is commonly suggested that translators working in this field should have two different types of competence: not only linguistic but also legal.[2]

Issues like these are crucial for the construction, interpretation and use of legal discourse across languages and legal systems. They are especially relevant in international trade, which often involves contracts written in English but incorporating statutes and regulations issued by a third country. Indeed, in the great, rapid changes taking place all over the world, there is a tendency for a single global standard to evolve and dominate over all others – i.e. English. The position of English as the language for international communication is a very strong one and is to become even stronger, due to the need for a common global language. However, as has often been remarked, the adoption of a lingua franca may have important consequences on the approach adopted locally. Indeed, when the language chosen for the international arbitration procedure is English, there is a tendency to adopt procedures typical of common law countries: 'Frequently the presence of American (or British) lawyers in a procedure normally leads to the de facto use of US (or English) procedures' (Lazareff 1999: 37).

The influential role played by this language is much more significant now that English is so frequently used also in cases in which no native English-speaking party is involved. The frequency of this situation is confirmed by Taniguchi's testimony:

> There are very many different arbitral practices associated with different legal and commercial cultures. However, the world has been unmistakingly proceeding toward a single commercial culture. Japanese businessmen, for example, are negotiating business in the English language not only with English speaking businessmen but also Korean, European and middle eastern businessmen. This is one of the realities of international trade today. (Taniguchi 1998: 39)

The increasing role of English as a lingua franca can also be seen at the EU level, where the use of English has become prevalent. Indeed, at the

Translation Service of the EU, nearly three-fifths of the documents sent for translation are drafted originally in English. This is nearly double the quantity of material drafted in French, which for decades was the dominant language. The great increase in the use of English in this context is due to the fact that English is often adopted as a 'relay language' for translations between combinations of languages, such as the Baltic languages and almost any other, for which the EU institutions are unlikely to find enough translators who can bridge the gap directly: the first translation is into English and from this a text in another language is then produced.

In this way, English terms are creeping into local legal terminologies. For example, over the last two decades, because of the rapid internationalization of commerce, an increasing number of English legal terms (such as *leasing, factoring* and *franchising*) have been introduced into Italian legal language. In some cases the original word has been maintained as the concept itself did not exist in that context; this is the case of the term *joint venture*, the English expression commonly in use also because of the inaccuracy of the numerous translations that have been proposed.

4.2 International commercial arbitration

An excellent example of the globalizing process taking place in the legal system is constituted by international commercial arbitration. In the last few decades, all over the world arbitration has become more and more common as a legal instrument for the settling of commercial disputes. The high recourse to this mediating procedure has given rise to a widely felt need for greater harmonization of the procedures followed, which has led to the elaboration of the UNCITRAL document approved by the United Nations to be used as a model by most of the member countries in the construction of their own individual statutory provisions for commercial arbitration. However, in spite of the growing globalization of arbitration culture, the elaboration of the UN Model Law has not guaranteed complete uniformity among the various national legislations, as the different countries have used this model in different ways, depending upon their national requirements, concerns, cultures, legal systems, languages and other constraints. Indeed, in the process of adoption of this model, the English language text of the UNCITRAL document has often had to be translated into the local languages, a procedure which has implied not only the adaptation of the original discourse to the typical features and resources of the national tongues, but also its adjustment to the cultural needs and legal constraints of each specific country. In the following sections examples of discrepancy in the formulation of arbitration concepts in different languages will be taken into consideration so as to identify the various motivations that have determined such diverging outcomes.[3] The examples will be drawn from legislation on international arbitration based on the Model Law on International Commercial Arbitration (ML) and the UNCITRAL Arbitration Rules (AR) issued by the United Nations and later integrated into the laws of several countries with varying constitutional, sociocultural and economic conditions. In particular, a comparison will be made with Italian arbitration law from the Code of Civil Procedure (Arts 806–40) and with regulations drafted by the arbitration chambers of Milan, Bergamo and Venice.[4]

4.2.1 Globalizing trends

As has already been pointed out in several preceding studies (e.g. Mellinkoff 1963; Bhatia 1993; Solan 1993; Tiersma 1999), normative texts have to conform to a double constraint: 'the law must simultaneously be both general and specific enough' (Hiltunen 1990: 66). Indeed, on the one hand they have to be very precise in defining the obligations they are meant to impose or the rights they confer; this is why permission and prohibition must be stated in a clear and unambiguous way. On the other hand, such rules have to refer to a very wide and sometimes unpredictable range of possible applications they may involve; to comply with this need, they have to be as all-inclusive as possible (Bhatia 1993: 102). However, this need for all-inclusiveness may determine some vagueness and indeterminacy in the wording of the texts themselves (Endicott 2000; Bhatia et al. 2005), mainly due to the adoption of general terms conveying wide semantic values, with the result that their meaning in the context of those provisions is not as clear as expected. Moreover, this ideal of all-inclusiveness implies the adoption of appropriate choices to be made not only at a lexical level, but also as regards syntactic and textual features, with the frequent use of indefinite expressions, *and/or* coordination, indeterminate reference (Mellinkoff 1963: 305–21; Hiltunen 1990: 70, 82; Solan 1993: 38–55; Tiersma 1999: 79–86) and even hedging expressions (Gotti and Dossena 2001), with the result that the use of these expressions creates a degree of vagueness and uncertainty of decodification in normative texts, which may cause serious problems when translating these texts into other languages (Šarčević 2000; Gotti and Šarčević 2006).

Like most normative texts, the Model Law aims to be all-inclusive and cover the widest range of possible applications and critical situations. This is determined, in particular, by the broad scope of this set of provisions, which targets the whole international community and is meant to be adopted in almost every context throughout the world. This strong purpose of global applicability can be perceived in the definition of 'arbitration agreement' given in the Model Law, which is formulated in such a way as to include any kind of formal arrangement (from *an arbitration clause* to *a separate agreement*) applicable to any sort of legal relationship (*whether contractual or not*), referring to all types of disputes (both *all* and *certain*) and covering the whole temporal gamut (*which have arisen or which may arise*):

> (1) 'Arbitration agreement' is an agreement by the parties to submit to arbitration *all or certain* disputes *which have arisen or which may arise* between them in respect of a defined legal relationship, *whether contractual or not*. An arbitration agreement may be *in the form of an arbitration clause in a contract or in the form of a separate agreement*. (ML 7.1, emphasis added, as in all quotations in this chapter)

Another example of the more general applicability of the UNCITRAL texts is offered by Art. 4 of the Arbitration Rules, which deals with representation of the parties:

> (2) The parties may be *represented or assisted* by persons of their choice. The names and addresses of such persons must be communicated in writing to the other party; such communication must specify whether the appointment is being made for purposes of *representation or assistance*. (AR 4)

The choice of the AR provision to use two lexemes to refer to the same concept – *representation* and *assistance* – points to the drafters' decision to include the possibility of assistance also by a non-lawyer and their willingness 'to ensure that the rule would have the same meaning in different legal systems' (Dore 1993: 5–6). As Garzone (2003: 205) has pointed out, the use of this binomial has no counterpart in the other texts she has examined. The text of the International Chamber of Commerce Court of Arbitration uses the word *representative* only. Similarly, Art. 18 of the text of the London Court of International Arbitration states that 'Any party may be *represented* by legal practitioners or any other *representatives*.' The more extensive wording of this point in the AR proves to be more effective in a wider and more diversified range of situations and contexts, offering a greater range of possibilities of counsel in support of the parties.

The intention of covering as many specific cases or interpretations as possible is particularly noticeable in definitions and explanations, where the extended applicability of the norm is stated explicitly:

> (3) Where a provision of this Law, other than in articles 25(a) and 32(2)(a), refers to a claim, *it also applies* to a counter-claim, and where it refers to a defence, *it also applies* to a defence to such counter-claim. (ML 2.f)

The all-inclusive purpose of the Model Law is often clearly signalled in the text by the use of the verb *to include*:

> (4) Where a provision of this Law, except article 28, leaves the parties free to determine a certain issue, such freedom *includes* the right of the parties to authorize a third party, *including* an institution, to make that determination; (ML 2.d-e)

This verb often appears in the expression *include(s), but is/are not limited to*, which is meant to introduce a number of interpretations to be given to a specific term. However, such a list does not cover the semantic field in an exhaustive way. See, for example, the definition of the term 'commercial':

> (5) The term 'commercial' should be given a wide interpretation so as to cover matters arising from all relationships of a commercial nature, whether contractual or not. Relationships of a commercial nature *include, but are not limited to*, the following transactions: any trade transaction for the supply or exchange of goods or services; distribution agreement; commercial representation or agency; factoring; leasing; construction of works; consulting; engineering; licensing; investment; financing; banking; insurance; exploitation agreement or concession; joint venture and other forms of industrial or business co-operation; carriage of goods or passengers by air, sea, rail or road. (ML 1.1.note)

This incomplete definition of *commercial* has led to different interpretations in different countries, with the result that this term has sometimes been submitted to strict delimitations of meaning in a few cultural contexts. In some countries, in particular, this definition has been interpreted according to the *expressio unius est exclusio alterius* principle, which says that if something is not included in a list, it is thereby excluded. Thus, the attribution of a limited semantic value to the term *commercial* led an Indian party to contend that its agreement with Boeing, an American company, to provide consultancy services for the promotion of the sale of Boeing aircraft in India could not be regarded as a 'commercial' transaction. The dispute resolution judgment instead opted for the broader meaning of that expression (Pathak 1998: 182).

Despite the recurring claim that precision is a prominent feature of legal discourse and one of its distinctive qualities, there are several exceptions to this rule. One of the least consistently precise areas is lexis, which may be to a certain extent referentially fuzzy. Indeed, legal English sometimes appears to tolerate insignificant differences (cf. 'tolerance principle', Endicott 2000: 1) and deliberately uses 'weasel words' (Mellinkoff 1963: 21), i.e. words and expressions which have flexible meanings. Very frequent are indefinite adjectives, which are particularly gradable and vague because of their 'borderline indefiniteness' (Fjeld 2001: 644). Examples commonly pointed out are *reasonable, substantial, satisfactory, negligent, unconscionable* (for more examples cf. Mellinkoff 1963: 21–2). Such terms allow judges to use their own discretion in deciding on their applicability in the circumstances. Tiersma (1999: 83) provides the example of the deliberately vague expression *prudent investor rule* in use in many states of the USA to refer to the requirement that a trustee in charge of investing money for somebody else should behave like a *prudent investor.* Also the drafters of the Model Law in several sections have been careful to adopt vague terms in order to allow the arbitrator greater freedom. For example, in the following quotation the discretionary powers of the judging authority are guaranteed by expressions such as *the necessary measure,* where the evaluation of what is to be considered a 'necessary measure' is left to the arbitrator(s) who is/are going to take it:

> (6) any party may request *the court or other authority* specified in article 6 to take the *necessary measure,* unless the agreement in the appointment procedure provides *other means for securing the appointment.* (ML 1.4)

As can be seen in the quotation above, also the limit to the intervention of the judging authority is qualified quite vaguely with the expression *other means for securing the appointment,* where the adjective *other* cannot be decoded in a specific way as it is linked to a referent of uncertain meaning. Moreover, the reference to the legal body that is to solve any possible dispute is not stated explicitly but indicated with the vague expression *the court or other authority*. This is due to the fact that the text is meant to be a Model Law to be applied in various contexts, and therefore it is left to the single national laws to indicate who the judging body is to be. This 'openness' of the text is clearly visible in the formulation of Art. 6 of the Model Law, in which the sentence is left purposely incomplete:

> (7) The functions referred to in articles 11(3), 11(4), 13(3), 14, 16(3) and 34(2) shall be performed by... [Each State enacting this model law specifies the court, courts or, where referred to therein, other authority competent to perform these functions.] (ML 6)

Many of the indeterminate adjectives used in the UNCITRAL texts concern quantification, which is often left open to arbitrariness; indeed the decodification of the semantic value of adjectives such as *substantial* or *sufficient* is very subjective. Other indeterminate adjectives (or their adverbial forms) are used to refer to time. One of these is *prompt(ly)*. At times, a flexible word occurs in clusters with other weasel words such as in the expression *as promptly as possible*:

> (8) The appointing authority shall, at the request of one of the parties, appoint the sole arbitrator *as promptly as possible*. (AR 6.3)

This adverbial phrase gives the appointing authority the liberty to fix the period of time in which the appointment is to be made. The rationale behind the use of such a flexible phrase is that – as the parties have not been able to reach an agreement on the appointment of the arbitrator within the time limit specified by the rules themselves (Art. 6.2) – the choice is handed over to an 'appointing authority', whose decisional powers are envisioned as indisputable since no binding time limit is set for this task. This is considered the most reasonable solution to a problem which the parties have not been able to solve. Weasel words are also used to refer to the behaviour of the parties, which is to be governed by common sense; indeed, the use of adjectives such as *appropriate, reasonable* and *justifiable* is quite frequent. The reference to common sense and shared views is not at all surprising, as it is in line with the idea itself of arbitration. In line with this presupposition, it is therefore legitimate for the arbitrator to decide what is appropriate or inappropriate according to his own discretion:

(9) Unless otherwise agreed by the parties, either party may amend or supplement his claim or defence during the course of the arbitral proceedings, unless the arbitral tribunal considers it *inappropriate* to allow such amendment having regard to the delay in making it. (ML 23.2)

As has been seen, the presence of vague textual formulations in the UNCITRAL texts is due to several reasons: like all normative texts (cf. 'indeterminacy claim', Endicott 2000: 1), the Model Law and the Arbitration Rules aim to be as all-inclusive as possible in order to be valid in the widest range of applications; thus they make use of general terms conveying wide semantic values, with the result that their meaning in these provisions is not as clear as expected. This need for all-inclusiveness is particularly strong in these provisions, as the main objective of the drafters of the UNCITRAL texts is to keep the scope of their application as broad as possible; indeed, these texts are not related to any specific, geographically based arbitral organizations, but they are meant to be truly international in their perspective so as to achieve 'the desired harmonization and improvement of national laws' (ML n. 2). Moreover, in many cases the text is worded in a vague way so as to allow the parties involved more freedom. This high degree of flexibility can be noticed, for example, in the following quotation drawn from the UNCITRAL Arbitration Rules, in which the possibility of avoiding the application of the official regulations is presented as deriving from any modifications that 'the parties may agree in writing':

(10) Where the parties to a contract have agreed in writing that disputes in relation to that contract shall be referred to arbitration under the UNCITRAL Arbitration Rules, then such disputes shall be settled in accordance with these Rules *subject to such modification as the parties may agree in writing.* (AR 1.1)

Another motivation for the vagueness of the UNCITRAL texts is that the drafters have been careful to adopt weasel words in order to allow the arbitrator greater freedom and to guarantee the maximal use of the discretionary powers of the judging authority to decide what is appropriate or inappropriate. This arbitrariness is in line with the idea itself of arbitration, which is a less formal procedure of dispute resolution based on the presupposition that the parties are willing to accept the arbitrator's personal opinion and final judgment. A further reason for the 'openness' and flexibility of the UNCITRAL texts is that they are meant to be a model to be used by most of the member countries to produce their own individual statutory provisions for commercial arbitration.

4.2.2 Local identities

In the last two decades the UNCITRAL provisions have been used as a model by a large number of countries. As the Model Law and its connected Arbitration Rules were created with the purpose of achieving the highest degree of harmonization, the single countries have been recommended to make as few changes as possible when incorporating them into their legal systems. However, the adoption of this Model Law has not guaranteed complete uniformity among the various national legislations, as this process has implied not only the adaptation of the original discourse to the typical features and resources of the national tongues, but also its adjustment to the cultural needs and legal constraints of each specific country.

4.2.2.1 Cultural constraints

Even from a very superficial analysis of arbitration practices, it is easy to realize that the cultural environment greatly influences the outcome of the arbitration procedure. This is clearly visible in those cases in which the national legislation imposes specific obligations in compliance with local customs and traditions: for example, some countries such as Korea and Saudi Arabia uphold requirements of nationality and/or residence for a person to serve as arbitrator (Jarvin 1999: 60); Saudi Arabia also requires arbitrators to be male and of the Islamic faith (Saleh 1992: 549). These criteria impose serious restrictions on the choice of arbitration in an international dispute and are usually taken into consideration by foreigners when they have to fix the site of an arbitration case with a party residing in one of those countries. But even when cultural differences are not so evident, it is impossible to guarantee a perfectly homogeneous process, as the various legal patterns of the countries involved will re-emerge in some of the procedures described or in a few of the principles set out. Such professional traits will not only characterize the written texts, but will be present in the minds of the arbitrators themselves, who – no matter how neutral and culturally open they wish to be – will be conditioned by their own specific legal philosophy. This emergence of the arbitrator's educational and professional background may create problems in the assessment of the parties' behaviour and originate negative consequences on the outcome of the proceedings themselves, a risk international arbitrators are fully aware of:

> [A]n arbitrator, without relinquishing the most impartial frame of mind, may nonetheless remain very distant, in educational and cultural terms, from the particular party or its counsel. In such a case, difficulties are likely to arise which have nothing to do with the probity of the arbitrator in question. They are due solely to the fact that said arbitrator reveals a greater intellectual propensity to grasp every detail of the arguments put forward by one party, while encountering objective and honest difficulties in understanding the submissions of the other(s) in the same way. Albeit unwillingly, the conduct of the arbitrator may thus adversely affect the equal treatment of the parties. (Bernini 1998: 42)

A similar opinion is expressed by Lalive, who remarks:

> [Participants in international arbitration] have different origins or places of business, different educations, methods, reactions or *Weltanschauungen*. In short, what has perhaps struck me more than anything after many years of arbitral practice, either as advocate or as arbitrator, is the capital role played by what may best be called '*conflicts of cultures*' between the parties (as well as their respective counsel) and, as a result, by difficulties of 'communication' between them and arbitrators. (Lalive 1992: 80, italics in the original)

In spite of the growing international arbitration culture, the national influences traced in the arbitrators' behaviour may prove particularly harmful and often rely on the arbitrators' unfamiliarity with one of the parties' site rules and practices. This is the reason why in recent legislation on arbitration there is a growing tendency to offer the parties a more comprehensive set of procedural rules rather than leaving the conduct of the proceedings completely to the discretion of the arbitral tribunal, an approach in line with the UNCITRAL Model Law. This process of harmonization, however, is very hard to carry out, and even if all the procedures were to be unified, some differences would still remain in their perception at a local level. The reason for this is to be found in the underlying professional background: 'Our own legal cultures remain, for the time being, in certain areas, an important limiting factor to harmonisation because [...] the application of the same rule may lead, despite all good intentions, to strikingly different results' (Lazareff 1999: 36).

One of the main features of the common law system is the greater degree of autonomy enjoyed by the judge (cf. Borris 1994). Similarly, in the arbitration process the arbitrator plays a very active role due to the fact that no jury is involved in the proceedings and that the majority of the disputes in international commercial arbitration are of a technical and complicated nature. Moreover, the arbitrator often makes proposals for an amicable settlement of the dispute if he sees any feasible solutions. It is important, therefore, that the decision-making process should be totally transparent and that the arbitrator should be impartial and independent. This need is particularly felt in the Italian context, where the custom of non-standard arbitration has often been regarded as too sensitive to the parties' interests and pressures, and provides an explanation for the specific rules that several Italian arbitration chambers have laid down to regulate the conduct of appointed arbitrators. In particular, the regulations laid down by a few arbitration chambers contain specific codes of conduct concerning such important issues as the arbitrator's competence, impartiality and independence, which are largely modelled on the Criteria of Arbitral Ethics *(Criteri di Deontologia Arbitrale)* enacted by the Italian Arbitration Association in 1999 (cf. Bartolini and Delconte 2001). In the UNCITRAL text, instead, this issue is considered in very general terms:

> (11) In making the appointment, the appointing authority shall have regard to such considerations as are likely to secure the appointment of an independent and impartial arbitrator and shall take into account as well the advisability of appointing an arbitrator of a nationality other than the nationalities of the parties. (AR 6.4)

The codes of conduct included in the Milan Arbitration Chamber (MAC) and the Bergamo Arbitration Chamber (BAC), instead, consist of 15 articles, covering various aspects connected to the problem of arbitrators' impartiality and independence and regulating the conduct of arbitrators in a very detailed way, from the moment they accept the appointment throughout the entire arbitration procedure. Also the Venice Arbitration Chamber (VAC) has a specific article (Art. 13) stating in an explicit way that the appointed arbitrator is expected to send a written statement expressing his independence and impartiality and declaring he has no connections with the parties involved in the arbitration process. Moreover, BAC also includes the need for a Roster of Arbitrators (Section 6) and outlines in detail the characteristics of a potential arbitrator and of the application procedures. The specification of a Roster of Arbitrators stresses the wish of this arbitration chamber to exercise strict control over the competence and reliability of prospective arbitrators. Also as regards the procedure for challenging an arbitrator, AR indicates the grounds for challenge in general terms, only mentioning 'justifiable doubts as to his impartiality or independence' (Art. 10). BAC (Section 8.1), instead, makes a clear reference to the reasons for challenging an arbitrator and refers to a precise external source of jurisdiction for their specification:

(12) The party may reject the arbitrator *in the cases specified in Section 51 of the Italian Code of Civil Practice.* (BAC 8.1.2)

Also in the Arbitration Law of the People's Republic of China the grounds for challenging the appointment of arbitrators are stated in very specific terms, and are exemplified in the mention of a close relationship with any 'one litigant' or 'the attorney', 'private meetings with the litigants or with their attorneys' or acceptance of 'invitation of the litigants or their attorneys to dine' or acceptance of 'gifts' (Bhatia et al. 2001: 10). This implication of possibilities of bribery or influence may be prompted by particular sociocultural factors specific to that country, a hypothesis which finds confirmation in the words of an expert on Chinese law, Professor Jerome Cohen from New York University, quoted by Jane Moir in an article in the *South China Morning Post* (5 October 2001):

> The longer my experience as either an advocate or an arbitrator in disputes presented to Cietac [China International Economic and Trade Arbitration Commission], the graver my doubts have become about its independence and impartiality. [...] At a minimum, I would surely no longer advise clients to accept Cietac jurisdiction unless the contract's arbitration clause required the appointment of a third country national as presiding arbitrator. (Quoted in Bhatia et al. 2001: 8)

4.2.2.2 Social constraints

The socio-economic environment in which legal provisions are introduced may also influence the style adopted in drafting the normative texts. An example can be seen in the regulations enacted in the Italian context by the Milan, Bergamo and Venice Arbitration Chambers. These institutions are situated in one of the most highly industrialized areas in northern Italy, where a large number of small enterprises operate successfully on foreign markets. Their sets of rules are intended for a number of business people running small and medium-sized companies and wanting clear indications on how to resolve commercial disputes without recourse to ordinary justice. This explains the higher degree of user-friendliness encountered in their texts, which can be noted in several cases. One instance is the fact that two of them (BAC and MAC) include standard arbitration clauses – such as the clauses for a sole arbitrator, for an arbitral tribunal and for a multi-party arbitration – which can be adopted verbatim and completed easily by the reader, as can be seen from the following examples:

(13) *Arbitration agreement* [(a)]
The undersigned [(b)] ... ... and ... ...
considering that a dispute has arisen on the subject [(c)] ... ...
agree to defer this dispute to the decision of [(d)] ... ...
to be appointed in accordance with the Rules of the National and International Arbitration Chamber of Bergamo, which the parties expressly declare they know and which they accept in full.
The arbitrators / the sole arbitrator shall decide according to the rules and regulations ... ... / fairness (specify what is relevant).
The language of the arbitration shall be ....

Notes

(a) The arbitration agreement is a document that is stipulated when the dispute has already arisen between the parties and in the absence of a precautionary arbitration clause.
(b) Specification of the name and residence, or in the case of companies, the head offices of the parties.
(c) Reference, also expressed in general terms, of the subject under dispute, with possible reference to the contract out of which the dispute originated.
(d) Specification of the number of arbitrators (one or three). (BAC, Arbitration agreement)

(14) *Clause for sole arbitrator*

All disputes arising out of the present contract[(1)], including those concerning its validity, interpretation, performance and termination, shall be referred to a sole arbitrator according to the International Arbitration Rules of the Chamber of National and International Arbitration of Milan, which the parties declare that they know and accept in their entirety.

The sole arbitrator shall decide according to the norms ... [(2)].

The language of the arbitration shall be ...

Notes

(1) Where the arbitration clause is contained in a document other than the contract to which it pertains, the contract referred to shall be indicated.

(2) The parties may indicate the norms applicable to the merits of the dispute; alternatively, they may provide that the arbitrator decide ex aequo et bono. (MAC, Clause for Sole Arbitrator)

The texts above have the form of ready-to-use specimens and are thus very easy to copy and complete. Instead, the UNCITRAL Arbitration Rules, on which the Italian texts are modelled, are mainly informative and imply some sort of adaptation on the part of the user of the clauses presented:

(15) *Model arbitration clause*

Any dispute, controversy or claim arising out of or relating to this contract, or the breach, termination or invalidity thereof, shall be settled by arbitration in accordance with the UNCITRAL Arbitration Rules as at present in force.

Note

Parties may wish to consider adding:

(a) The appointing authority shall be ... (name of institution or person);

(b) The number of arbitrators shall be ... (one or three);

(c) The place of arbitration shall be ... (town or country);

(d) The language(s) to be used in the arbitral proceedings shall be ... (AR 1)

AR's adherence to a more traditional legal style is also demonstrated by the lengthy and complex structure of most of its sentences, in line with

Table 4.1 Average sentence length in the corpus analysed (from Belotti 2003: 33)

	Average sentence length
AR	43.1
MAC	37.0
BAC	34.4
VAC	29.8

Table 4.2 Distribution of sentence types (from Belotti 2003: 34)

	AR		*MAC*		*BAC*		*VAC*	
Simple	5	17%	9	19%	15	28%	4	33%
Compound	1	3%			2	4%	5	42%
Complex	24	80%	36	77%	37	68%	3	25%
Complex-compound			2	4%				

Table 4.3 Type and number of occurrences of archaic words (from Belotti 2002: 132)

	AR	*MAC*	*BAC*	*VAC*
Forthwith		1		
Hereinafter	1			
Therefore	2	2		
Therefor	2	2		
Therein		1		
Thereof	2	3		3
Thereon	2			
Thereto	2			
Total	11	9	0	3

the features of legal discourse (Gustafsson 1975; Tiersma 1999; Gotti 2005). As can be seen from Table 4.1, the average sentence length is higher in AR than in the other three texts.

The more complex structure of legal discourse in AR is confirmed by the data concerning sentence types. As Table 4.2 shows, AR has more complex sentences than the Italian texts; MAC, BAC and VAC, on the contrary, contain more simple and compound sentences.

The shorter sentence length and the higher average number of simple and compound sentences determine a positive impact on the level of readability of the Italian texts and make them easier to process, which strengthens their greater degree of user-friendliness. This greater attention to reader's competence and expectations is confirmed by the use of lexis. Indeed, AR contains many Latinate and French forms, some of which already found in ML: *ex aequo et bono, amiable compositeur, de iure, de facto, ipso iure, in camera*. These, instead, do not occur at all in some of the Italian arbitration rules (such as BAC) or are very few in others (MAC and VAC). The same can be said for archaic words, as can be seen in Table 4.3.

4.3 Conclusion

As has been seen, the recent strong moves towards globalization have implied relevant consequences in sociocultural and communication terms. Indeed, the formulation of legal concepts in normative texts in a multilingual/multicultural context is greatly conditioned by specific sociocultural and economic factors strictly depending on the different cultural, linguistic and legal environments in which it takes place. The investigation of the process of adaptation of the international legislation to different national realities has pointed out several cases in which the source text offers the input on the basis of which new autonomous texts are created taking into consideration the needs of the final users. The analysis of arbitration texts has shown that, although the Model Law has been created with the purpose of achieving the highest degree of harmonization, total harmonization has not been realized, with the consequence that it is no longer unanimously perceived as a final and attainable goal. Indeed, the current prevalent interpretation of the harmonization process emphasizes a common understanding of the meaning of terms and practices rather than total adoption and blind acceptance of proposed models (Borris 1999: 11). In spite of the desire to make international arbitration procedures 'unbound' (Paulsson 1981) by local constraints, cultural aspects still represent an important conditioning factor on the construction and interpretation of the legal discourse concerning this mediating practice.

In particular, cultural constraints have proved to be detectable in texts which are the result of a translation or a rewriting process such as those deriving from the process of adjustment and adaptation of a text issued by an international organization to the legal and sociocultural features of the various national target users. These international documents have been shown to possess clear traits of 'hybrid' (Trosborg 1997: 146) discourse; indeed, the differentiations between the source and the resulting texts are the outcome of the conscious and deliberate decisions taken by the drafters of the local documents, and their final form shows that they 'are arrived at as an outcome of negotiations between cultures and the norms and conventions involved' (Trosborg 1997: 146).

Notes

1. This also applies to different contexts using the same language. As Nadelmann and von Mehren (1967: 195) rightly exemplify, 'Even in the same language the meaning of a legal term may differ from system to system. Thus, "domicile" has one meaning in English law and quite different meanings in American jurisdictions.'
2. For example, the Court of First Instance and the Court of Justice of the European Communities have 11 translation divisions (one for each of the Community languages) averaging 15 'lawyer/linguists' each (cf. Weston 1995).
3. The analysis presented here derives from an international research project entitled 'Generic Integrity in Legislative Discourse in Multilingual and Multicultural Contexts' (http://gild.mmc. cityu.edu.hk/). The project has investigated the generic integrity of legislative discourse by analysing the linguistic and discoursal properties of a multilingual corpus of international arbitration laws drawn from a number of different countries, cultures and sociopolitical backgrounds, written in different languages, and used within and across a variety of legal systems. Some of the results of the project are presented in Bhatia et al. (2003a, b, 2007).
4. The texts taken into particular consideration are: Arts 806–40 of the Code of Civil Procedure (CCP, available at http://www.camera-arbitrale.com/codice.htm; an English translation, offered by the Milan Chamber of National and International Arbitration, is available from http://www.camera-arbitrale.com/eng/rifarb.htm; it is the version referred to in this chapter), UNCITRAL Arbitration Rules (AR, available at http://www.uncitral.org/english/texts/arbitration/arbitrul.htm.), the United Nations Model Law on International Commercial Arbitration (ML, available at http://www.uncitral.org/english/texts/arbitration/ml-arb.htm), the regulations enacted by the Milan Arbitration Chamber (MAC, available at http://www.mi.camcom.it/eng/arbitration-chamber/reging.htm), the regulations enacted by the Bergamo Arbitration Chamber (BAC, available at http://www.bg.camcom.it/camera_arbitrale), and the regulations enacted by the Venice Arbitration Chamber (VAC, available at http://www.VAC.it/rules.htm).

5
The Status and Position of Legal Translation: a Chapter in the Discursive Construction of Societies

José Lambert

5.1 Basic goals

Symposia, articles, books from many countries and continents, within linguistics but also in law studies, seem to indicate that language is more or less at stake within the world of legislation. Why exactly? Language and languages have always been part of the legal curriculum worldwide. First of all, as a didactic tool: knowledge of Latin (and French) was needed in most West European (and in many other) countries as a kind of an entrance ticket to the world of legislation. In our contemporary age, English has been added to the foreign languages that lawyers worldwide need to master before they are to be admitted to the world of experts. In recent times, it has also become obvious that 'law' is, first of all, a given kind of 'language use', it is 'discourse', and as a particular kind of institutional discourse, it deserves to be positioned somewhere between the various discursive traditions of any community. And citizens of the entire world have become aware of the power games that discourses of all kinds, including legislation, may disseminate.

In the discussion essay that follows, I am focusing nevertheless on a very different kind of linguistic and discursive problem linked with legislation. It seems that the many legal traditions worldwide have always had and maintained and developed linguistic relationships with 'other' (neighbouring?) legal traditions. Such relationships have often been made active and dynamic with the aid of translation(s), sometimes also with the aid of 'lingua franca' rules. The question of translation is well known to lawyers and theoreticians, it is even part of the curriculum, the training package of future lawyers. However it tends to be approached in a strongly reductionist way. It is generally speaking approached as a 'tool', as a service. And scholars dealing with translation as part of the (very young) discipline called 'translation studies' often tend to do the same: having entered translation studies via translation training (hence via business entries), as happens to be the case, they also tend to reduce 'the question' of translation to a few limited questions, mainly linked with the perspective of the translator. It will be shown that the translation issue (and the language issue) cannot be reduced to a few limited perspectives, neither in modern times nor in the study of the past. And it will become clear that translation often plays an active and organizational role in the planning of societies. Societies often seem to start first as 'discourse', and in the planning of new discursive communities, translations seem to have often played a central role from the very beginning. This may tend to be more the case in modern times and in the era of communication societies and global/virtual societies.

To the extent that 'language' is – until now, in the academic canonical traditions – supposed to be (just?) a component of legislation and legal traditions, it is not surprising at all that 'translation' tends to be treated as – just – an interesting but marginal component in the various programmes devoted to law. In recent times the globalization (internationalization) phenomenon has influenced and enlarged the linguistic agenda of law studies. The interpreter happens to be better treated than the translator by the representatives of international and global legislation, but his role is also seen as (only) a fragment in the entire legal process. And generally speaking, it is mainly within one given (national) language that legislations are scrutinized in terms of linguistics.

It will be stressed time and again in this contribution that legislation, while being institutionalized first and mainly within individual societies (later called 'nations'), has always been a very 'international' (intercultural) matter through the ages and that it tends to be more so than ever in the age of globalization. And this may be the very origin of recent discussions on law and language/translation: language appears to be a problem for law in/because of the age of globalization. It is one of the underlying initial assumptions in this discussion essay that the question of the language(s) of legislation itself cannot just be reduced to 'language/languages', and that 'translation' can never be reduced to – just – language. This is what the (new) discipline called 'translation studies' demonstrates:[1] translation always involves more than – just – language, it generally also involves more than one language since large fragments of all constitutions have been imported (and translated) from previous bodies of texts, if not from well-known 'models' like the *Code Napoléon*. Before being able to read and understand the Flemish–Dutch version of the Belgian constitution, Flemish lawyers need to have at least a limited knowledge of the other Belgian language that was used as the model (French). Throughout the history of Europe, knowledge of Latin helps most lawyers, for similar reasons; and many African citizens and experts need French in order to understand the linguistic substrate of their own African constitution; in the case of citizens in Burundi (Bigirimana, this volume), being familiar with the official language (Kirundi) is not enough, not even among intellectuals, to be able to read the Kirundi formulation of their constitution; and being fluent in French is not enough either, since Belgian (in fact Flemish) missionaries have translated the oral *coutumes* from Kirundi into the legal habits and terminology of the French-Belgian constitution. Such multilingual strata may be particularly complex in the Burundi (and Congo) area of Africa, but they remind us of the linguistic multilayeredness of most European constitutions, in particular within minority cultures. They clearly reflect the underlying linguistic and sociocultural strategies from so many different moments and spaces in the European (and in other) legal traditions. It has only been a few years that translation studies discovered how particular 'intercultures' of language mediation groups provide insight into the dynamics of 'translation' (Pym 1998a).

One of the interesting illustrations of the ambiguous functions of language and translation in legal discourse is the fact that the EU is – no doubt – the biggest employer of translators in the history of mankind, first of all for legal reasons (Fishman 1993). What exactly is the (verbal) status of international legislation, and how does its formulation relate to 'local'/national legislations and constitutions? It is a familiar phenomenon – among lawyers – that legal discourse is invaded by loan words, loan structures and interferences: even Indian lawyers have problems, not just with English words, but also with Latin, Roman (*sic*) and French idiomatic trends, which explains why internationalization nowadays generates a campaign in favour of 'plain language'.

On the basis of the paradox(es) noted so far, I would like to list additional questions that deserve to be part of any research (programme) on law and language:

- what kind of language register is selected/in use/accepted as the language of legal discourse, in any constitutional environment (and where, when exactly; why, etc.)?
- to what extent is the language of legislation the result of translation (and can it be recognized as translated discourse or not?)? Is it 'visible' (Venuti 1995)?

- to what extent are given legislations (in any society) dependent on import/export operations, and how/why exactly?
- are the visible features of imported/translated texts experienced as part of the political power games, as part of colonial planning and organization (Lambert 1995), either at the very moment of their distribution (in synchronic terms) or afterwards (in diachronic terms)?
- how parallel was the dissemination of legal texts into a large number of languages in Central Europe, first in the case of Marxist models (from the Soviet Union), then in the case of the EU?
- to what extent are constitutions worldwide (now) submitted to international innovation and to globalization, how exactly does this work, and is this verbal internationalization experienced by the user as a chapter of another colonization?

Such questions all tend to position language and translation as part of an interdisciplinary research programme that is both theoretical and (inter)cultural: as long as there has been no explicit research on the many links between language(s) and law, there is no possibility of any strictly theoretical answers (by yes and/or no), since European and/or Latin American and/or Asian responses are not supposed to be relevant a priori for other continents (or nations). The history of legislation may so far have overlooked such questions. The fact is that they are not necessarily relevant for legislation only, since law and legislation are part of society: the issue of legal language has good reasons for being recognized as part of the dynamics of any society, but also as part of the dynamics of language anywhere. Where do our constitutions come from, after all?

Last but not least: given the well-known globalization phenomenon, researchers and intellectuals (maybe also politicians or sociologists) may be convinced by the relevance of language and translation issues in contemporary legislation, but there are no serious grounds for excluding that language and translation – in particular – have also played a substantial role in the establishment of legislation (and constitutions) in the past. Would this simply and only have occurred 'by accident', or would it also be, as in our contemporary age, part of a (pre-) planned extension movement, long before the execution has taken place? Has legal translation been organized as a technical service, as it is supposed to be nowadays, or as part of an organization and institutionalization wave? And how has it been 'integrated' into various waves of colonization throughout the ages? One can assume that, for and from a given society, it is never an innocent decision from which language and society and social system given rules are going to be borrowed and transplanted. Legal translation, whether (pre-) planned or not as just described, is an inevitable moment in the integration/rejection tendencies that have always oriented cultural interactions.

For any culture on our globe, the question becomes whether legal translation really plays a more strictly technical, or a rather more strategic (social, political, cultural) role in the planning and organization of societies. It may be part of pre-planned power games, it may also become part of power games afterwards, and nothing excludes that power games evolve differently from their initial conceptualization (Lambert 1993; Burke 2004).

5.2 One constitution, never one language

Our initial assumption, i.e. the assumption that the attention given to the language(s) of law in the programme of scholarly symposia is influenced by the internationalization of societies and by the necessity to plan interaction between societies and their organization, is rather trivial: it is supported by institutional arguments, i.e. by the observation that financial support is being provided by one of the most visible international organizations, the EU. Given the particular development of technologies and societies over many centuries (Ong 1982; Hobsbawm and Ranger 1996), given also the development of national cultural and legal policies, the question of language(s) has become a crucial issue in the formulation of laws and constitutions (Fishman 1999; Šarčević 1997; Busekist 1998).

In recent times, the interaction between societies and nations, the development of communication societies (Even-Zohar 1997, 1998; Lambert 1998; Pym 1998b) tend to reshape legal traditions from an international point of view. It seems that the role of translation in such a new configuration needs fundamental clarification. It is not at all certain that principles and models used in traditional historical situations still apply to 'virtual societies', and one of the obvious reasons for change is simply the 'deterritorialization' phenomenon, which disconnects the concept of 'society' from 'territory' (Lambert 1998, forthcoming).

One of the paradoxes of legislations and constitutions seems to be, on the one hand, the need for one single and institutionalized basic formulation (within given borderlines) – the idea of the *one only* constitution, even in the case of bilingual and trilingual nations – and, on the other hand, the unavoidable interference between several legal traditions (interactions) with one or several neighbour systems: how autonomous are legal traditions, and how exactly do they (verbally/linguistically) interact with others?

The very recognition of one single constitution, in a monopoly position, which is common to most nation states, also implies its contradiction, i.e. the possible coexistence of a given number of constitutions in several different languages (as in Belgium, Switzerland, Canada or South Africa): the very (Western) tradition of the constitution tends to be linked with a monopoly policy in which one language only is supposed to apply to one given territory. In principle, citizens do not have a choice: the 'ethnolinguistic policy' is an innovation of the EU (Fishman 1993). The strange thing has been, since the 'Déclaration Universelle des Droits de l'Homme', that (1) the universalistic view on language has been compromised in – exactly – the country with the most explicitly monolingual ambitions in the Western world, i.e. France; and that (2) modern sociolinguistics (and translation studies) demonstrates that there are/can be no strictly monolingual societies, which implies that the language of the legislator is not necessarily the language of the user, and that multilingualism and/or translation is unavoidably linked with translation, even within one given society or nation state.

Let us explain: the French paradox is due to the historical language map, where the French *patois* were strongly established and where the 'universalistic' language of the Revolution was in use among the social and intellectual elites; it has become known in Western historiography in relation with the activities of l'abbé Grégoire, who started struggling against *les patois* on behalf of legal universalism: French citizens subjected to the new constitution of the French Revolution appeared to be unable to understand their own (universal) rights.

The idea that societies are monolingual is due, not to linguistic evidence (on the contrary: notwithstanding much linguistic evidence), but rather to the normative developments of societies (in the Western world), on the basis of national(istic) concepts that have become dogmatic and dominant little by little within the 'invention of tradition' (Hobsbawm and Ranger 1996).

As can be illustrated by the prototypical French situation, the ideological (monolingual) basis of constitutions is in conflict with the dynamics of languages and the use of languages in society. The *Code Napoléon*, which Napoleon himself always considered to be one of his most basic performances, is heavily inspired by the idea of standardization and homogenization: all in one movement the dispersed legal traditions were meant to be unified in one single formulation that became a model of the French community. The fact was that changing legal formulations and documents on behalf of authority was not a sufficient solution for the user, for the citizen, who was supposed to be a basic and universal concept in the new legislation itself. But neither the *Code Napoléon* nor the *Declaration of Human Rights* were accessible to the real population that was object of the new legislations, since the French language was not at all the exclusive 'mother tongue' of French citizens, neither in 1790 nor in 1800 nor even say in 1850. And this is why the *Human Rights* have immediately needed to be translated into the various dialects of the French geographical areas (whatever their name has become) (Lambert 2004).

The linguistic crisis in the age and the country of revolution, the crisis from the so-called new era of civilization, seems to have been much less exceptional than it looks: legislations, constitutions tend to be reductionist and monolingual; as the first principles of sociolinguistics, 'use' and 'variables' (Fishman 1999) indicate, societies are never monolingual in their actual use of language(s). This is also one of the results of the confrontation between (socio)linguistics and legal traditions: the language of law is never just 'the language' of a given community. It was not only for internal (French) reasons that the *Code Napoléon* and the *Human Rights* were immediately used in more than one single language: an English version was distributed pretty soon after, and the interaction between legal texts on the New and the Old Continent became a well-known chapter in the history of Western society. By definition, language and translation have been an important moment in the systematic confrontation of two legal worlds. Nowadays it is easy to find the *Code Napoléon* in many, many languages on the Internet. Constitutions and languages are not simple pairs. But other particular constitutions have been submitted to multiplication on the basis of translation. In the Belgian case (Busekist 1998), the bilingual, then trilingual formulation of the constitution has required time; it has been the result of political and cultural struggle, but has finally been accepted. One constitution in three languages, it exists, but not without specific conventions as far as the legal status of translation is concerned: it is not compatible with the Belgian legislation to select one of the three versions, the one that fits best, in order to support a given legal option, all three versions are supposed to be 'equal'.

The fact is that the idea of legislations formulated in more than one language can hardly ever be considered to be unproblematic. This is at least a preliminary observation, easy to be deduced from the more or less 'universalistic' claims of the 1789 French Revolution.

5.3 Linguistic heterogeneities

In theoretical terms, there is an unavoidable conflict between, on the one hand, the willingness to provide a given society with legal texts in one single formulation, and, on the other, a well-known historical and sociolinguistic observation: the recognition of the dynamics and heterogeneity of linguistic landscapes, within given territories as well as beyond their borders. Sociolinguistics has greatly investigated the fundamental features of linguistic instabilities, while ignoring (too much, until recently) international instabilities of a similar kind.[2] Historiography has established how the various European nation states have developed: according to Eric John Hobsbawm's state of the art, hardly any among the European nations (except for Germany?) has been conceptualized on the basis of a pre-existing national language, which implies the inevitable conflict between linguistic heterogeneity on the one hand, and the various legal formulations that have been proposed/imposed a posteriori, like an ideal (or like an imposed) model (Hobsbawm and Ranger 1996; Hobsbawm 1990, 1996).

It is one of the implicit goals of any legal formulation to propose (impose) norms, hence to impose language/discourse as a *normative model*, like a normative grammar of (social and) legal behaviour. Given the lack of linguistic uniformity in European societies during the pre-national period, the very idea of the monolingual constitution generates a structural conflict with the very idea of 'citizen', as the French case has clearly demonstrated. The fact that French politicians have been obliged to produce the *Human Rights* in the (many) languages (*patois*) of French citizens simply confirms the linguistic gap between newly written laws and populations. It is clear by definition that the success and efficiency of normative models depend, and can only depend, on the citizen's willingness to respect the (at least partly) new legal constraints. This was the case around 1800, it seems also to be the case in international environments around 2000.

Constitutions pop up at a given moment in the history of mankind. Even at this very moment, in 2006, they have not really been adopted as a necessary or universal basis, since some countries prefer their ('British') 'common law' to the (French, more 'continental') idea of 'civil law'. Focusing on the twentieth century, the sociological approach to language has stressed the innovative rules underlying the language policy of the EU while calling it 'ethnolinguistic democracy' (Fishman 1993). According to Fishman, this is the first time in the history of mankind that the individual citizen has been allowed to ignore regulations if they have not been made available in his/her language: within the EU, citizens can select their language. Hence the 'ethnolinguistic' basis of this new kind of 'democracy': democracy depends on language and discourse. But the entire ethnolinguistic construction would collapse without one particular large-scale organization: the systematic and parallel translation of the basic texts into the various languages. And in the specialized discussions on language policy it is mainly the result (the 'output') of this language policy, the so-called multilingualism, that is under discussion, whereas the exact strategies adopted, e.g. the use of specific translation strategies or of 'lingua franca' options, are not really the object of discussion. 'Worüber man nicht spricht'? Why exactly?

5.4 Recognizing (more) languages and idioms

In many countries, the coexistence of different languages and/or the complexity of linguistic societies have been recognized in a progressive and gradual, but still restrictive way. When founded as a bilingual nation in 1830, Belgium waited for several decades before translating its (French) constitution into Dutch. And even now, quite a few components of national legal reforms are not (immediately) available in translation (Busekist 1998). Since the beginning of the twentieth century, German has been accepted as the third Belgian national language, but its treatment has never been in full parallel with the two ('first') national languages. During the – almost – two centuries of its existence, Belgium (like most other bilingual or multilingual nations?) has always had an obvious tendency of reducing the number of languages to be used for interaction with its citizens. But such appear to be features of any linguistic community, including even the EU.

5.5 The illusion of linguistic democracies

One of the ambiguous conventions (implicit rules) of public bilingual and multilingual communication is that languages and discourses are displayed side by side, without (too many) explanations, i.e. in their final result of juxtaposition. As in the case of Belgian bilingual street names, the exact relationships between the different names/messages/discourses are not made 'explicit' nor 'public' (official): the user very often wonders about the exact link between both 'names': has one been translated from the other? It is not at all certain that 'bilingual text editions' exhibit any translation…What is meant exactly when a given text is displayed in two languages, one on the left, one on the right? The very identification of the translated origins of a given message would/does imply that one of the/both texts is 'first', earlier than the other one(s); and being first in chronological terms seems to mean that Text 1 is a model ('norm'), whereas Text 2 is referring (hence secondary?) to it. *Ay, there's the rub!*

In almost all literature referring to the Belgian constitution, the very idea of 'translation' is rather systematically avoided: the item 'traduction' does not pop up in the thematic index of the basic book by Astrid von Busekist on 'La Belgique des langues et la politique de l'Etat' (Busekist 1998; Lambert 2004). Any reference to translation appears to be *un pis-aller*, 'a necessary evil', even in its Dutch formulation, which has been entirely, for many decades, the output of a translation process. As can be illustrated by many instructions about bilingual/trilingual revisions of particular fragments from the same Belgian constitution, the idea of 'translation', when popping up (e.g. on the Internet), is used almost exclusively in one or two different reductionist ways, i.e. in order to stress that 'translation is (absolutely) required' in a given number of cases, or in order to mention that cases of ambiguity (and conflict) are due to incorrect (bad) translation: translation tends always to have a pejorative connotation. The normative assumption is that translation itself ought to be in principle – for legal reasons, after all – an unproblematic issue. Unfortunately, as footnotes may explain in commentary, there happen to be cases of 'bad translation', which of course (would) need to be avoided. Bilingualism or multilingualism are no shame at all, they are even made visible (in their juxtaposition of supposedly parallel texts), but translation tends to be made public verbally mainly as the origin and explanation of damage(s). From the moment translation is the object of legal discussions, it becomes a negative concept. Translators and translation experts are well aware of the difficulty: they know that the actual use and institutionalization of given translation solutions are the best protection against quarrels, but they also know that new legal terms and, more particularly, large bodies of imported legal regulations as well as new political situations almost inevitably generate new interpretation problems. In fact the givenness of simple *one-to-one* translations appears to be(come) an illusion: by *one-to-one* translations, we mean the kind of formal correspondence that the first handbooks from the *Stylistique comparée* in the Vinay and Darbelnet (1977) tradition had in mind, and that implied the possibility to render two, three, four terms in the original language by two three, four terms in the target language, more or less in the same order and with parallel or identical syntactic functions. As long as no quarrels start, translation seems to function well, the relationship between two/more texts is supposed to be unproblematic, one text being (taken as) the equivalent of the other, in both directions (Dutch–French and French–Dutch). Just an illusion? Translation scholars are familiar with such conventions: they know that translation is never symmetrical, that back-translation is an illusion, and that the 'history' of any translation solution is always the history of reductions that are never fully repetitive. In principle, for the man in the street, languages are supposed to be unproblematic, and if translation is in contradiction with such rules, the implicit legal idea is that it must be 'by accident', the translation must just be bad, it is in fact 'no real translation', since translation is required to provide unambiguous texts. For translation scholars, any translation equivalence (for the concept of equivalence, see Baker 1997–2000 and Frank et al. 2004) is dependent on conventions, even on the illusion of similarity, equivalence, sameness or whatever you call it, and any translated text/discourse refers to 'another text', explicitly or implicitly (it is either anti-illusionnistic or it is illusionnistic: Levý 1969), but from the moment legal texts refer to models in another language, they are compromised as part of their (monolingual) institutional position.

One of the fascinating consequences of this analysis of legislation (and constitutions) is the observation that historical (West) European legislation is closely linked with an international tradition of law – or rather: with several traditions – from which the various (national) traditions have been transmitted – in translation: 'Worüber man nicht spricht?' – The *Code Napoléon* itself is heavily indebted to Roman legal traditions, which themselves have been borrowed from previous legislations: how could the (West European?) legal traditions have been established without translation? Experts will reply that no constitution (nor law) could be reduced to translation: translation scholars are familiar with such paradoxes, they know that translations can never fully be explained by their 'original', by their 'model'. But how exactly do legal translations work out, and what exactly is (not) translation?

Re-examining the (European) past with the aid of contemporary models for linguistic and cultural research would require an enormous framework and large-scale testing: it seems that the history of legal translations has to be written, just like many other chapters in the historiography of translation. Before scrutinizing our common traditions, we have good reasons for first observing large-scale contemporary situations.

5.6 The European Union and its new member states

The EU offers a larger framework, particularly in its recent developments. From the moment we focus on approaches in progress within the EU, it is basic to recognize that translation within this (new kind of) institutional framework is by definition (more and more) multilingual, but on the basis of explicit rules (Coulmas 1991).

One of the privileged moments in both the political history and the translation history of the EU is/was the political – and legal – preparation of the fifth enlargement of the EU (Cyprus, the Czech Republic, Estonia, Hungary, Latvia, Lithuania, Malta, Poland, Slovakia and Slovenia), which became official in 2004 and which had begun in the mid-1990s. In fact such a preparation process had been planned with the aid of explicit rules since 1995, as established in the Treaty of Accession in 2005). It is on the basis of the institutionalization of such rules that our analysis of the accession process deserves to be accepted as the analysis of an institutional approach.

It is the planning of the legal basis for the fifth extension of the EU that will now be the object of study. The information collected was available within seminars planned by the EU itself as part of their training and supervision programme for translators.

The planning and supervision priorities adopted within this training and supervision programme were indeed highly indicative of a set of strategic views on translation, and the planning of translation previous to accession and as part of the preparation phase was/is a clear illustration of the strategic planning of legal texts within the overall EU organization.

While about 12 new states were candidate members of the enlarged Union, the preparation was intended to convince the citizens of the potential member states to accept their membership (citizenship). Whatever the procedure within the individual countries was going to be (either an individual referendum, or votes/decisions on behalf of Parliament and/or representatives), the individual would-be new citizens were given access to the key rules of the EU before they were invited to decide: hence translation was part of a promotional movement. In the 'prehistory' of their membership in the new Europe, all citizens in the (future) new member states were invited to study and to accept their future status within the enlarged framework with the aid of the more than 100,000 legal pages called the *acquis communautaire* (the exact contents of the *acquis* are now part of a standardized procedure, available on the websites of the EU). In the 'jargon' of the EU, both the EU itself and its translators simply used the imported technical term in French as a loan word, and even the BBC has domesticated the concept in English (since the fifth enlargement) as 'The entire body of European laws... [, i.e.] all the treaties, regulations and directives passed by the European institutions as well as judgements laid down by the Court of Justice.' In the jargon of the translation teams, it was obvious that the 100,000 pages were going to be translated into the language of the new citizens, and that accession to the EU was going to be possible only afterwards and – only – on the basis of that requirement (the set of 'requirements' is also mentioned in the contents of the *acquis*). No translation, no membership, no extension. And via this – first – verbal integration process, the various populations were – then – going to be invited to accept or to reject the invitation round while entering/not entering the international community, on the basis of the specific procedure (individual vote or referendum vote in Parliament, etc.) selected by each of the potential member states. Which means no more nor less than the idea and fact that participation in the EU depended on votes – by citizens or Parliament – directly dependent on the translation campaign prepared and worked out for months by the competent services.

The symbolic meaning of such a vote leaves no doubt about the functions fulfilled by translators and translations. The entire set of legal texts being the result of translation, it was – partly – the efficiency of the expected approach to the translation of legal texts that was going to decide about the extension/non-extension of the EU. Before becoming new member states, the Baltic States, Poland, the Czech and Slovak Republic, etc. had to design their future on the basis of the verbal description of their own new society. The very construction of the new society was going to rely on (translated) discourse, which was borrowed from the traditions, from exactly those pages and values that had already been established and canonized by the first partner countries. Experts in translation studies are familiar with the instruction procedure, i.e. with the briefings ('translation briefs', see Nord 1997) given to translators before they really start their job. It is easy to understand, however, that in larger collective (and institutionalized) enterprises such briefing movements are more explicit than in average situations. This was the more obvious within the series of seminars organized by the employer, the EU itself, with the aid of experts. During such seminar sessions as well as during the discussions, some of the most basic rules appeared to be well known, though not really available in writing, in particular the 'invisibility' rule, which is also one of the (unwritten) rules among interpreters: when answering on behalf of his customer, the interpreter is supposed to speak in the I-form ('I did so and so...') instead of making use of indirect speech ('My client says he did so and so...'). To the newly trained (legal) translators of the EU, it is/was recommended not to make translation (too) 'visible' (for the visibility/invisibility concept, see Venuti 1995), hence to produce 'natural' texts, i.e. texts looking like average political and legal instructions in the language of the (new) target country. For any average reader of legal documents, such recommendations and rules ('norms') do indeed sound natural; lawyers and politicians experienced in reading similar documents do know however that in the more innovative (and in the more fashionable or international) chapters of these regulations it may become extremely difficult to avoid looking/sounding 'exotic', i.e. to leave the features of imported discourse (and certain languages, e.g. Finnish and Hungarian, have structural features where it is more complicated to conceal the foreign origins of imported documents). Whether easy or not, whether applied in a consistent way or not, such an approach is called a 'domesticating' approach or strategy: its first purpose is to offer the various basic rules, which are supposed to be more or less innovative, as 'normal' and familiar discourse, if not as rules and constraints that avoid inspiring exotic feelings in the target audience. Too many new rules offered without any acculturation might indeed work like a threat. As many translators know, translations are not supposed to read like...translations, they are supposed to be compatible with the illusion(!) of feeling at home and at ease.

The ambiguities of any (legal) translation are known, generally speaking, to translation scholars and often also to the translators themselves (who may however concentrate on the prospective position and use of their texts). Whatever the central(ized) instructions may be, the reception process is never simple, it is never static; it may change after several months or years, often under the impact of particular cultural or linguistic (or political) events. By definition, the reception and perception process always has a good chance of being different from country/language to country/language, and some particular chapters or concepts or set of documents may influence the entire integration process.

As such, integration processes in society, hence also in texts or discourse, are not an unknown problem in contemporary societies; on the contrary, they are not at all specific to discourse, but they are well known from discursive situations (e.g. in the case of features in pronunciation, or in the use of foreign words). In political and social environments or situations, they can generate strong reactions on behalf of our West European societies. And for just such reasons, legal (translated) texts distributed by the EU are politically delicate almost by definition. The integration of such texts is/was just one sensitive moment in a long process of social and political change: whether or not politicians and/or citizens were going to answer 'yes' or 'no', – that was the challenge, directly linked with the rhetorics of persuasion. The number of loan words, and English or 'franglais'-looking concepts, as such, have influenced the position of texts and readers in the European political climate. By definition, it is no shame either for translators or for politicians to sound too English, too American or too German from the moment the target reader is unaware of it, or from the moment the reader is not worried. The success of such a political (translated) communication has to do with persuasion and credibility, to the extent that EU style, language, acronyms and terminology may become familiar, part of everyday jargon. Almost every citizen is aware of the foreign roots of the many documents and messages that the EU will distribute. How exactly particular features of this material give hints of particular ideas or values or words, that is the question. As has been established by translation scholars, values and value systems are inevitably but often unconsciously related with translations and with the reshuffling of value systems. In the case of the EU, such shifts in terms of value systems are the more pervasive since they are part of multilateral planning, even part of globalization, in this case on behalf of Western Europe rather than North America: for the future members of the fifth enlargement, who had experienced contact with foreign military powers since the Second World War, the language(s) of the new international partners could hardly appear as an innocent value system.

This kind of consideration is not often linked with translation, and certainly not with legal translation, not even in the case of research (as even the most sophisticated *Handbuch der Übersetzungswissenschaft* tends to indicate: see Gémar 2004; see also the works by Sarcevič): even within translation studies, 'legal translation' still tends to focus on the questions asked by the translator ('How to… translate well/efficiently?') rather than on the position that will be given now or later or by certain groups within the entire body of legal texts, within a given political or linguistic community. In such terms, translation is envisaged from the point of view of a future task to be fulfilled ('How should/can I translate?' 'Is this word translated correctly?' etc.). However, from the point of view of politics, of culture, in terms of language evolution and in terms of communication, the massive transfer of texts, rules and terminology has been envisaged as a pervasive and organized movement of know-how from a limited number of countries and people (the Brussels 'Eurocrats') into the Central European belt with its post-communist world view. Translation is a technical service, indeed, but it is also and inevitably much more, it is – in the case of the EU – also a political, a social and a cultural large-scale operation.

From this perspective, whatever the intentions and intentionality of the political managers and their staff may be/have been, translation is one of the decisive keys to the construction of a new social, cultural, political, cultural, maybe even religious world. To the extent that translation, and also the whens, whys and hows of translation are concerned, it is one of the parameters that decides whether whole populations will/will not become part of a new world. It is one of the institutional and strategic elements that is supposed to condition the response towards the question of belonging to a new society. Legal translation, at least in this case, is leading far beyond – just – legal issues. It is (also) about identity, about entering a new world, first of all in terms of discourse, then (later) in terms of rights and commitments.

5.7 Future, past and present in the legal landscapes

It has been said and written time and again that the fifth enlargement of the EU was by far the most impressive one. Which implies that not all enlargement processes within the EU have had exactly the same features within the realm of legislation and discourse as the fifth one.

However, the approach to language and translation within the EU has developed step by step, and the basic rules have been established much earlier, and maintained up to the present. The approach described has obvious institutional and pre-planned features. Which means that the translation of legal and organizational discourse is part of the construction of the new EU society. This is less the case when isolated documents are under observation: it is more the case, by definition, from the moment the enormous *acquis communautaire* is at stake.

There is no reason, however, for assuming that, from the perspective of the target audiences, only the EU is involved in this internationalization process of legal discourse. International organizational rules established and disseminated by the United Nations, Unesco or the World Trade Organization seem not to function much differently.

The main difference is that the managers or decision makers as well as their translators, the languages involved (and the basic language policy: cf. Fishman 1993) are not (exactly) the same, hence the institutionalization process is not identical with the integration processes within the EU. From the moment the dissemination of communication is worked out on the basis of a 'lingua franca' policy (in English, in a high percentage of cases), the underlying mechanisms are not fundamentally different: they imply the progressive integration of people and their discourse into other/new communities. Such integration movements may take place in English, in the well-known lingua franca. But to become legal within a given community/nation, translation will be required.

In parallel with the extension of (legal) texts within the EU and other communities, international business communities are spreading out their uninterrupted flow of messages via different channels, partly via the Internet, partly within the so-called localization industries. Specific organizations distribute such commercial messages in more than say 7000 languages. In principle, the dissemination of legal texts by the EU and other international organizations has nothing to do with the continuous flow of business communication. The question is, however, to what extent the perception of the target groups really distinguishes between the various channels of international communication. The general environment may have its impact on the legal body of texts issued by Brussels and supported by national governments. And translators, in their translation process as well as in the instructions they are supposed to assimilate, may very well be aware of contemporary internationalization processes.

5.8 Back to the past: legal discourse in traditional societies

The description of the EU text strategy within the planning of extension may look like one of the patterns of internationalization and globalization. To what extent would it teach us anything about the distribution of legal discourse (and terminology and models) in the past? To what extent was the establishment of legal traditions, the canonization of the nation state constitutions linked with similar patterns?

One of the first distinctions to be made has to do with size, with small-scale v. large-scale planning: bilingual (Belgium, Canada) or multilingual (Switzerland, South Africa) countries do not rely on large-scale institutional networks, hence the premeditation of translation planning has less chance of seeming too pervasive. In the case of South Africa, however, the movement really started in the Mandela era, and was supported by external know-how (including the bilingual/multilingual Belgian one). It was much earlier, in the nineteenth century, that Belgium itself was obliged by political pressure to start up its translation movement with some urgency, and the Dutch version of the Belgian legislation exhibits many ideological features that remind us of... recent EU experiences, especially because of its heavy francophone linguistic infrastructure. For Belgian citizens, the origins of the initiative had clear political colours: when using the Dutch version of the Belgian constitution, Flemish users/citizens were (and are) almost obliged to know French (legal terminology and idioms) in order to understand the legislation in their mother tongue. Lawyers and the Flemish institutions become part of the Belgian traditions simply while using their constitution in Dutch: these texts require linguistic competence that citizens from the Netherlands can hardly ever acquire. The Dutch version of the Belgian constitution is – also – a strategic tool of Belgian citizenship: non-Belgians are excluded, Flemish speakers on the other hand would be more or less in trouble when ignoring this kind of discourse, or they need to pay lawyers to translate their own legal language into their everyday speech. Such rules apply in particular to the institutional terminology (the concept 'federal' is used in the German version of the Belgian constitution, but it has no institutional status in the German used in Germany). And almost by definition, they are also one of the requirements of the German legislation in Belgium, where key concepts (related to federalization, 'communities'/*Gemeinschaft*, etc.) are incompatible with the language used beyond the German border.

Internationalization was also part of the distribution of the *Code Napoléon*, hence of legal discourse as such, long before the EU developed new legal networks. This is why lawyers and experts in legal administration have needed Latin for centuries, not just in order to understand Latin texts from the Middle Ages, but first of all in order to understand legal traditions in their (various) mother tongues. One of the consequences was that their own mother tongue was less developed in its legal traditions. After all, some of the warnings against the language of Eurocrats in the twentieth century may be instructive as a basis for understanding of language developments in intellectual areas through the ages in (Western?) Europe: translation has been both an instrument leading into new territories of national discourse all over Europe; on the other hand it has also reduced such extension movements while keeping visible the common origins of many legal traditions. And such traditions are not even confined to the Old Continent.

5.9 Legal colonization cultures and beyond

On the basis of their national history from the nineteenth and twentieth centuries, Belgian intellectuals may have a sufficient experience in legal matters to hypothesize how legal traditions were established in Congo/Zaïre during those times: the various phases in the development of the Flemish constitution suggest patterns for the analysis of how the legal formulation in Congo may have started and developed somewhere in the twentieth century. And bilingualism is probably one of the first paradoxes of constitutions all over Africa: the predominantly monolingual legal model of Western Europe seems to have exported itself as a mainly bilingual/multilingual model into Africa, while becoming for example one of the platforms for post-apartheid South Africa.

The very fact that constitutions in Africa are to a large extent the result of translations is not a real paradox from the European point of view, since the Roman and the *Code Napoléon* substrate could be simply accepted as one of the (covert) layers in the dissemination of European legislation. In the previous traditions, the translation model was less visible, it was not displayed on the left of the Code books, but the various users could hardly become familiar with the actual legislation without reading the foreign origins of their *own* laws through and within their modern texts: translation was not fully invisible, not even in the monolingual traditions of legislation.

The systematic investigation of some – in Europe – well-known areas of Africa deserves to be considered as test cases for our language–law investigation. As Jean-Baptiste Bigirimina (Chapter 11 this volume) demonstrates in his panoramic presentation of the Burundi constitutions during the twentieth century, translation is and has been the heart of the matter since the very beginning of any constitutional effort in that country. And the very first step was anything but canonical in European terms, since it was bilingual – as in Belgium – in French and…Dutch: the text tradition was treated as it would have been in a Belgian province. At least until 1960–61. Sticking to the model of the bilingual constitution from then on – as in Belgium – Burundi also adopted a very typical feature of West European bilingual writing while displaying its own language(s) – Kirundi – on the left and while 'leaving' the so-called translation on the right: in fact it is obvious that the legal translations had been worked out the other way round, i.e. from right to left rather than from left to right. But the deepest colonial trend in the various constitutions published in the Burundi bulletin is the play with the patchwork of legal models: almost all articles and items have been translated, either from the Zaïre/Congo model, hence also indirectly from the Belgian model, or from the Brazzaville model in the other (French) Congo across the river. To the extent that the final result, i.e. the Burundi constitution, is as much the result of negative decisions against various constitutional models as it is of a positive selection from actual neighbour models: the new constitution is the result of positive and negative selection processes, within a limited repertoire of models.

5.10 The chicken and the egg

The basic lesson to be deduced from an analysis of legal discourse as translated discourse may be a remarkable illustration of Benedict Anderson's *Imagined Communities* (Anderson 1983). Instead of being the reflection of cultural, legal and institutional autonomy, constitutions are one of the critical moments in the institutionalization (Anderson calls it *vernacularization*) of autonomy with the aid of a selection of imported discourses, fragments and models.

One of the paradoxes of nationalism, according to its historians, is its international origin(s): international and intercultural traditions have helped shape the various national traditions and nation states – and vice versa. International traditions are much older than national ones, and this is why the establishment of particular national traditions deserves to be envisaged as vernacularization. It is obvious that both movements, internationalization and vernacularization, are heavily indebted to translation and to particular translation strategies. How exactly, on the basis of what kind of selection processes and models, that is what specific historiographical ('descriptive') research needs to establish. But it would be difficult to assume that the 'making of the nation' and its symbolic cultural goods could be transparent without an analysis of the verbal interactions with neighbouring and fostering systems. It is our feeling that the contribution of translated discourse to the planning and construction of societies in the past and present has so far been greatly underestimated by interdisciplinary research on the dynamics of cultures.

Notes

1. Our basic concepts on translation and translation studies refer to Frank et al. (2004), the journal *Target*, key books such as Toury (1980, 1985), where the concept 'descriptive translation studies' is central, and Hermans (1985, 1999).
2. See Lambert (forthcoming). Sociolinguistics and pragmatics tend systematically to pay attention, nowadays, to the globalization process, but so far questions such as translation tend to be further excluded from their object of study.

Part II

Handling Legal Discourse in the Modern World

6
Translation at the Court of Justice of the European Communities

*Karen McAuliffe**

6.1 Introduction: the multilingual nature of EU law

While other international organizations appear to function smoothly using only a few official languages,[1] the EU today uses 20.[2] There are numerous historical and political reasons for this multilingualism. It must be remembered that the institutions of the European Community were created in the aftermath of the Second World War. The founders of the Community were motivated by a desire to avoid such a tragedy ever reoccurring. This was a Community that would peacefully unite the peoples of Western Europe (or at least their states' economies), which in the past were so often in conflict. (Perhaps more importantly, the founders of the Community were also motivated by 'une certaine idée de l'Europe' of a federal nature.) Thus, the very first regulation of the European Council concerned the linguistic regime of the European Economic Community and stipulated in its first article that the official and working languages of the institutions of the Community would be German, French, Italian and Dutch – four languages covering the six founder members of the Community.[3] Those four languages remained the only languages of the Community until 1972; however, that figure has grown, and, as noted, there are today 20 official languages of the EU.

In recent years 'language in the European Union' has become something of a hot topic, gaining ever more coverage in the press and other media throughout Europe and the rest of the world (especially in relation to the onward march of English as a lingua franca for the EU).[4] Yet, such coverage rarely, if ever, stretches to an in-depth discussion of law and language in the EU; and the issue of translation is generally reported from an economic point of view, focusing on the cost and logistical problems associated with producing translations of various EU documents.

However, the multilingual nature of EU law is often highlighted by academics and practitioners, in particular when discrepancies between language versions of EU legislation arise. Numerous cases have been brought before the Court of Justice as a result of discrepancies or ambiguities between different language versions of EU legislation, and many commentators have seized those opportunities to liken the EU to a modern-day 'tower of Babel'. Each new enlargement of the Union brings with it a flurry of publications concerning law and language in the EU (the accession of ten new countries – and the introduction of nine new official languages – in 2004 was cause for the greatest concern and interest in the issue of law and language in the EU to date – see, for example, Creech (2005); Cunningham (2001: 22); Fidrmuc and Ginsburgh (2004); Harlow (2002: 199); Heutger (2003); Phillipson (2003) and Toscani (2002: 288).

Although the multilingual nature of EU law is frequently criticized by academics and practitioners, there have been few or no substantive studies of the important linguistic element in EU law (most writing focuses on the logistical problems of multilingualism or only very briefly touches on the legal effects of that multilingualism) and its implications for the understanding and application of that law.

Unlike international organizations such as the United Nations or the Council of Europe, whose resolutions are addressed to governments only, the activity of the EU institutions is such that it creates a whole new 'EU law' in the form of regulations, decisions and recommendations, which is applicable in each member state, to each citizen and legal person. As a result, it is necessary for such texts to exist in the national languages of the states concerned, that is, in a language spoken and understood by each citizen to whom they apply. However, much of the 'constitutional law' of the EU is contained not in the founding treaties (which have been described as the European Community's 'constitutional charter'[5]) but in the judicial pronouncements of the Court of Justice of the European Communities.

While much scholarship on language and EU law has focused on the Court of Justice (indeed many such pieces of work are written by members of that court – see, for example, Edward (1995: 539); Jacobs (2003: 297) and Mancini and Keeling (1995: 397)) – it tends mainly to involve questions of language policy and regime, interpretation of multilingual legislation and pragmatic or logistical translation concerns. To date there has been no study that has focused on the fact that the court's judgments, as presented to the outside world, are, for the most part, translations.

6.2 Language regime at the Court of Justice

Article 217 of the Treaty of Rome states:

> The rules governing the languages of the institutions of the Community shall, without prejudice to the provisions contained in the Rules of Procedure of the Court of Justice, be determined by the Council, acting unanimously.

The Council fulfilled its responsibility under that article in the very first regulation that it issued.[6] Article 2 of that regulation firmly establishes the right of citizens to communicate with the European institutions in the language of their own state and puts an obligation on the institutions to answer them in the same language. Article 3 states that:

> Documents which an institution of the Community sends to a Member State or to a person subject to the jurisdiction of a Member State shall be worded in the language of such State.

Article 6 of the Regulation stipulates that Community institutions may determine internal language regulations in respect of specific administrative practices. Doc A3–169/90[7] provides that any such internal guidelines introduced by the institutions must comply with the doctrine of linguistic equality.

While the Court of Justice is subject to the general linguistic guidelines set out in that regulation, under Article 7 it may develop autonomous rules in respect of language use for proceedings. Chapter 6 (Articles 29–31) of the Rules of Procedure of the Court of Justice deals with language use at the court and Chapter 5 (Articles 35–7) of the Rules of Procedure of the Court of First Instance covers language use at that court.[8]

For every action before the Court of Justice and Court of First Instance there is a language of procedure (there are, at present, 21 such languages: the 20 official languages of the EU, and Irish – however, up until now Irish has never been used as the language of procedure in a case and judgments and references for a preliminary ruling are not translated into Irish), which must be used in the written pleadings or observations submitted and for all oral pleadings in the action. The language of procedure of the case must also be used by the court in any correspondence, report or decision addressed to the parties in the case. Only the texts in the language of procedure are authentic.

In direct actions before both courts, the language of procedure is chosen by the applicant. However, where a defendant is a member state or a natural or legal person holding the nationality of a member state, the language of procedure is the official language of that state.

In references for a preliminary ruling the language of procedure is the language of the national court that has made the reference. In appeals, the language of the case is that which was used before the Court of First Instance.[9]

Member states are entitled to use their own language in their written statements and observations and oral pleadings when they intervene in a direct action or participate in preliminary reference procedures.

Unlike the other EU institutions the court operates using a single internal working language – French.[10] The Rules of Procedure provide that a judge or advocate-general may request the translation of any document into the language of his choice.[11] However, the members have been obliged to forgo that possibility in order not to increase the workload of the translation service.

Clearly then, translation plays a significant role in the working of the Court of Justice and it is not difficult to imagine how the translation burden can affect the court's output.

6.3 Lawyer-linguists at the Court of Justice

Article 22 of the Rules of Procedure of the Court of Justice states:

> The Court shall set up a translating service staffed by experts with adequate legal training and a thorough knowledge of several official languages of the Court.

The Translation Directorate of the Court of Justice of the European Communities is the largest directorate within the court, employing 788 people – almost half of the entire staff of the court. The directorate is managed by a director, with the assistance of his secretariat and two deputy directors (who share responsibility for the language divisions between them). Directly under the director is the 'Organization and Methods' department, which is basically a development section, responsible for training and information; organization and methods of work; development of new translation/management tools, and so on. There is a separate translation division for each of the 20 official languages.[12] As well as those language divisions there is also a General Services division, which is responsible for the management and planning of individual translations at the court (distribution of work, etc.); textual analysis; creation of matrices; documentary and terminology research; management of the archives; provision of background documents for lawyer-linguists and management of freelance work. Of the translation directorate's current 788 staff, 553 are *lawyer-linguists* (the remainder being made up of administrative staff and managers of the various divisions). Lawyer-linguists are responsible for the translation of the judgments of the Court of Justice as well as all of the various other internal, outgoing, and documents received by the court.[13] There is no specific training available or vocational course that must be followed in order to qualify as a lawyer-linguist. To obtain such a position in the court's translation directorate one must pass a 'competition',[14] which consists of a written translation exam (translation of legal texts from two foreign languages chosen by the candidate into his/her mother tongue[15]) followed by an 'oral examination' or interview. As a result of the rather vague language used in Article 22 of the Rules of Procedure, the criteria for lawyer-linguists at the Court of Justice are not set in stone and can vary from competition to competition. Candidates for a competition for lawyer-linguists at the Court of Justice are typically required to possess a perfect command of their mother tongue and an in-depth knowledge of at least two other official Community languages. The definition of 'adequate legal training', for the purposes of such competitions has, however, changed over the years. Nowadays, in order to qualify for a competition, candidates are usually required to hold a law degree awarded in the state or states the languages of which is that for which the recruitment is organized and, generally, to have two years' professional experience.[16] In the past the criteria have included holding a degree 'with a law component' or having a 'professional legal qualification'.

To the outsider it must seem that the role of the lawyer-linguist is purely translation or translation-related; however, upon closer analysis it becomes apparent that the role of lawyer-linguist is far more complex and difficult to define than that. In order to be able to translate legal concepts from one language to another, lawyer-linguists need a comprehensive knowledge not only of their own legal systems but also the legal systems of other member states, as well as a thorough understanding of the law of the EU and the jurisprudence of the Court of Justice. They are responsible for dealing with legal issues that may arise because of *linguistic* ambiguities in texts. In short, the work of a lawyer-linguist is much more than translation – it is the manipulation of the law as language and language as law.

While dealing with the classic problems of translation on a daily basis, the translators at the Court of Justice also appear to be trying to balance a dual professional identity – that of lawyer *and* linguist. It is the struggle to successfully merge those two professions that sets those who work in the court's translation service apart from both lawyers and translators.

Interestingly, all of the lawyer-linguists interviewed for the present research were quick to disassociate themselves from the profession of translating – even those who described themselves as translators immediately qualified their statement by pointing out that as translators of judicial texts, with law degrees, they are 'much more than simply translators'; others claim that they are lawyers who work exclusively with a particular sphere of law. All insist that they could not do the job without legal training and that 'that sets us apart from "mere" translators'. The role of lawyer-linguist requires expertise in law *and* expertise in languages, and the majority of lawyer-linguists at the Court of Justice find it very satisfying to be able to 'tie up' their interest in law and their love of languages. As one Italian put it: '... my job at the Court of Justice is the perfect synthesis of a lawyer and a linguist'.However, in spite of such job satisfaction, there is an undercurrent of feeling misunderstood and sometimes underappreciated on the part of lawyer-linguists at the Court of Justice of the European Communities.

Within the legal community, and indeed in general society, a number of negative attitudes towards translation prevail (see Berglund 1990: 145; Kaseva 2000: 72). The lawyer-linguists at the Court of Justice are quite defensive about their profession and seem to feel that they must continuously justify their role. This may be due to their perception of negative attitudes within that institution towards the importance of their work and indeed towards their profession.[17] In spite of their relatively high salary scales, there is a feeling among the lawyer-linguists that they are at one of the lowest levels within the hierarchy of the Court of Justice. The majority feel that their work is underappreciated, in particular by the judges and advocate generals and their staff. Many lawyer-linguists feel that those who draft the judgments and advocate generals' opinions do not appear to appreciate the complexity of their task and seem to think of translation merely as part of the administration process, forgetting that while they may be drafting the word of law, that word of law only becomes so through translation. Some feel that translation is often considered to be 'nothing more than typing with dictionaries'! During the course of my interviews, countless anecdotes were recounted in which lawyer-linguists recalled brusque statements made in speeches by judges and advocate generals, irate memorandums exchanged between judges and heads of various language divisions within the translation directorate and offhand comments made by judges and their staff at various functions or informal occasions, concerning the lawyer-linguists' work – including one particular comment by a judge who stated: 'I can't understand why a translator translates only seven pages a day when I can read more than one hundred pages a day'!

At best the lawyer-linguists at the Court of Justice feel invisible to the rest of the court. They feel that they are seen as a 'translation machine' and that the judges and advocate generals and their staff probably only think about translation when it goes wrong.[18]

Such contradictions, experienced by the lawyer-linguists in their daily working lives, point to the paradox that is the very essence of their role: the reconciliation of the notions of 'law' and 'translation'. It is generally accepted that translation of any kind, including legal translation, involves some measure of approximation (see Šarčević 1997). This concept of approximation in translation, however, does not sit easily with traditional notions of law – an authoritative force, necessarily uniform throughout the jurisdiction within which it applies, in particular in the European legal order where the principle of uniformity has formed the basis for the most important doctrines of EU law introduced by the Court of Justice.

6.4 EU law as approximation

The majority of those working in the multilingual, multicultural environment of the Court of Justice of the European Communities are very much aware that there is always some approximation involved in translation; and they all acknowledge that approximation exists in legal translation in general and at the Court of Justice in particular:

> Translation is not a precise science – since legal concepts in various legal systems differ, it's not easy to find an exact translation that conveys the context;
>
> Of course there is approximation in translation – and that approximation increases many-fold in the Court of Justice – the final judgments delivered by the Court have gone through many different permutations of translation out of and into various languages.

Some approximations between different language versions of EU legal instruments and Court of Justice judgments cannot be avoided. For example, where words or concepts exist in a number of different languages but do not necessarily have the same meaning in each language because of differences between legal systems (see further McAuliffe 2006a). Other language and translation problems can be caused as a result of poor drafting by lawyers who must work in a language that is not their mother tongue (since the working language of the court is French – see above), or from a failure by such lawyers to use clear, uncomplicated language.[19] Approximation in translation at the Court of Justice can also arise from the fact that those who draft judgments, etc. are often constrained by the wording of EU legislation from which they cannot derogate.

Thus, approximation is inherent in EU law in general and at the Court of Justice of the European Communities in particular. How then can the 'uniform application' of EU law be ensured? How can the jurisprudence of the Court of Justice be, on the one hand, multilingual (and therefore subject to the approximations of translation) but on the other hand uniformly applied throughout the EU?

It must be remembered that the production of the jurisprudence of the Court of Justice of the European Communities involves much more than the application of the relevant law(s) to a given situation: it involves the drafting of texts (in a language which is not necessarily the mother tongue of the person drafting such texts), relying on multilingual law and other translated sources, which are subsequently translated into up to 19 other languages. The unique situational factors in the production of that jurisprudence have led to a *hybridization* of law and language. While it is accepted that there is approximation involved in translation and thus in EU law, it is also accepted that those who use that law will acknowledge that exact transpositions of concepts are impossible to achieve, yet will understand the 'EU meaning' of those concepts – that is, EU law is, quite simply, a *new* legal language. That new legal language was, famously, expressly acknowledged by the Court of Justice in CILFIT, in which the court stated that:

> ...even where the different language versions [of EU legislation] are entirely in accord with one another ...Community law uses terminology which is peculiar to it. Furthermore, it must be emphasized that legal concepts do not necessarily have the same meaning in Community law and in the law of the various Member States.[20]

It seems that the Court of Justice functions in the way that it does, producing case law in 20 different languages to be 'uniformly' applied in 25 different member states, quite simply because the actors within that court, in particular the lawyer-linguists, are aware that EU law is a legal system built from approximations of law and language from different legal cultures and different legal languages, which come together to form a new supranational legal system with its own language.

However, during the course of my fieldwork for the present research, I discovered that the notion of concepts being created in the language of the case law of the Court of Justice and subsequently being 'fed back' into a hybrid language of EU law does not always work well in practice. In most cases the language or phrasing used is drawn from the legal language of a particular member state. Difficulties arise where concepts are then to have a distinct 'EU meaning' – this can even lead to incorrect translations being used throughout proceedings before the court. One such example can be seen in the order of the Court of First Instance of 3 June 1997 in Case T-60/96.[21]

This case concerned an application for the annulment of certain Commission decisions refusing authorization by a number of EU member states to take protective measures with regard to Spanish pharmaceutical products. The language of the case (that is, the authentic version of the order) was English. According to the normal procedure of the Court of First Instance, the order in question was drafted in French and subsequently translated into the other EU official languages. Paragraph 44 of that order referred to 'un droit subjectif préexistant des titulaires des brevets en cause'. However, 'un droit subjectif' is a legal concept that exists in civil law jurisdictions but not in EU common law jurisdictions and thus has no equivalent in English (the authentic language of the order in question). This problem was brought to the attention of the judges at the Court of First Instance who deliberated over it for a considerable period of time and eventually decided that the phrase should be changed and that, in English, it should refer simply to 'a pre-existing right of the patent holder'. However, it appears that the original French language version of that order was never amended and, to this day, refers to 'un droit subjectif'. The danger in this case, according to those who consider approximation in translation to be a problem for EU law, is that, since only the English language version of the order was amended, the right referred to in that order could be understood differently in member states with common law legal orders than in member states with civil law legal orders, thereby potentially jeopardizing the 'uniform application' of EU law. While the actors within the small legal community of the European institutions are aware that the language of EU law is a multilingual one, based on compromise and approximation, there can be no guarantee that everybody dealing with EU law in each member state will be aware of this. The question thus remains as to whether there can really be 'uniform application' of EU law. As one advocate general stated:

> ... even internally in the Court, from the introduction of a case to its closure with the delivery of the judgment, concepts, ideas and phrases go through a kind of 'Chinese whispers' effect and emerge in a slightly different form or as an approximation of the original issue or question. That judgment is then translated into [20] different languages, to be interpreted within [25] different legal orders – discrepancies in the application of EU law are therefore almost unavoidable...

That issue recently arose in a series of cases before the Competition Appeal Tribunal in the UK[22] (the replica sports kit cases) in which the applicants sought to rely on the wording of the English language judgment of the Court of First Instance in Case T-25/95,[23] which sets out the requirements for a concerted practice. Paragraph 1852 of the English language version of that judgment states:

> In order to prove that there has been a concerted practice, it is not necessary to show that the competitor in question has formally undertaken, in respect of one or several others, to adopt a particular course of conduct or that the competitors have colluded over their future conduct on the market. It is sufficient that by its statement of intention the competitor should have eliminated, or at the very least, substantially reduced uncertainty as to the conduct *to expect of the other* on the market (my emphasis).

However, if one considers the French language version (that is, the original judgment drafted), which states:

> Il suffit que, à travers sa déclaration d'intention, le concurrent ait éliminé ou à tout le moins substantiellement réduit l'incertitude quant au comportement *à attendre de sa part* sur le marché (my emphasis).

it seems that, for a concerted practice to exist, it is sufficient that two competitors (A and B) meet and that A receives information about B's likely conduct; whereas the English language version implies that A has to indicate his own conduct to B.[24] That case was relatively unusual in that there were nine languages of the case and therefore nine equally authentic language versions of the judgment (Spanish, Danish, German, Greek, English, French, Italian, Dutch and Portuguese). As a result, the Competition Appeal Tribunal compared four of those language versions of the judgment (French, German, Italian and Spanish) and concluded that they were indeed 'translated slightly differently' from the English language version,[25] the correct rendering of which should be:

> In order to prove that there has been a concerted practice, it is not ... necessary to show that the competitor in question has formally undertaken, in respect of one or several others, to adopt a particular course of conduct or that the competitors have colluded over their future conduct on the market ... It is sufficient that, by its statement of intention, the competitor should have eliminated or at the very least, substantially reduced uncertainty as to the conduct [on the market to be expected on his part][26] (in other words, the Competition Appeal Tribunal agreed with the respondent that the French language version was correct).

Therefore, it appears that discrepancies and approximations in translation at the Court of Justice can indeed have consequences for the application of EU law at a member state level. In the latter example there were a number of authentic language versions of the judgment in question; however, would the ruling of the Competition Appeal Tribunal have been any different had the English language version of Case T-25/95 been the only authentic version of that judgment? How realistic is it to expect member state courts and tribunals to compare up to 20 different language versions of a Court of Justice judgment before interpreting that judgment, in particular where that court officially declares only one of those language versions authentic?[27]

6.5 Conclusion: the impact of the 2004 enlargement

May 2004 saw the greatest increase in membership of the EU to date. Ten new member states joined the 'club' of 15, bringing the total number of member states to 25 and the population of the Union to almost half a billion. One of the more practical consequences of that enlargement was that each institution of the EU had to recruit a significant number of administrators, lawyers, interpreters, translators and other professional and general staff from the new member states. For the Court of Justice this meant a huge influx of people to staff new divisions in the research and documentation and press and information services, 20 new judges' *cabinets* (ten at the Court of Justice and ten at the Court of First Instance) and nine new language divisions in the translation service, as well as a number of administrators, etc. working in various other parts of the court. Preparation for the May 2004 enlargement at the Court of Justice began as far back as the late 1990s. The introduction of such a large number of 'new' official languages was considered the most significant aspect of that enlargement for the court and so the initial focus was on training lawyer-linguists in those languages. Later on, the logistical problems of enlargement, such as space and management policy, became more relevant. In 2002 the decision was made to introduce, on enlargement, a 'pivot-translation' system alongside the direct translation system already in use (see further McAuliffe 2006a). That pivot translation system has been in use at the court since May 2004 and is actually a mixed translation system – where possible direct translation is used instead of translation through a 'pivot language'. There are five 'pivot languages': French, English, German, Spanish and Italian. Because French is the working language of the court, the French translation division provides translation from all of the 'new' official languages while each of the other four pivot language divisions are 'partnered' with two 'new' official languages[28] (Maltese has not been assigned to a pivot language division – since English is Malta's second official language, it is assumed that the Maltese lawyer-linguists are able to provide English translations of documents drafted in Maltese).[29]

With such dramatic changes in the structure and sheer size of the Court of Justice, the question that immediately arose was whether the May 2004 enlargement would represent a qualitative or merely a quantitative change in the functioning of that institution: would the nine 'new' languages ultimately be absorbed into the existing multilingual working methods at the court? Or would the introduction of those nine new official languages and ten new cultures mark a shift in the dynamics of the linguistic regime itself? Would it be a case of more meaning less, in the sense that the incapacity of the system to cope meaningfully with 20 languages would lead to a progressively greater de facto privileging of one, two or a few of those languages?

Before the accession to the EU of Austria, Finland and Sweden in 1995, a 'mild panic' was felt throughout the Court of Justice and in particular within the translation directorate. That panic is reflected in a number of articles that appeared around that time, in which it was speculated that the translation directorate of the court (or indeed those of the Commission and Parliament) would not be able to cope with the addition of a further two new official languages and that the language regime of the court would have to be significantly changed (see, for example, Barents 1997: 49; Coulmas 1991; Haarmann 1991; Koch 1991; Usher 1998: 222). In fact, the translation directorate 'absorbed the new languages with minimal fuss or problems' (no doubt aided by the fact that there was a 'gap' of approximately two years between those states joining the EU and actually bringing cases before the Court of Justice; as well as the fact that, with that accession, a de facto system of pivot translation began to be used at the court since it was extremely difficult to find Finnish and Swedish lawyer-linguists capable of translating from all of the other official languages of the EU). However, that feeling of mild panic experienced within the Court of Justice before the 1995 enlargement of the EU seems to have been a mere drop in the ocean in comparison with the general panic that was swelling within that court prior to the most recent EU enlargement. The accession of ten new states to the EU would not only require skilled management from a logistical point of view, but would also introduce to the court new cultures and legal traditions that would necessarily change the dynamics of that institution. Whether they felt that the only problems enlargement would bring would be logistical:

> ...it will be almost impossible to find enough people in the accession states qualified and with the linguistic abilities to come and work in the [EU] institutions ... even if that isn't a problem it will be extremely difficult to organize such a huge expansion from the point of view of management...;

or that the main problems would be linguistic and would have consequences for the application of EU law:

> the inherent problem with enlargement for the Court is a linguistic one ... there is the danger that, as a result of the 'Chinese whispers' that will increase with pivot translation, there will be discrepancies and differences between language versions of judgments, which could then be applied differently in various Member States;

all were agreed that 'enlargement will change the way that the Court works'. One lawyer-linguist even described the forthcoming enlargement in terms of chaos theory: '... everything will become so awful that it will all explode and then, only in the aftermath, a solution will be found!'

The reality, however, was far from such predicted chaos. Recruiting lawyer-linguists and other staff from the new member states was easier than had been anticipated,[30] judges appointed from the new member states have, for the most part, a good working knowledge of the

French language, and so on. On top of such factors, as a result of the amendment of the court's Rules of Procedure, significant changes have been made to the working methods of the court[31] and there has been a considerable reduction in the amount of pages published (and translated) in the European Court Reports. The pivot translation system has not, as yet, caused particular problems – although it remains a little early to tell just how successful that system will be.

One change that has been noticeable has been the use of language in day-to-day life at the court. While French remains the sole working language, it is now much more common to hear English than it is to hear French used in the corridors and canteens of that institution. In-house training seminars and programmes are now largely held in English rather than in French. Also, a number of judges and their staff admit to having recourse to English in order to discuss cases with colleagues (officially such discussions are held in French and the secret deliberations of judges continue to be conducted in French).

It remains far too early to notice any major changes in the dynamics and working of the Court of Justice as a result of the May 2004 enlargement – the changes so far have only been incremental. Nor is the new cohort of staff at the court going to have any major impact in the very near future. However, the changes in the use of language at the lower levels within that court are interesting to note, particularly in the light of the increasing outside awareness of the way that French is challenged in the other European institutions. Are we seeing the beginnings of a de facto privileging of the English language at the Court of Justice? And if so, is that a step towards a more significant change in the use of language within that institution? In 2007 Bulgaria and Romania joined the EU, adding a further two languages to the list of official EU languages – thereby doubling the number of official EU languages in the space of three years. The question of whether enlargement represents merely a quantitative change or a qualitative one for the production of EU jurisprudence remains; and it will be interesting to discover whether doubling the number of official languages will have any implications for the way in which EU law works – can an infinite number of languages continue to be absorbed by the language regime of the Court of Justice?

Notes

* This chapter (written in 2006) is based on the results of periods of participant observation at the Court of Justice of the European Communities undertaken in 2003, 2004 and 2005 as part of fieldwork research for my PhD thesis (2006);

all comments/criticisms are welcome (k.mcauliffe@exeter.ac.uk). Unless otherwise indicated all quotes are taken from interviews with members of the court, their *référendaires* or with lawyer-linguists at that court.

I would like to thank Dr Robert Harmsen of the Queen's University of Belfast for his support and valuable comments. I would also like to thank my former colleagues at the Court of Justice in Luxembourg for their assistance with this research, in particular Mr Alfredo Calot-Escobar and Ms Susan Wright.

Any errors are mine alone.

1. For example, the United Nations uses six (Arabic, Chinese, English, French, Russian and Spanish); NATO, with 26 members and the Council of Europe, with a current membership of 46, use only two languages – English and French; EFTA uses only English, a foreign language for all four of its members.
2. These are, in English alphabetical order: Czech, Danish, Dutch, English, Estonian, Finnish, French, German, Greek, Hungarian, Italian, Latvian, Lithuanian, Maltese, Polish, Portuguese, Slovakian, Slovenian, Spanish and Swedish. The official order of these languages is to list them according to the way they are spelt in their own language. Maltese is an official language of the EU; however, because of the lack of qualified translators of the Maltese mother tongue, the Council has adopted a 'partial derogation' whereby not all acts of the EU institutions (including judgments of the Court of Justice) will be drafted or translated in the Maltese language (Council Regulation (EC) No 930/2004 of 1 May 2004 on temporary derogation measures relating to the drafting in Maltese of the acts of the institutions of the European Union). After a transitional period of three years this derogation will be reviewed. Until June 2005 Irish was regarded as an official language only where primary legislation (that is, the treaties) were concerned, however, on 13 June 2005 Irish was granted full status of an official language of the European Union – this came into effect on 1 January 2007, with a partial derogation in place whereby only key legislation must be translated into Irish. After a transitional period of four years, this derogation, known as the 'Maltese Derogation', will be reviewed.
3. EEC Council Regulation No 1/58 determining the languages to be used by the European Economic Community (JO 17, 06/10/1958, pp. 385–386; English Special Edition: Series I Chapter 1952–58, p. 59).
4. *Le Monde* in France, *La Gazzetta di Mantova* in Italy and *The Economist* in the UK are only a few of the European newspapers that regularly publish articles on EU language policy, the use of language in EU institutions, the status of minority languages and the rise of English within the EU, etc.
5. Case 294/83 *Parti Ecologiste 'Les Verts'* v. *European Parliament* [1986] ECR 1339.
6. See *supra*, note 3.
7. OJ C 19 28/01/1991, p. 42.
8. Any amendment to those Rules of Procedure requires the unanimous approval of the Council. See Arts 225a and 245 EC.
9. Likewise, in appeals to the Court of First Instance from the new Civil Service Tribunal the language of procedure is that which was used before the Civil Service Tribunal.

10. Note: Art. 9(5) of the Rules of Procedure of the Court of Justice and Art. 35(5) of the Rules of Procedure of the Court of First Instance state that:

    > The President of the Court and the Presidents of Chambers in conducting oral proceedings, the Judge Rapporteur both in his preliminary report and in his report for the Hearing, Judges and Advocates General in putting questions and Advocates General in delivering their opinions may use one of the [official] languages other than the language of the case

    – in practice the language used is French.
11. See Art. 30 of the Rules of Procedure of the Court of Justice and Article 36 of the Rules of Procedure of the Court of First Instance.
12. There is no need for an Irish language translation division, since Irish has never been used in submissions before the Court of Justice. Whether this will change with the change in status of the Irish language (see *supra,* note 1) remains to be seen.
13. Sometimes, owing to time pressures, the press and information division of the Court of Justice will produce their own translations of press releases, notices, website information, and so on.
14. The court, through the European Personnel Selection Office (EPSO), organizes open competitions at regular intervals in accordance with the needs of each language division. The competition notices are published in the *Official Journal of the European Communities*. The conditions governing each competition tend to be roughly the same, but may be adjusted to take account of the specific needs of the division concerned. Such adjustments principally concern the age and linguistic knowledge of the candidates.
15. These translations must be done without dictionaries. Candidates may sometimes sit an optional test involving translation from a third language.
16. It is not clear whether this refers to translating experience or other professional experience. From various interviews with lawyer-linguists and my own participant observation, however, it appears that prior translating experience is not necessarily a prerequisite for the job of lawyer-linguist at the Court of Justice.
17. Whether or not such attitudes are actually present within the court is irrelevant since, if the lawyer-linguists believe that they are, the consequences will be the same nonetheless.
18. From interviews carried out with lawyer-linguists from the accession states one year following the May 2004 enlargement it appears that such feelings of underappreciation are *not* experienced by those lawyer-linguists from the 'new' member states. This is due in a large part to the fact that, owing to difficulties in recruitment of heads of division and because of the lack of an EU terminology in the 'new' official languages, those lawyer-linguists worked very closely with the judges from their respective states in order to translate the Rules of Procedure of the Court of Justice and Court of First Instance and to develop a new EU terminology in their respective languages (see further McAuliffe 2006a).
19. A frequent complaint voiced by the majority of lawyer-linguists interviewed during the course of fieldwork research is that often the lawyers drafting the legal instruments in question use 'complicated language' or 'legalese' that is not easily translatable. Indeed in some cases the wording used is a 'legalese' understandable only to lawyers working within EU institutions!

(See further: Bellier's discussion of a 'Eurolanguage' within the European Commission: Bellier, 1997: 91.)

20. Case 283/81 *CILFIT* v. *Ministry of Health* [1982] ECR 3415, paragraph 19.
21. *Merck and Others* v. *Commission* [1997] ECR II-849..
22. Case numbers: 1019–1022/1/03 *Umbro Holdings Ltd* v. *Office of Fair Trading; Manchester United PLC.* v. *Office of Fair Trading; Allsports Ltd* v. *Office of Fair Trading; JJB Sports PLC.* v. *Office of Fair Trading* [2005] CAT 22.
23. *Cimenteries CBR and Others* v. *Commission* [2000] ECR II-491.
24. In the case before the UK Competition Appeal Tribunal there had been a meeting where the JJB witness claimed that he had received information about other competitors but did not tell them what he intended to do.
25. Case Numbers 1021/1/03 and 1022/1/03 *Allsports Ltd* v. *Office of Fair Trading* and *JJB Sports PLC.* v. *Office of Fair Trading* [2004] CAT 17, paragraph 159.
26. Ibid.
27. Note: under Art. 234 EC member state courts and tribunals may refer questions to the Court of Justice on matters concerning the interpretation of EU law. The danger pointed out by many lawyer-linguists is that if a member state court or tribunal reads only one language version of a judgment and finds that a version to be clear and precise then some questions will never be referred to the Court of Justice and the application of EU law will not, in fact, be uniform.
28. The German language division provides translation from Polish and Estonian; the English language division from Czech and Lithuanian; the Spanish language division from Hungarian and Latvian and the Italian division from Slovak and Slovenian.
29. For a detailed explanation of how the mixed-translation system at the Court of Justice works, see McAuliffe (2006a).
30. Although recruitment of staff from new member states was not without some problems – see further McAuliffe (2006a).
31. In order to 'counteract the expanding average length of proceedings' a series of measures were put into practice progressively from May 2004. Those measures included adopting a stricter approach to granting extensions of time limits for submitting pleadings; decreasing the size and content of reports for the hearing and ceasing to produce a report of the judge-rapporteur in cases that do not require an oral hearing. The court also reassessed its practice of publishing judgments in the European Court Reports and adopted a policy of selective publication (*Court of Justice of the European Communities Annual Report 2004, I-A(1.3)*).

7

Drafting or Translation – Production of Multilingual Legal Texts

Agnieszka Doczekalska

Introduction

Legal multilingualism – characteristic of multilingual states,[1] international[2] and supranational organizations[3] – is based on the principle of equal authenticity of all language versions of a legal act. The principle means that each of the authenticated language versions has the force of law and must be considered by a court during the interpretation process when the meaning of a legal act is sought. In order to assure that all language versions are treated as equally authentic and none of them prevails for interpretation purposes, the principle presumes that all language versions have the same meaning and consequently the same legal effect.[4] Hence drafting of multilingual law, which involves search for identical equivalents in two or more languages, is a challenge for lawyers and legislators. On the other hand, particular circumstances of multilingual law production cause some theoretical and conceptual difficulties for linguists and translation theorists. Translation studies that deal, *inter alia*, with semantic equivalence between source and target texts, could offer useful tools and methods for drafters of multilingual law. However, before such methods can be used in legal drafting, first of all the question whether translation studies can be applied for investigation of multilingual law, especially in the analysis of the drafting process, should be examined. In order to answer this question I consider whether drafting of multilingual law and products of that process can be regarded as translation. Before I analyse this subject, I shall draw attention to some issues characteristic of legal multilingualism.

Firstly, while examining whether the term 'translation' can denote process and products of multilingual legal drafting, it should be kept in mind that from a legal standpoint the term 'translation' cannot be used either in reference to the authentic language versions of a legal act or to the process of their drafting. Even when language versions of a legal act are in fact prepared by translation, in legal language it is still nevertheless improper to use the term 'translation' (Šarčević 2000: 64). This is a consequence of official multilingualism that consists not only in the coexistence of two or more languages but also in the equality of these languages (Wagner et al. 2002: 1). It means that legally, according to the principle of equal authenticity, all language versions have equal power and authority. Consequently, none of them can have a status of translation. Moreover, a translated text is usually considered to be inferior to an original (Yuhong 2000: 24), therefore one language version of a legal act cannot be regarded as a translation of the other one. Hence, from a legal standpoint, all authentic texts are originals regardless of the way they were produced. This statement is the main assumption of the theory of original texts (Šarčević 2000: 20, 64). It can be stated that the aforementioned assertion of this theory is a legal fiction (Wagner 2000: 2). However, it should be kept in mind that from a legal standpoint it is not the manner of creating language versions that is important but their authentication (Sullivan 2004: 1006). Language versions are usually authenticated when they are enacted or adopted by a proper body. It is also possible for a language version that has not been enacted to be declared authentic by legislation or constitutional amendment (ibid., fn. 102).[5] Nevertheless, language versions become authentic, due to their enactment or adoption, when the drafting process is completed.[6] Hence, the manner of their drafting does not matter for their authentication and legal force as long as they are authenticated in a prescribed way. Consequently, the word 'authentic' conveys the meaning of 'legally valid' rather than of 'original' (Wagner et al. 2002: 8).

Secondly, as far as the application of translation studies in drafting of multilingual law is concerned, it should be taken into account that translation is not the only method of multilingual legal drafting. Since translation is often regarded as flawed and inferior, in order to achieve semantic equality and true authenticity, new methods of drafting of multilingual law (so-called co-drafting techniques) have been put forward and applied. Hence the question of employment of the term 'translation' and translation studies to multilingual legal drafting is raised not only in reference to translation but also to co-drafting techniques.

Finally, as regards legal multilingualism, it should also be borne in mind that new types of text evolve and new relations between source and target texts appear. It has already been mentioned that the theory of original texts (applied in the domain of law) can change the meaning of the original text as understood in translation studies. Moreover, due to the development of international and intercultural communication, a source (original) text is often drafted in more than one language and incorporates elements of various cultures. Consequently, a new type of text – called hybrid text – can be recognized.

Bearing in mind the above-mentioned observations, in order to analyse the subject of the chapter the following issues are considered:

1. Translation vs multilingualism
2. Translation from one legal system into another vs translation within one legal system
3. Translation vs co-drafting methods
4. Source and target texts vs hybrid text – a lack of a 'proper' source text.

7.1 Translation vs multilingualism

Since I would like to consider whether multilingual legal drafting can be regarded as translation, I should, first of all, explain what I mean by 'translation' and 'legal multilingualism'. Although translation studies are quite a new academic discipline, various definitions of translation have already been proposed. The term 'translation' is very broad and sometimes an ambiguous notion. One of such ambiguities results from the confusing meaning of the term 'translation', which can be regarded as a product (a text that has been translated) or as a process (translating). Throughout the chapter, the term 'translation' is mainly used in the meaning of a process.[7] Needless to say, translation involves a written text, as opposed to 'interpretation' or 'interpreting'. The meaning of the term 'translation' depends on the theory and the approach being considered. I will leave aside the description of different definitions of translation. For the purpose of this chapter, it will suffice to quote the definition proposed by Nida and Taber (1969: 2): 'translating consists in reproducing in the [target language][8] the closest natural equivalent of the source-language message, first in terms of meaning and the second in terms of style'.

In translation we always deal with 'texts-in-situation and in culture' (Schäffner 1998: 83). In typical circumstances the source text is produced in the primary communicative situation in the source culture in order to fulfil a specific purpose or function. The primary communicative

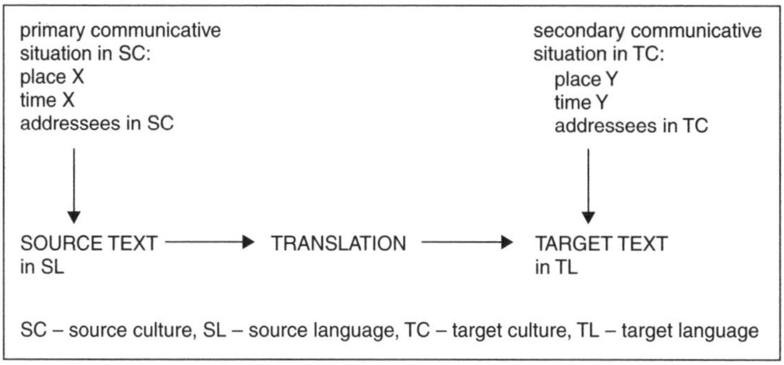

Figure 7.1 Schema of translation (based on Schäffner 1998: 84)

situation comprises a particular place and space and addressees for whom the source text has been produced. The addressees have a specific knowledge, experience and expectations. The target text should fulfil the same function but in the secondary communicative situation and for addressees in the target language and culture (ibid.). This model of translation is depicted in Figure 7.1.

Hence according to the traditional translation studies approaches, when we deal with translation, source and target texts are produced in different languages, in different places and at a different time, in different cultures and for different addressees who have specific knowledge and experience.

In the case of legal multilingualism, we face a different situation. The phenomenon of multilingual law stems from official multilingualism, which usually requires not only that the law should be enacted in all official languages, but also that texts of a single legal instrument expressed in official languages be treated as equally authentic. It means that legally all language versions have equal power and authority. Consequently, official multilingualism consists in the coexistence of two or more languages and in the equality of these languages (Wagner et al. 2002: 1). MacDonald (1997: 119) contrasts legal bilingualism with legal dualism and warns against a risk of legal bilingualism being transformed into a legal dualism that, in this context, means that bilingual law is supposed to be completely understood by referring to only one of the official texts (ibid.: 129).

Accordingly, multilingualism evokes the co-presence of two or more languages, whereas translation is rather a substitution of one language for another (Grutman 1997: 157). In multilingual legal systems, different language versions of a single legal act coexist, they do not substitute for each other. They are at the same time independent and mutually dependent on each other because they contribute to the meaning of the single instrument (Šarčević 2000: 64).

The next section explains how translation is applied within a multilingual legal system and how it differs from translation that involves different legal systems.

7.2 Translation from one legal system into another vs translation within one legal system

This chapter tackles multilingual legal drafting methods that embrace translation as well. Therefore the distinction between legal translation from one legal system into another and translation within one legal system should be pointed out. The latter occurs in multilingual settings as a drafting method. The comparison of these two models of translation should help to find out whether translation as a drafting method can be treated as a translation from a translation studies' standpoint.

Different names have been proposed to denote these two types of legal translation. This terminological controversy is demonstrated by Susan Šarčević (2000: 15), who notes that, for instance, Didier distinguishes *transposition juridique,* which involves different legal systems, from *traduction juridique,* that is, a transfer of a legal message within one legal system, but from one language to another (1991: 9). However, the terms used by Didier are unfortunate, because a narrow definition of *traduction juridique* implies that *transposition juridique* is not a translation. On the other hand, Crépeau (1995: 207) proposes the term *transposition linguistique 'simple'* to denote legal translation within the same legal system and *transposition linguistique 'complexe'* or *transposition juridicolinguistique* to denote legal translation from one legal system into another. Due to this terminological controversy, I use descriptive compounds, that is, 'legal translation from one legal system into another' and 'legal translation within the same legal system'.

What we traditionally understand by legal translation is translation from one language into another that involves different legal systems. The model for this type of translation is illustrated in Figure 7.2. The main problems of this kind of legal translation are related to the fact that it is not only translation from one language into another but also from one legal language to another legal language and from one legal system into another legal system. Legal translation used to be regarded as a mechanical process of transcoding one language into another. Nowadays, as a result of a shift in the main emphasis in translation

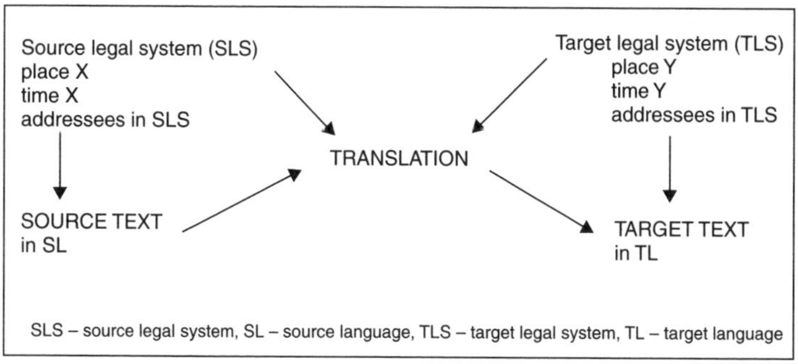

Figure 7.2 Schema of legal translation from one legal system into another

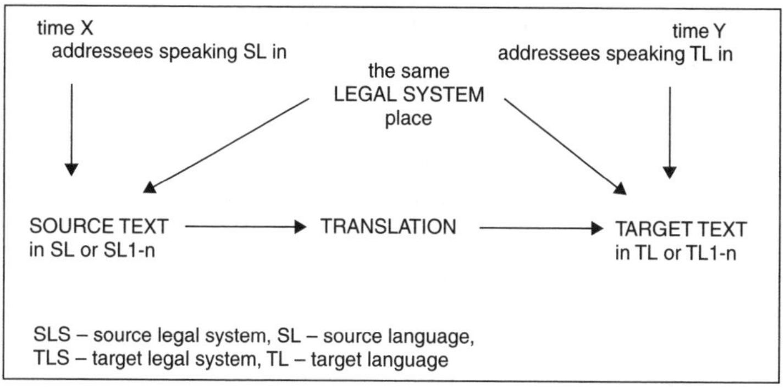

Figure 7.3 Schema of legal translation within one legal system

studies from interlingual to cultural transfer (Šarčević 2000: 2, 5, 209), legal translation is regarded as a cross-cultural event (Snell-Hornby 1988; Šarčević 2000). Legal terms have meaning only in the context of a legal system. Hence the elements of one legal system cannot be simply transposed into another legal system. Consequently, the legal terminologies of different legal systems are for the most part conceptually incongruent. Furthermore, all legal systems contain a number of terms (so-called system-bound terms) with no counterparts in other legal systems. System-bound terms designate concepts and institutions peculiar to the legal reality of a specific system and very often are considered as untranslatable (Šarčević 1985: 127–8).

The scheme of this type of legal translation (Figure 7.2) overlaps the translation scheme proposed by Schäffner (Figure 7.1).

On the other hand, the scheme of translation within one legal system has much fewer overlapping elements (see Figure 7.3). This stems from the fact that the source and target legal systems are one and the same.

Consequently, all official languages share the same system of reference, that is, the signs in each language refer to the same objects (Šarčević 2000: 15, 230–1). The situation can be more complicated in multilingual legal systems that are characterized as mixed (for example, Israel, South Africa) or bi-jural (Canada). Force of law in such a system is derived from more than one legal tradition or family (Tetley 2003: 182).[9] Consequently, drafting multilingual law in a mixed or bi-jural system, where each language usually corresponds to a particular legal tradition (as in the case of bilingual and bi-jural Canada where English corresponds to common law, but French to civil law) and all language versions should reflect the specificity of each legal tradition, is much more challenging and difficult than in legal systems based on one legal tradition. This issue, although an interesting one, falls outside the scope of this chapter.

It should be taken into consideration that translation is not the only method of drafting law in many languages. In some multilingual legal systems, co-drafting methods are used instead of or in addition to translation. Aiming at the elimination of the distinction between original (source text) and translated text (target text), co-drafting methods coordinate time and place of production of a legal text in all official languages, whereas source and target text produced by means of classical translation are drafted at different times and places. The next section describes various co-drafting techniques and discusses whether translation studies can be applied to research on co-drafting methods.

7.3 Translation vs co-drafting methods

Translation is the most traditional and the most often used method of drafting in multilingual settings. Usually, a legal act is drafted in one language and then translated into other languages. Drafting by means of translation has, however, several linguistic and legal drawbacks. For the sake of brevity I will mention only some of them. The linguistic weakness of translation as a drafting method results from the fact that, when a text is first drafted in one language (the source language), that is usually a dominant one, and then translated into other official language(s), the translation (the translated text) is not always produced in the spirit of the target language(s).[10] Drafting in the spirit of all official languages upholds the principle of language equality and language rights. Accordingly, it is, nowadays, commonly acknowledged that legal translation that results in producing multilingual law should be idiomatic[11] or free[12] rather than literal. However, it is still hard to decide how closely translation must follow the source text. It is difficult not only to write authentic texts in the spirit of all official languages, but also to convey the same meaning in all language versions. When there are discrepancies between language versions, sometimes the opinion – in contradiction to the principle of equal authenticity – is articulated that the real intent of the legislator is expressed in the original version. Hence, within the scope of law, the main weakness of drafting by means of translation has to do with the problem of the reliability of a language version that has been translated. When translation is used as a method of legal drafting, the court sometimes gives priority to the original text during interpretation of a legal act. Lawyers and judges often doubt the interpretative value of a text that has been translated (that is, whether the intent of a single instrument was preserved). The interpretative value of an authenticated language version depends on the situational factors of its production, such as time and place (Rosenne 1983: 759–84). Therefore, attempts have been made to find a new multilingual legal drafting method that would coordinate the time and place of the production of authentic texts.

As a result, several co-drafting methods[13] have been proposed. They coordinate the place and time of the production of authentic texts and combine translating and drafting in various ways and degrees. Table 7.1 gives an outlook on different types of co-drafting techniques. For the sake of simplicity, only pairs of texts (only two texts) are examined. This is plausible because in practice even when they are employed in multilingual settings, for instance, in Switzerland, they are usually used solely for the purpose of bilingual (and not multilingual) drafting.[14] In the area of international law, the activity of the Drafting Committee of the Third United Nations Conference on the Law of the Sea (UNCLOS III) can be pointed out as the unique example of multilingual co-drafting.[15]

As demonstrated in Table 7.1, apart from double entry drafting, there are two drafters, or to put it a better way, 'co-drafters', involved in the drafting process. Both drafters should be fluent in both languages an act is drafted in and have a perfect knowledge of at least of one of them.

The first indicated co-drafting method is parallel drafting. First of all, a detailed bilingual outline of the act to be drafted is prepared. Then the co-drafters draft a large part or the entire act in their mother tongue and then they meet in order to compare and coordinate texts. After that they leave again in order to modify their versions. Co-drafters work simultaneously yet independently and separately (Covacs 1982: 93; Šarčević 1998: 283; 2000: 102). Parallel drafting was used in the German and

Table 7.1 Comparison of co-drafting techniques

Type of co-drafting	*Number of drafters*	*Separate or joint work of drafters*	*Drafting elements*	*Translation elements*	*Practical use of drafting method*
Parallel drafting	2	Separate	Drafting of the whole act in two languages	–	In canton of Berne (Switzerland) drafting in German and French cantonal bill on Official Publications
Alternate drafting	2	Separate	Some parts of the act are drafted in language A, some in language B	Parts drafted in one language are translated into another language	At the federal level in Switzerland drafting in German and French; in canton of Berne (Switzerland) a revision of the Constitution of the Canton of Berne
Shared drafting	2	Separate	Half of the act is drafted in language A and half in language B	Drafted halves are translated into another language	Theoretical solution
Double entry drafting	1	–	Drafting of the whole act in two languages	–	–
Joint drafting	2	Joint	Drafting of the whole act in two languages	–	Canada, Hong Kong

French bilingual canton of Berne (Switzerland) when the cantonal bill on Official Publications was prepared (see Caussignac and Kettinger 1991: 79–81; Šarčević 2000: 102).

The second method indicated in Table 7.1 is alternate drafting, which is a combination of drafting and translating. Two persons participate in the preparation of a bilingual legal act, each fulfilling the role of co-drafter as well as the role of legal translator. First, the co-drafters-translators decide which parts of an act are to be prepared in language A and which in language B. Second, they leave and draw up the designated parts. Third, the co-drafters-translators exchange drafted parts and translate them into one another's language. Finally, the translated parts are revised by the co-drafters (Covacs 1982: 93).

According to Šarčević (1998: 283; 2000: 101), the term 'alternate' refers to the fact that the source text is not always the same (that is, it refers to the fact that the source text alternates), not to the way it is drafted (that is, not to the alternate use of drafting and translating).

This method of bilingual legal drafting was used in Canada at the federal level (Covacs 1982: 93) as well as in the province of New Brunswick and in Switzerland at the federal level as well as in the canton of Berne (Šarčević 2000: 102). For instance, in the Swiss bilingual (German and French) canton of Berne, a revision of the Constitution of the Canton of Berne was prepared using the alternate drafting method.[16] Moreover, in Switzerland the most important federal laws are drafted in accordance with alternate drafting (in Switzerland called *Koredaktion*), or at least such an attempt is made.[17]

The next method, denoted as shared drafting, is very similar to alternate drafting. Two co-drafters, who are also the translators in the process of drafting, prepare the outline of an act, divide the act into halves and decide which part is to be drafted in language A and then translated into language B, and which one will be drafted in language B and then translated into language A. Thus, the only difference between alternate drafting and shared drafting is that according to the former, parts of an act are alternately drafted and translated, whereas according to the latter, half of an act is drawn up in one language and the other part is drafted in another language and then both halves are translated (Covacs 1982: 93; Šarčević 2000: 101). Shared drafting is so far only a theoretical solution. It is not used in practice probably because it would create too great a risk of discrepancy (Covacs 1982: 93).

As far as double entry drafting is concerned, only one person participates in the process of drafting of a bilingual legal act. The same person draws up both language versions (both texts), preferably part by part in correlation. This method was proposed for drafting bilingual legislation in Canada and theoretically it seems to be ideal (Covacs 1982: 93). The advantage of this method is that drafting of an act by the same person guarantees the unity and coherence of both language versions and makes the source and target texts – or in other words, the original and translated versions – indistinguishable.[18] However, in practice it is very difficult to find a bilingual person whose linguistic abilities in both languages are perfect. Moreover, bilingual persons usually favour one language. As a result, a version written in the second language is not linguistically pure and consequently a target text can be distinguished. Furthermore, in bilegal countries like Canada it is also difficult to find a person who is educated in both legal systems (that is, in civil law and common law, as in the case of Canada) (ibid.).

The solution offered by joint drafting differs from the above-presented bilingual drafting methods. In all the drafting methods described so far, when co-drafters-translators draw up legal texts of a single instrument, they work separately. Co-drafters only come together when they draft the outline of a legal act, and later on when they compare and revise both language versions jointly. In joint drafting, in contrast, the co-drafters work together at all stages of the drafting process. This process of drafting is similar to or even the same as the one applied in parallel drafting. Both language versions are drafted; none of them is translated. The co-drafters prepare an outline jointly and then jointly draft (usually part by part), compare, revise and correct both language versions. On the other hand, joint drafting avoids the pitfalls and disadvantages of parallel and of double entry drafting (Šarčević 2000: 102). In parallel drafting, the main difficulty concerns the unity and consistency of the two language versions. Due to the constant cooperation of the co-drafters during the drafting process this demand can be achieved when joint drafting is employed. Doubly entry drafting ensures the unity of thoughts but involves the difficulty of finding a bilingual person who writes in the spirit of both languages and – regarding bilegal countries – is trained in both legal systems. When the joint drafting method is applied, the drafting is made by two drafters who are able to write linguistically pure texts in their mother tongues.

With the aid of these methods a greater equality of official languages should be achieved. All texts of a single legal instrument should be linguistically pure. Moreover, there ought to be inter- and intratextual coherence. Finally, it should not be possible to distinguish between source and target text, or, in other words, between original text and translation (translated text). Consequently, the priority in interpretation would not be given to one language version because this version was drafted first, is original and better expresses the will of the legislator.

At this point the question arises whether co-drafting methods can be considered as a special case of translation and whether translation studies' methodology can be used to find out the best multilingual legal drafting method.

From a legal standpoint, as was explained in the introduction to this chapter, it is presumed that all authenticated language versions are originals regardless of the manner of their drafting. However, in order to find out whether translation studies' methodology can be useful in the study of co-drafting techniques, we should look for the answer in translation theories. The answer is not as forthcoming as when the legal perspective is used. There are many approaches to and definitions of

Table 7.2 Possibility of the distinction between source and target text in co-drafting methods

Co-drafting techniques	*Holistic analysis of entire texts*	*Atomistic analysis of text segments*
Parallel drafting	–	–
Alternate drafting	–	–
Shared drafting	–	–
Double entry drafting	–	–/+
Joint drafting	–	–

– distinction between source and target texts is not possible.
+ distinction between source and target texts is possible.

translation. However, it is traditionally accepted that the source and target texts are always produced at a different time and place. Usually the process of producing the target text starts only after the source text is completed. As Steiner (1977: 334) has noted, 'every act of translation (...) is a transfer from past to a present'. This statement is in contradiction to the main objective of the co-drafting methods, that is, a coordination of the time and place of production of parallel texts. For that reason, I verify whether two texts relate to each other as source and target texts. I conduct my analysis at two levels. First, I examine the production of the texts at the micro-level, that is, the production of text segments (atomistic analysis); and, second, I analyse the production at the macro-level, that is, the production of the whole text (holistic analysis). The results of these analyses are demonstrated in Table 7.2. I also refer to the stages of the translation process.

In the case of parallel drafting, it is impossible to identify the source text and the target one either at the micro-level or at the macro-level of production. Both language versions are prepared independently. Hence, as far as the relation between the two texts is concerned, neither an original text nor a translation can be indicated, either at the level of text segment, or at the level of the whole text. Consequently, both parallelly drafted texts are originals. Thus the theory of original texts, which presumes that all authentic texts are originals, regardless of drafting method, is not a fiction in this case.

The application of this two-level analysis to the alternate drafting and shared drafting methods proves to be very useful. When we examine the drafting process at the micro-level of a text segment (a half or a smaller part of a text), it is possible to point out which part is drafted in which language. As a result, a source text can be identified, and consequently a translated part can be recognized. Most importantly, the source text is not always the same, that is, it is partly (or a half) in language A and partly (or a half) in language B; in other words, it alternates. Therefore when the drafting process and the product of this process are analysed at the macro-level, we are not able to identify the source language of the entire text. However, as far as these two methods are concerned, it is possible to apply translation studies at all stages of translation. It should be pointed out, however, that the idea of alternating the source text and target text is new in translation studies (Šarčević 2000: 102).

In the case of double entry drafting, the same person drafts both language versions. Translation studies (especially of literary translation) recognize 'autotranslation' or 'self-translation', which is defined as 'the translation of an original work into another language by the author himself' (Popovič 1976: 19).[19] In some translation theories, autotranslation is not a variant of the original text but a true translation (ibid.). Thus, from the translation studies point of view, double entry drafting can be regarded as a translation process as long as parts of one text are used as the source text for the others. In order to find out whether this requirement is fulfilled, the process of drafting should be investigated from a psycholinguistic perspective. However, it should be borne in mind that according to the double entry drafting technique, the drafter ought to draft both language versions separately, not to draft one version and then translate it into another language. Accordingly, if this drafting method is applied correctly, both texts can be regarded as originals as in the case of parallel drafting. Even if a drafter prepares some parts in language A and some in language B and then translates them respectively into language B and A, when the entire texts are analysed, a source text and a target text are indistinguishable, similarly to alternate and shared drafting. Even if an entire text is drafted in one language and then used as a source text by the drafter who has a perfect knowledge of both languages, as long as he or she does not point out which text has been drafted and which one translated, it is not possible for others to identify the original and the translated text. A drafter who produces parts of or an entire text by means of translation does not follow proper double entry drafting methodology. But still, both a drafter who applies a 'pure' double entry drafting method and one who uses translation elements in drafting have to produce coherent and equivalent texts in two languages. Hence, the problem-solving strategies recommended by translation studies may be helpful to them whatever drafting method they use (involving translation elements or not).

The case of joint drafting is similar to the parallel drafting method. The difference, as mentioned above, is that during the latter co-drafters work separately apart from revision of drafted versions, while co-drafters – each of them responsible for his/her language version – who apply the joint drafting method not only revise but also prepare and draft texts jointly. Since both language versions are drafted at the same time and even in the same place, while using the joint drafting method one text does not serve as the source text for the other. Therefore it is text production rather than translation.

Each of the co-drafting methods described above includes comparison and necessary modifications of both language versions. This last stage of co-drafting resembles revision, which is recognized by many translation theories as the last stage of translation. The problem-solving techniques applied according to translation studies to revision can be used when language versions are compared and corrected by co-drafters. However, it should be taken into account that during revision, as defined in translation studies, only the target text can be modified, whereas during co-drafting changes and corrections can be included in both language versions.

To sum up, in some co-drafting techniques elements of translation can be identified whereas in others, especially in parallel and joint drafting, it is difficult to recognize translation aspects. The main difference between translation and co-drafting is the relation between the two language versions. Translators reconstruct what is said in a source text whereas each of the co-drafters produces, on the basis of the detailed outline of an act, a text that expresses what the legislator meant to say, thus preserving the original intent (Šarčević 2000: 102). However, while preparing texts, both translators and co-drafters share the same difficulty, that is, how to find equivalence and avoid a discrepancy between two language versions of the same legal act. Consequently, since equivalent and coherent texts in two languages are to be prepared and no two languages are identical, some translation problem-solving strategies (for instance, finding terminological equivalences, achieving intra- and intertextual coherence) can be of help. Furthermore, translation studies can be profitably applied in the examination of the drafting process, as well as in the analysis and comparison of the products of this process.

Nonetheless, drafting by means of translation in multilingual settings can pose some challenges to translation theories. Firstly, the new type of relation between the source and target texts that has already been discussed in section 7.2; and secondly, the new character of original (source text) that is to be analysed in the next section.

7.4 Source and target texts vs hybrid text – a lack of a 'proper' source text

Sometimes it can be observed that in multilingual settings target texts are produced by means of translation without the existence of a proper source language or a proper source text (Schäffner 1998: 87). The first situation takes place, especially in international organizations and in the European Union, when a text is produced by means of multilingual negotiation (that is, more than one working language is used) and then translated into other official languages. If two or more working languages have played a role in setting up the final version, then none of the working languages can legitimately be called a source language (ibid.: 87–8). In such a situation, the production of a text is influenced by several languages or a text is even produced in multiple languages.[20] Then the final text is translated into other languages. Legal texts produced within international organizations or the EU are multilingual and multicultural by nature. The source text as it is understood in traditional translation studies, that is, a text produced exclusively in one language and culture, does not exist in this situation. Thus, neither a source language nor a source text can be indicated.

A text produced in such a way is sometimes called a 'hybrid text'. A hybrid text results from the contact of two or more cultures and languages and it is a compromise between several cultures and languages (Schäffner and Adab 1997: 325). A hybrid text can also result from the translation process (see Schäffner and Adab 2001: 167). In other words, the target text can be a hybrid text. However, in multilingual legal systems, translation can even play a role of 'dehybridization'. According to Pym, in the EU, source texts are hybrid texts because of the intercultural and multilingual nature of the drafting process, whereas the role of translation is 'dehybridization'. In the words of Pym '[c]ontemporary professional non-literary translation in Europe is an agent of dehybridization for the simple reason that source-text generation processes are increasingly multilingual, whereas translational outputs are normally monolingual' (2001: 205).

As far as co-drafting methods are concerned, a lack of a 'proper' source text can also be identified when multilingual legislation is drawn up. This accords with the objective of multilingual drafting methods which avoid the use of translation and aim to produce legal texts in all official languages so as to preclude the possibility of distinction between the source and target text.

As already mentioned, according to the model relation between the source text and the target text, the source text fulfils its communicative function for its source-language addressees in the primary communicative situation, whereas the target text fulfils its communicative function for its target-language addressees in the secondary communicative situation. In the secondary communication, addressees are not the addressees for whom the text was originally created but instead a secondary target group intended as addressees of the translation (Trosborg 1997: 155). As far as the drafting of law in multilingual settings is concerned, there is neither a primary communicative situation in which the source text fulfils its communicative function nor a secondary one in which the target text fulfils its communicative function. On the contrary, both texts share the same communicative situation.

According to traditional translation studies, such translations as the one described above are not translations because there are no proper source texts (see Gutt 1990). Thus the traditional designation of 'source' and 'target' text cannot be applied here. However, in the opinion of some authors the meaning and status of the source language, and of the source language community, as well as of source text and the relation between source text and target text should be reconsidered in translation studies (Trosborg 1997: 155; Schäffner 1998: 87–90).

Some work toward this end has been done. For instance, Trosborg (1997: 155) proposes the term 'pseudo-text' to refer to 'a text which in itself does not fulfil a communicative function, but serves as a draft for translation'. Translations of pseudo-texts are close to the primary texts 'addressing a primary target group' (ibid.).

A different approach is taken by Šarčević. In order to identify a source text in parallel and joint drafting, Šarčević (2000: 107) tries to apply Holz-Mänttäri's theory of 'translatorial action' that 'dethrones' the source text. Holz-Mänttäri reduces the role of source text to the 'carrier of message'. As a result, traditional source text can be replaced by new forms, for example, briefings and agreements specifying the features of a new product can be treated as a source text. Although Holz-Mänttäri does not refer to legal texts, Šarčević suggests that in parallel and joint drafting, the outlines which form the basis for the production of parallel legal texts can be treated as source text for these drafted legal texts.

There is another opinion as to what translation is. According to this approach, translating can be seen as a modelling activity in that the result of the operation, that is 'the translated text, commonly claims, (...) to represent an anterior discourse in a way comparable to the representational function of models' (Hermans 1997: 156). It makes translation a representation, substitute or at least metatext. Thus, if translation claims to represent a source text and is accepted as such, it is a translation even if no prototype can be identified. As a result, in some cases translation can be recognized even if the source text does not exist (the so-called 'pseudotranslation'). However, according to this theory 'a translation that goes unrecognized as a translation is, functionally speaking, not a translation at all because its modelling aspects remain inoperative' (Hermans 1997: 156). Hence, authentic language versions of a legal act produced by means of multilingual legal drafting or even of translating cannot be treated as a translation, because they are not and should not be recognized as a translation.

Conclusion

To summarize, this chapter posed two theoretical problems. The first, whether it is correct to apply translation studies' terminology and tools to translation applied during the drafting of multilingual law in a situation when, from a legal standpoint, we should not speak about translation. The second, whether co-drafting methods can be analysed with the aid of translation studies.

As far as the first question is concerned, one should distinguish translation as a process (translating) and translation as a result of the translating process, that is, a target text (text that has been translated). Legally, it is inconceivable to denote one or some of the authentic language versions as translation (in a sense of a text that has been translated). However, language versions become equally authentic when the drafting process is finished and when they are authenticated, that is enacted, adopted or declared as authentic by a proper body. Consequently, before authentication when the principle of equal authenticity is not applied (although it should be taken into consideration during the drafting process), it is plausible to denote and treat the drafting process as translation and apply solutions and tools offered by translation studies.

As regards the second question, 'drafting or translating' should not be treated as a disjunctive alternative. Although the result of multilingual legal drafting should not be recognized as a translation, the drafting process sometimes involves elements of translation. Nonetheless, even though the process of production of multilingual law or its product (that is, legal texts) cannot be treated as a translation, we still deal with transfer from one language to another. No two languages are identical, even if they share a common system of reference. A lack of absolute correspondence between languages poses problems and difficulties for multilingual legal drafting. These problems can be analysed and solved by means of translation studies.

Moreover, due to the challenges posed to translation studies by the specific character of the translation and drafting processes within a multilingual legal system, the approach of translation studies towards legal translation should be modified. Some of such attempts have been already pointed out in section 7.4 of this chapter in reference to the relation between source and target texts. Another example which can be indicated is a modified approach proposed by Susan Šarčević who regards legal translation as an act of communication in the mechanism of the law (2000), and furthermore, suggests that the role of the translator in multilingual settings should be changed and become more creative (1998). If translators were treated as creators, then the inferiority of translations as a copy of originals could be reduced.

Notes

1. For instance, in Canada, section 18 of the Canadian Charter of Rights and Freedoms, 1982 provides that the English and French versions of the statutes are equally authoritative. In Hong Kong, since 1987 the Interpretation and General Clauses Ordinance in Part II A, section 10B(1) states that both the English and Chinese texts of an ordinance shall be equally authentic; moreover, section 10B(2) presumes the provisions of a statute to have the same meaning in each authentic language text.
2. See Art. 33 on interpretation of treaties authenticated in two or more languages (esp. paragraphs 1 and 3) of the Vienna Convention on the Law of Treaties of 1969 (United Nations, Treaty Series, vol. 1155, p. 331).
3. In the EU, although the Council Regulation No. 1 of 15 April 1958 determining the languages to be used by the European Economic Community does not state directly that all official language versions of a legal act are equally authentic, such conclusion follows from Art. 1 of the same regulation, that provides which languages have official and working status in the Community, and from Art. 4 stating that regulations and other documents of general application shall be drafted in all the official languages. Moreover, the European Court of Justice and the Court of First Instance confirmed in several cases that the different language versions are all equally authentic and that an interpretation of a provision of Community law involves a comparison of the different language versions (see esp. judgments in case 283/81 Srl CILFIT [1982] ECR 3415, paragraph 18; joined cases T-22/02 and T-23/02 02 *Sumitomo Chemical Co. Ltd and Sumika Fine Chemicals Co. Ltd* v. *Commission* [2005], ECR II-04065, paragraph 42). The term 'authentic' appears, however, in the final provisions of treaties; see Art. 314 of the Treaty establishing the European Community (consolidated text in *Official Journal* C 325 of 24 December 2002), Art. 53 of the Treaty on European Union (consolidated text in *Official Journal* C 325 of 24 December 2002), Article 13 of the Treaty of Nice (*Official Journal* C 80 of 10 March 2001). From the aforementioned provisions, it follows that treaties have been drawn up in a single original in all official languages and texts in each of these languages are equally authentic.

4. See Yuhong (2000: 5) who states that in order to achieve legal equivalence (denoted also as 'substantive equivalence' (Schroth 1986: 57)) or 'juridical equivalence' (Šarčević 2000: 48), the authentic language versions (denoted by Yuhong as 'parallel texts') of a legal act should lead to the same legal effect. Obviously, a condition for such legal equivalence is semantic equivalence among all language versions.
5. Sometimes a language version does not even exist when a legal act is enacted or adopted (a case of so-called subsequent translation). Such a situation is related to the expansion of the number of official languages. It takes place, for instance, within the EU after each enlargement as well as in multilingual countries or in international organizations when a new language is granted an official status (for example in Switzerland where Italian became a new official language in 1902; or in the United Nations where Arabic and Chinese were granted the status of official and working languages in 1973).
6. It is the usual and proper situation. However, sometimes due to practical or technical difficulties, a text in one of the official language(s) cannot be submitted before the adoption. Examples of such a situation are described in Šarčević (2000: 94 – case of Switzerland where Italian versions were not ready at the time of enactment) and Tabory (1980 – see on authentication after time of signature p. 193 and on authentication of non-existent texts, pp. 191–2, 194).
7. In this chapter, the term 'target text' is used to denote 'a text that has been translated', while the term 'translation' is used in reference to the process, unless otherwise indicated.
8. Nida and Taber use the term 'receptor language' in their definition. I replaced this term with the term 'target language' since the latter is generally accepted and more often used in translation studies. The term 'target language' is consequently used throughout the chapter.
9. For more details on the definition of 'mixed legal system' or 'mixed jurisdiction', see also Örücü (2004: 149) and Palmer (2001: 7).
10. As an example of such a situation, one can indicate the poor translation of Canadian federal legal acts from English into French before co-drafting methods started to be used in the late 1970s (Labelle 2000).
11. Idiomatic translation means that, while producing target text by means of translation, the conventions established in the target language are to be conformed to (Delisle et al. 1999: 144).
12. As a result of free translation, instead of preserving the source text wording intact, a naturally reading target text is produced (Shuttleworth and Cowie 1997: 62).
13. Terminology for denoting co-drafting methods has not yet been established. For instance, terms describing the bilingual drafting methods are not used in a uniform way by Swiss authors. Furthermore, different terminologies are used in Switzerland and Canada. Thus, no authoritative catalogue of bilingual drafting methods exists. However, Alexandre Covacs (jurilinguist in services linguistiques français, Section de la legislation, Ministère de la Justice du Canada) proposed such a catalogue for Canadian use. These terms are also used by Šarčević (1998, 2000). I too have decided to follow this terminology.

14. In Switzerland, where French, German and Italian are official languages, law is simultaneously drafted only in French and German, whereas the Italian version is added by translation. However, irrespective of the way they were produced, all three language versions are equally authentic. This hybrid way of drafting law in more than one language combining co-drafting and translation is applied as regards important legislation and only in certain departments (Wagner 2005: 19). For further details see ibid.: 18–20.
15. According to Rule 53 of the Rules of Procedure of UNCLOS III, the Drafting Committee could 'formulate drafts and advice on drafting', however, it could not alter the substance of the text. The Drafting Committee was responsible for ensuring that the same content is in all authentic versions, that is, in Arabic, Chinese, English, French, Russian and Spanish. In order to fulfil this task, six language groups – one for each authentic text – were established. As a result, the text of the UN Convention on the Law of the Sea was drafted at the same time in all official languages. All interested delegations were able to participate in the work of the language groups. Furthermore, each language group appointed a coordinator. Coordinators met regularly together and with the chairman of the Drafting Committee. For further details on the work of the UNCLOS III Drafting Committee, see Nelson (1986).
16. Swiss authors use the term 'parallel drafting' when they refer to the process of revision of the constitution. However, from the analysis of the drafting process one can conclude that it is an alternate drafting (as described by Covacs and understood in this chapter).
17. For further details see Šarčević (2000: 98–100) and Wagner (2005: 18–20).
18. As for the double entry drafting, both language versions of an act are or should be drafted, and for that very reason we should not even apply here such terms as 'source text', 'target text', 'original version' or 'translation'.
19. This definition is cited from Shuttleworth and Cowie (1997: 13).
20. See the example and analysis of the production of multilingually negotiated legal and political texts in Schäffner (1998: 87–9).

8
Legal Translation in Canada: the Genius of Legal Language(s)

Louis Beaudoin

8.1 Introduction

In bilingual countries like Canada, bi-juralism and official bilingualism represent considerable challenges for lawyers and translators. How does one translate common law concepts into French when they have evolved over the centuries in English? The Anglophone lawyer in Quebec, coping with a code directly inspired by the *Code Napoléon*, confronts a similar issue. This raises the question of the specific nature of the legal vernacular. In other words, must the common law be expressed only in English and the civil law only in French? In Canada, we hold to the belief – some would say naively – that translating legal notions from another legal system is not only possible, it is essential.

Legal systems (common law and civil law) and the languages in which they are expressed (French and English) are inextricably linked to the culture, history and social system of the country to which they belong.

In Canada, legal drafting and translation present additional difficulties because of the coexistence of two languages (French and English) and two legal systems (common law and civil law), which have undergone parallel development. Hence the necessity for beginning legal drafters and translators to acquire a firm grasp of the formal, conceptual, stylistic and organizational (apprehension of the world, genius of the language) differences between the two languages and between the two legal systems.

8.2 The history of legal translation in Canada

First, I would like to point out that the views I express are my own and not necessarily those of my fellow legal translators in Canada.

My perspective is primarily that of a Francophone jurilinguist who translates common law from English to French. With that in mind, let us get to the heart of the matter.

The fascinating history of legal translation in Canada began in 1759 when the British troops defeated the French army in the Battle of the Plains of Abraham. Under the Treaty of Paris signed in 1763, the French ceded to the British the vast territory occupied by present-day Canada and the entire area of North America west of the original 13 colonies, which would eventually form the United States of America.

Out of a spirit of generosity towards the inhabitants of the former New France or a desire to ensure their loyalty, the British conquerors granted them the right to preserve their language, customs, religion – Roman Catholicism – and legal system – the French system derived from the Romano-Germanic civil law tradition. It is interesting to note that besides Quebec, the only two other North American jurisdictions ruled by civil law are Louisiana and Mexico.

French civil law had narrowly escaped extinction. But for the next 150 years, it endured the assaults of the dominant language: English. More often than not, the coexistence of the two languages and systems has come at the expense of the quality of the French language, which has been 'contaminated' by numerous Anglicisms as well as syntactical and lexicographical calques. As Professor Jean-Claude Gémar (1982, 1995; see also Gémar and Vo 1997; Gémar and Kasirer 2005) has so rightly remarked: 'Language does not escape with impunity the clash of legal languages and systems.' The plight of legal French in Canada throughout the nineteenth century right up until the mid twentieth century is a perfect illustration of that statement.

Historians are unanimous in lauding the quality and purity of written and spoken French in New France at the time of the conquest. And yet, a few decades of British rule and the conqueror's initial determination to assimilate a population that was 99.28 per cent Francophone sufficed to bring about a decline in the quality of the language. The celebrated French historian, Alexis de Tocqueville, who witnessed the period, was perplexed at the language spoken by lawyers and witnesses at a trial he attended in Quebec City in 1831. He had this to say: 'I am more convinced than ever after attending [this trial] that the greatest, most irremediable fate that can befall a people is to be conquered.'

In 1867, the situation began to take a turn for the better with the adoption of the British North America Act. As a result of this legislation, provinces were formed and legislative powers were divided between the two levels of government: the federal Parliament in Ottawa (the capital) and the provincial legislatures. The province of Quebec was founded. A constitutional text established the equality of French and English. However, in reality, the equality of languages and legal systems was partial and territorial (bilingual civil law in Quebec (since 1774), bilingual common law at the federal level (since 1867), in Manitoba (since 1870), and in New Brunswick (not before 1969)).

From 1867 to 1969, when the Official Languages Act became law, French remained a language of translation. Literalism and even servility to the source language characterized the approach taken by translators who were assigned to establish the French version of the federal laws when they translated bills conceived and drafted in English.

There resulted considerable interference from English: witness the profusion of Anglicisms that peppered French legal texts, doctrinal works and casebooks of the time. A few examples will illustrate this point: *offense* instead of *infraction, acte* instead of *loi, papiers-nouvelles* (from the English word *newspaper*) instead of *journal, mérite* (in English, *merits*) instead of *fond, évidence* (in English *evidence*) instead of *preuve*, etc.

Interestingly enough, the reverse is also true: English has also been subjected to assaults by Quebec's dominant language. In fact, the 1866 version of the Civil Code of Lower Canada reveals numerous gallicisms, heavy, awkward phrases and calques on French words and expressions. The following are only a few:

Article 501 of the Civil Code of Lower Canada

Les fonds inférieurs sont assujettis envers ceux qui sont plus élevés à recevoir les eaux qui en découlent naturellement sans que la main de l'homme y ait contribué.	Lands on a lower level are subject towards those of a higher level to receive such waters as flow from the latter naturally and without the agency of man.

The revised English version of this provision is a model of clarity and simplicity:

Les fonds inférieurs sont assujettis envers ceux qui sont plus élevés à recevoir les eaux qui en découlent naturellement sans que la main de l'homme y ait contribué.	Water must be allowed to flow naturally from higher land to lower land.

There are many borrowings in English civil law: *rent* (from the French *rente*), instead of *annuity*. Other loanwords are *hypothec, procès-verbal, cadastre, acte en minute, pari mutuel, délibéré, delay* (from the French *délai*, instead of *time limit, period*), *mandatory delay* (calque of the French expression *délai de rigueur* instead of *absolute deadline*) and so on.

If we take another look at the state of French in federal legislative texts, we are forced to admit it was only in the last 30 years that the federal legislator has made a solid effort to rectify the situation. Literalism was shelved; even translation has been jettisoned in favour of a system of bilingual co-drafting of the laws. A team of jurilinguists consisting of Anglophone and Francophone lawyers and legal language specialists has been charged with drafting the bills. This method has the remarkable advantage of affording co-drafters the opportunity to persuade colleagues who have written the bill in the other official language to improve and even modify their texts. Their input is valuable, even indispensable.

With regard to the courts, only since the adoption of the Official Languages Act in 1969 have all decisions by federal courts – the Supreme Court of Canada, Federal Court of Canada and Tax Court of Canada – been published in both languages.

8.3 Challenges facing legal translation in Canada

As we have already seen, bi-juralism and official bilingualism represent considerable challenges for legal translators in Canada.

The translator *weighs* the acceptations of a term and then selects the one that faithfully renders the meaning of the original text. I will cite only a few of the most glaring problems posed by the translation of legal texts from one legal system to another (from common law to Romano-Germanic law) and from one language to another (from English to French).

8.3.1 The absence of universal operational referents

Law is not an exact science. As we have seen, it is entirely dependent on discourse and hence words. To produce a good legal translation, translators must, therefore, deploy their entire art, possess a thorough knowledge of the source language and, above all, a mastery of the target language, be familiar with its many resources, riches and subtleties and know where to find the clarifications they need to render the meaning of the text they are translating. These elements are not unique to Canada. They are the building blocks of translation.

8.3.2 Stylistic and lexical preferences

In the exercise of their profession, legal translators who work from English to French become aware, as they go from one language to the other, that not only do the concepts and words change, but the relationships between them change as well. Each language favours certain forms, syntactical or stylistic processes, and terms.

In Canada, legal drafting and translation present additional difficulties because of the coexistence of two languages (French and English) and two legal systems (common law and civil law), which have undergone parallel development. Hence the necessity for beginning legal drafters and translators to acquire a firm grasp of the formal, conceptual, stylistic and organizational (apprehension of the world, genius of the language) differences between the two languages and between the two legal systems.

From its very beginnings, legal English has been a more technical, more highly specialized language than legal French. One explanation for this is the development of parallel notions issued from *law French* and common law (hence the plethora of doublets such as *last will and testament*). Today's legal English is the fruit of the evolution of law French (that is of Anglo-Norman), which was used in England until about 1400 by jurists, legal writers and the courts as a result of the Norman Conquest by William the Conqueror, the Duke of Normandy, at the Battle of Hastings in 1066. Even now, we sense the influence and presence of law French in common law. Many common law terms, concepts, locutions and expressions derive directly from law French (*en ventre sa mère, cestui que trust, semble, autrefois acquit, mortgage, plaintiff, defendant, profit à prendre, voir dire, tort, chose, lien, chattel, parole*).

Over time, common law jurists have developed parallel concepts by combining French terms and English terms, giving rise to a plethora of doublets in legal English (*last will and testament, breaking and entering, fit and proper*). At other times, two different terms were employed (one French and one English) for the same concept: *buy/purchase, have/possess, child/infant*. This parallelism makes the modes of expression in common law heavier and more complex. Undoubtedly, this is one reason why our Anglophone colleagues felt compelled to simplify legal language and produce clearer legal documents long before we Francophone civilians did. So the *Plain Language Movement* came to prominence in the English legal world.

The technical nature of legal English is due only in part to its lexicon. In fact, there is a greater distance between common law texts and English vernacular than there is between civil law texts and the French vernacular. There are more Latin words and heavy or archaic structures are more common as well. Sentences are long and often clouded by bewildering punctuation and grammar. The style is often turgid, verbose, cumbersome and fuzzy.

8.3.3 Legal French and legal English

Modes of expression peculiar to legal French and legal English attest to the genius of each language. As a rule, French employs deduction, beginning with principles and then applying them to concrete cases (from the general to the particular, the understanding level). English, on the other hand, prefers induction, inferring principles from particular cases or using analogy (the reality level).

It is often said that English functions with images and intuition at a concrete level while French, more abstract and more logical, operates at a conceptual level. The assumption is also valid in the field of legal language, in which Francophone lawyers' natural impulse is to resort to a greater degree of abstraction than their Anglophone counterparts. This is best illustrated by the importance that law deriving from the Romano-Germanic tradition gives to codified law, which constitutes the principal source of the law, and the paramount importance that common law ascribes to jurisprudence and judge-made law.

These differences also apply to dictionaries. The prevailing mode of expression of civilian dictionaries reflects an appreciation of meaning in law which is at once objective, historical and unified, which traits are, in turn, deeply embedded in the civilian imagination. As Nicholas Kasirer (2003: 387) remarks so aptly: 'Arguably, dictionaries play a different role in the Civil law methodology than in the Common law and this *fossé épistémologique* is felt in the way in which civilians cast definitions as generally applicable abstract ideas as opposed to the words and phrases constrained by facts in the Common law tradition.'

To illustrate theses differences, let us compare the definitions of the legal terms *delivery/livraison* as we encounter them in common law and civil law dictionaries respectively:

> *Delivery*
> The act by which the res or substance thereof is placed within the actual or constructive possession or control of another. (Garner 2004)
>
> *Livraison*
> Opération juridique par laquelle le transporteur remet, au destinataire qui l'accepte, la merchandise transportée. (Cornu 2000a, b)

which can be translated as: 'Legal operation by which property is placed at the disposal of the person who is entitled to it.' Very abstract indeed...

This said, civilian dictionaries offer a representation of reality that sometimes fails to take into account the diversity of meanings of terms encountered in the legal community.

In the exercise of their profession, legal translators who work from English to French become aware, as they go from one language to the other, that not only do the concepts and words change, but the relationships between them change as well. Each language favours certain forms, syntactical or stylistic processes, and terms.

English legal language abounds in catch-all words like *issue, policy, basis, case* and others such as *forum* and *jurisdiction*. French legal language demands greater precision, although it also resorts to all-purpose words such as *mesure, instance* or *justifié* for which English possesses more precise equivalents (for example there is a fortunate distinction in English between *right* and *law*, key words in the basic legal vocabulary for which French has only one word, *droit*, which is qualified (*droit objectif/droit subjectif*) or clarified by the context in order to express the various meanings).

Furthermore, legal English is more hospitable than French to qualifiers (e.g. clear, relevant, reasonable, trite, learned) while legal French, the descendant of Roman law, is more circumspect about adjectives, using them in general when they have legal value (*faute lourde, question sérieuse à juger, bon père de famille, personne raisonnable*).

The problem most often arises when we translate sayings, time-honoured adages that have acquired a particular lustre over the years. The following examples will illustrate these points.

8.3.4 A greater degree of abstraction

When the Supreme Court of Canada ruled on the legality of same-sex marriage, the newspapers made a feeble attempt to translate the justices' remark, 'La Constitution est un arbre vivant' as 'The Constitution is a living tree', taken from a judgment by the Privy Council in 1930 (*Lord Sankey L.C. from Edwards* v. *Attorney General for Canada*).

Such a hopelessly literal rendering may seem childish, hardly unusual in slavish translations from English. French demands a greater level of abstraction (Vinay and Darbelnet 1977).

8.3.4.1 The Chancellor's foot

Nineteenth-century English critics derided the discretion of the equity courts to enforce legal rights by complaining that the only standard by which to measure its authority was the size of the Chancellor's foot.

The image of the Chancellor's foot is used in common law to signify the inherent power of courts having jurisdiction in equity (recalling England's Court of Chancery in days gone by) to grant relief at their discretion in cases not provided for by common law. The standard regulating this type of relief is the size of the Chancellor's foot, a trope traditionally employed to evoke the sovereign power of equity courts. Gradually taking on a rather pejorative connotation, the expression could be rendered, in many contexts, by *norme arbitraire* or *pouvoir discrétionnaire absolu*. The meaning of this expression centres on the notion of the *arbitrary*, the *capricious (abusive discretionary power)*. Only in a work in which the historical context is significant would the translator use the image of the Chancellor's foot:

> [...] Des auteurs anglais du XIXe siècle ont tourné en dérision le pouvoir discrétionnaire des tribunaux siégeant en *equity* en lui reprochant le fait que le seul critère permettant d'en mesurer l'étendue était la taille du pied du chancelier.

If the context does not imply this idea of arbitrary power, the translator will simply use expressions like

> cas d'ouverture à l'application des principes d'equity
> (availability of equitable principles)
>
> A man's home is his castle.

A literal translation of this adage would fail to respect the genius of the French language. A better rendering would be *le principe de l'inviolabilité du domicile* or *du caractère sacré du domicile*.

Translators need to keep a critical distance from the text they are working on; they should not be obsessed by it. For instance, rendering some figurative English expressions (thin skull doctrine) requires a greater degree of abstraction in French (*théorie de la vulnérabilité de la victime*).

8.3.5 Word combinations – co-occurrents

As we have seen, the unique vehicle of law is language. The law has only words at its disposal to decree, formulate, apply and interpret the rule of law. In common law as in systems inspired by the Romano-Germanic tradition, the conceptual system is entirely dependent on discourse. And in this discourse, phraseology occupies a privileged place. Hence the importance of co-occurrence. Language is of paramount importance in law and, therefore, in legal translation, whatever the combination of languages in question.

Legal translators can count on few works to guide them in their difficult task of finding the appropriate co-occurrent, phrase or idiomatic expression. Jurilinguistics is still relatively unexplored territory. Bilingual lexicons abound. Terminological databanks – Termium, Eurodicautom – proliferate; there is no shortage of vocabularies, glossaries and lexicons (e.g. Beaudoin 2004; Beaudoin and Mailhot 2005; Crépeau 1991; Baleyte 1995; Mel'cuk 1984; Roland and Boyer 1983; Meertens 2002; Vincent and Guillien 1995; Dubois 1999; Elliott 1998; Didier 1990; Bissaron 2002; Beauchesne 2001). But much remains to be done in terms of bilingual legal phraseology. Though it is relatively easy to locate in specialized glossaries and dictionaries the exact right word to translate one's thought, it is more difficult to choose word combinations – co-occurrents – to create an idiomatic, elegant and precise phrase. For example, in French, is the correct usage *juger l'accusé coupable* or *déclarer l'accusé coupable*? How do we find a more precise term for the generic French word *admettre* (*une demande, une preuve, un pourvoi, une prétention*) and its English equivalent *to grant*? What is the English equivalent of the sanctioned expression *ester en justice*?

8.4 Conclusion

Legal translators must be taught to keep the reader in mind when drafting their texts. Their readers may not necessarily be legal experts. But the real challenge facing language instructors attempting to teach translation students and future jurists to write better is first to teach them how to think, and then to show them how to draft precise, simple, intelligible and pellucid texts informed by the latest principles of readability. In a bilingual and bi-jural country like Canada, they must be sensitive to the structural and cultural differences between the coexisting legal languages and systems.

These thoughts inevitably give rise to the following question: what is the place of jurilinguistics in our law faculties? Of what avail is our legal knowledge if we cannot transmit it?

To be a legal translator is to embark on a passionate adventure, a never-ending dialogue between two cultures, two ways of thinking, two world views. I would like to conclude by saying that legal translation is the most intense, most arduous, but also the most passionate of dialogues. We are privileged, indeed, to practise this stimulating, constantly evolving profession.

Part III

Concrete Problems in Legal Translation

9
Pitfalls of English as a Contract Language

Volker Triebel

9.1 The growing predominance of English as a contract language

9.1.1 English – the universal language of business and finance

The language spoken by business people in our globalized world is generally also the language used when they enter into contracts. Thus, there is a natural progression from the language used in business to the language used for conducting negotiations and, ultimately, the language used for contracting. Regardless of whether or not one believes the British Council's estimate that *one out of four of the world's population speaks English to some level of competence;...* [1], it cannot be denied that a substantial share of the business transacted in our global economy is handled in English. After all, nearly half (approximately 227) of the companies listed in the Fortune Global 500[2] are headquartered in an English-speaking country (Australia, Britain, Canada (not counting Quebec), Ireland or the USA).

Furthermore, two of the world's main financial centres are firmly seated in English-speaking territory – London, the traditional centre of finance, and New York. Even where neither London nor New York plays a role in a particular financial transaction, the English language frequently still does. The following example where none of the players involved is a native English speaker illustrates this.

A German company financed by a German lead bank/arranger acquires a target company in Germany. The German bank, eager to share the credit risk with other banks, brings in other lenders (this is called syndication). The facility agreement for the German acquiring company, often also the working capital of the German target, will be syndicated in Luxembourg. Any attempt by the German company to insist on the

German language being used for the documentation would be flatly refused with the *floodgate* argument, that is allowing German to be used would lead to allowing lots of different languages to be used. As a result, syndication in Luxembourg is only possible in English although it is a foreign language for all of the parties concerned!

9.1.2 English – the language of convenience

Many European lawyers like drafting contracts in English since it is a cosmopolitan language in which they feel at home even though it is not their first language. Many naturally feel some closeness to their native tongue. Germans and northern Europeans feel at ease with the Germanic grammatical structure and many Germanic words in the English language. Our French colleagues detect French roots in many English words,[3] especially in English legal terms.[4] Italian and Spanish lawyers are happy to discover the common Latin roots of English legal terms and also find terms and maxims in Latin.[5] Indeed, half of the English vocabulary is derived from Latin, be it directly or indirectly through French (Baugh and Cable 2002: 11).

Other foreigners are attracted to English due to its inflectional simplicity and natural gender without realizing the price they have to pay for it, namely greater ambiguity[6] which can only be avoided by a rigid word order.

Languages of Continental Europe have lost the battle for the prevailing contract language to English. The dominance of legal English and common law is increasing. The battle for the governing contract law has been discontinued in Europe, since Anglo-American firms have merged with continental firms. But common law is still outside the gates of Continental Europe.[7] More importantly, the largest player in the global economy, the USA, and the two most prominent financial centres, New York and London, are English-speaking and are governed by common law.

Nolens volens civil law lawyers have to accept that English is the international contract language. And common law lawyers have to become accustomed to their civil law brethren drafting and negotiating contracts in a type of English which is different from the English they are accustomed to at home.

As a warning to civil law lawyers, it must be said that it is a fallacy to think English is an easy language. It may well be easy to gain quickly a modest – au pair – level of proficiency in English, but in fact English, in particular written English, is rather a difficult language. This is all the more true when it comes to legal English.

9.2 Unity of language, forum and law

This essay puts forward the following propositions:

1. English as a contract language is difficult to master, even for common law lawyers. Problems exist even where there is harmony between language, forum and law, that is to say where a dispute arising under a contract written in English and governed by English law (or the law of another common law jurisdiction) is brought before common law judges or common law arbitrators.[8]
2. Even more difficulties are encountered in those situations where there is no unity of language, law and forum. There will be a higher degree of uncertainty and a greater scope for misunderstandings where a contract written in English and governed by English law is to be adjudicated by civil law judges or arbitrators who have to decide how the contract should be construed or which meaning of an ambiguous term should prevail.
3. The situation is even more precarious where the governing law of a contract written in English is that of a civil law country. Additional ambiguities will arise where an English term of art or an ordinary word may have another meaning under a civil law system. Civil law lawyers using English as a contract language must be on guard, even when their native law governs the contract. But common law lawyers also encounter difficulties in understanding a contract written in their native language but drafted by civil law lawyers.

Each of these three situations is dealt with in detail below. In this essay, English law has been chosen among the common law systems and German law among the civil law systems.

9.3 English contracts under common law

9.3.1 English contract language and historical common law

Legal English is inseparable from common law

Civil law lawyers should be warned: an English contract governed by English law can only be understood within the context of English law. English law, like common law in general, developed in England after 1066 and is a historical law. Legal English and common law grew up together. Many English legal terms and concepts can only be understood against a common law background. Only common law jurists know their full significance. Without a thorough knowledge of common law and contract practice, it is impossible to fully grasp the full content, ambit and proper use of these terms of art and concepts.

Here are examples from land law.[9] The meaning of the term *fee simple* cannot fully be conveyed by using the term *property*, as the Roman concept of *dominium* was never received into English law. *Mortgage* cannot be considered identical with the German *Hypothek*. In the case of an English mortgage there is a transfer of an interest in land subject to an equity of redemption.[10] A *Hypothek* is just a legal (not an equitable) charge on the immovable property of another. A lease under common law gives the lessee an interest in the leased property, not merely a contractual licence (like a *Mietvertrag* under German law).

Equity is a set of rules developed by separate courts in England. It is important to know whether rights and remedies derive from equity or law because the requirements for and the legal consequences of the two are different.

Common law terms with no equivalent in civil law

There are many English legal terms of art, words with a special legal meaning,[11] for which there is no equivalent in civil law systems. There are many others which cannot be translated into another language at all or only as broad approximations even if these terms originated from Norman French or from Latin.[12] Many common law legal terms have a forensic and not a scholastic origin since they were developed by the courts and not as the result of abstract considerations in academic circles.

To name but a few examples where there is no civil law equivalent:

- *Deed*: a deed is a written document that must be signed, sealed and delivered. A deed must make it clear on its face that it is intended to be a deed and validly executed as a deed. Before 31 July 1990, all deeds required a seal in order to be validly executed. This requirement was abolished by the Law of Property (Miscellaneous Provisions) Act 1989. A promise contained in a deed is a covenant and is binding even if not supported by consideration. The advantage of a deed over an ordinary contract is that the statute of limitations period is 12 rather than 6 years and no consideration is required in order for the deed to be enforceable.
- *Trust* is the ingenious invention of the concept of equity. Rights and obligations arising out of a trust find no equivalents under civil law.
- *Consideration* is the benefit to the promisor or detriment (loss or disadvantage) to the promisee. Consideration is an essential part of a contract under common law, unless the contract is made in the form

of a deed. Reference to it in the recitals under common law is ineffective and superfluous. Reference to consideration under civil law is pointless because there is no equivalent for it in civil law: *in consideration of...* does not mean *with regard to...* and *in consideration of* should not be translated in the sense of *having regard to*.
- *Registered office* is a concept of English company law denoting an address where certain documents must be kept for inspection by the shareholders and where documents may be served (cf. Sect. 287 Companies Act 1985; Triebel et al. 2006: 20–1). German company law does not yet[13] have an equivalent to this concept, but has developed the notion of *seat (Sitz)* which is the place of a municipality.

Lawyers use many common law words that they invest with a special meaning. This can confuse the layman or foreign lawyer. However, many of these legalese terms will be given up for the sake of clarity and plain English.

The procedural nature of some common law terms poses interesting issues of categorization: how will a German court deal with a procedural common law term whose equivalent under civil law is a matter of substantive law? Many common law terms have their background in procedural and not substantive law. These include:

- *Remedy* is a term of procedural and not of substantive law. It is noteworthy that in common law contracts the clause following *Representations and Warranties* is generally a provision headed *Remedies for Breach* and not *Rights for Breach*.[14]
- *Specific performance* is a discretionary secondary remedy developed in equity to grant performance of a contract in circumstances where damages are not adequate.
- *Limitation* is a procedural defence and not a matter of substantive law. It is the remedy and not the substantive right which becomes time barred upon expiration of the limitation period.
- *Interest* is classified under common law as a matter of procedure and not of substance.

Common law contract style

The style of common law contracts is influenced by a variety of factors including the legal tradition of judge-made law, the lesser emphasis on codifications and the rigid rules of construction developed by the courts.

Contracts are mostly drafted in more concrete terms than their civil law counterparts: with general parts and general concepts as civil law systems have developed them; with only a few types of contract with yielding statutory provisions thus necessitating writing into contracts many details; more rigid rules of construction. Since they may end up being void for uncertainty if drafted too broadly, it is no wonder that common law contracts tend to be more concrete and less abstract. Thus, the court in *National Trust* v. *Midlands Electricity Board* ([1952] Ch. 380) held that the omission of any concrete criterion made the contract uncertain and void:

> No act or thing shall be done or placed or permitted to remain upon the land which shall injure, prejudice, affect or destroy the natural aspect and condition of the land except as hereinafter provided.

Common law lawyers seldom draft a contract from scratch, but avail themselves of form books, standard forms, precedents[15] and model contracts.[16] The common law world is drowning in such precedents. They give common law lawyers a degree of security: by using tried and tested standard forms, common law courts will presume that the parties relied on the established practice and interpretations by the courts.[17] However, they should be used judiciously and sparingly and should not be the draftsmen's masters,[18] rather their servants. Simply slavishly copying and pasting without giving each sentence due consideration can be fatal (Butt and Castle 2001: 7–12).

The traditional structure of English sentences in contracts is different from that of German ones. The structure of an English contract goes back to land law with deeds dealing with conveyancing, leases and trusts. These deeds set the pattern of contract drafting in the common law world. Following an old legislative tradition,[19] the confining circumstances for an action and the conditions come first followed by the subject and the action (Daigneault 2005: 58–61; Asprey 2003: 111–15). The order of the typical English sentence in contracts is: where/when A[20] – and if B – then (C = legal subject + D = legal action), such as: 'Where the Buyer has not paid the purchase price by and if the Seller has set a time limit in writing for payment and the Buyer has not complied with it, (then) the Seller may rescind the contract except when E and F.'[21] As translators from English into German will know, a typical German sentence begins with the statement followed by the circumstances, conditions, qualifications and limitation.

Clarity

The Plain English Campaign also encroached upon legal English in all parts of the common law world culminating in Clarity, an international organization of lawyers devoted to improving legal drafting (Butt and Castle 2001: 61; Asprey 2003: 11–78). The effects have been felt over the full range from procedure[22] to consumer and commercial contracts.

Many traditional common law terms should be replaced by familiar words, for example:

- *Alienate* by *transfer*
- *Avoid* by *cancel*
- *Execute*[23] by *sign a contract*
- The archaic *joint and several*, though still widely used, by *together and separately*
- *Instrument* by *legal document*
- *Of course* by *as a matter of right*
- *Provided*[24] *that*, as it is used, is often ambiguous: it may introduce (a) a condition where it should be replaced by *if*; (b) an exception where it should be replaced by *except* or *however*; (c) a limitation where it should be replaced by *in any event*; and (d) an addition where it should be omitted
- *Quiet enjoyment* by *uninterrupted possession*: when a landlord promises a tenant *quiet enjoyment* he promises he will not default under the mortgage or do anything else that might cause some third party to try to remove the tenant
- *Restraining order* by *injunction*
- *Save* by *except*.

9.3.2 Ordinary English as the contract language

Words and phrases judicially defined

Not only English legal terms, but also ordinary English words in contracts may give rise to problems. This is reflected by the fact that common law courts have often been called upon to interpret English words and phrases which are not terms of art. Thus, the courts have given many words of ordinary English a special, often more precise, meaning. Many common law lawyers are lulled into a feeling of precision when they see how a court has construed a word or phrase. For the precise meaning not only of legal terms, but also of ordinary English expressions, there are voluminous books such as *Words and Phrases Judicially Defined (*Burrows 1943–46); *Words and Phrases* (1940–73).

Vague words and phrases

There is a difference between ambiguity[25] and vagueness. Ambiguity arises when a word or a phrase may have two or more inconsistent meanings. This should be avoided at all costs in contract drafting since certainty is the ultimate aim. Vagueness, however, is a matter of degree (Child 1992: 304). Too much vagueness may render a contract void. Vague words receive their contents from their context and the circumstances of the case without the sanction of nullity.[26] There are many of these that common law lawyers use both because of, and in spite of, their flexibility, well realizing that complete precision cannot be achieved.

Needless to say, vague words and phrases are constantly litigated. Here is a sampling of vague words lawyers use:

> about, adequate, as soon as possible, due, excessive, fair, few, just, forthwith,[27] immediately and without any delay,[28] material, substantial,[29] sufficient, necessary, on demand (Asprey 2003: 177), practicable, proper, reasonable (alone or in its many combinations, like *reasonable doubt, beyond a reasonable doubt, consent not be unreasonably withheld* (Mellinkoff 1963: 301–4ff.), reputable, satisfactory, suitable, whenever possible.

Auxiliary verbs[30]

The proper use of auxiliary verbs is a constant source of confusion:

- *Shall*[31] can be present imperative (*You shall do as I say*) or future indicative (*I shall contact you shortly*). In legal documents *shall* is generally not used to express future time but to express obligation. However, there is authority that *shall* necessarily implies futurity. Thus, there is ambiguity (Butt and Castle 2001: 99–104). In Wydick's eyes *shall* is the biggest troublemaker; he recommends: 'Don't use *shall* for any purpose – it is simply too unreliable' (Wydick 2005: 63, 64). For the future tense, *will* and not *shall* should be used (Butt and Castle 2001: 150–2).
- Lawyers tend to use *shall* all the time without thinking, just in case the present imperative is the appropriate one. In fact the present tense and not *shall* is appropriate in definition clauses because a declaration is being made.
- *Must* denotes all required actions, whether or not the subject of the clause performs the action of the verb. Hence, *Notice must be*

given within 14 days and *The employee must give notice within 30 days* (Garner 1987: 941). *Must* is sometimes preferable to *shall* since it clearly imposes an obligation.

- *May* is permissive and conveys discretion. Hence, *The seller may ship by air, truck or rail.*
- *May not* can express a prohibition, but is ambiguous: *May not transfer shares* may mean (i) may possibly not transfer, (ii) is authorized not to transfer, and (iii) is not authorized to transfer (Adams 2004: 36). Thus it is better to use *must not.*
- Use of the correct tense – language of performance: when drafting a document, it should not be overlooked that documents normally become operative on execution by both parties or on exchange. At the time of drafting the document the action covered by it is in the future. However, the document should speak in the present tense regarding matters happening at the time of exchange or execution. The agreement to buy or sell, or to lease, or mortgage, is a present agreement at the date of execution. It is easy for the draftsman to express these in the future tense when drafting the document, for example *the mortgagee will agree to lend the sum of $10,000.* The correct expression should be *agrees to lend,* as that is occurring on execution of the document. Similarly, where an agreement deals with a period of time commencing from its date of execution and continuing throughout its operative term, it is preferable to use the present tense. For example, in a partnership agreement, in defining the partners' mutual obligations, it is better to say that they agree to be honest and faithful, rather than that they *shall be honest and faithful.* That obligation operates from the moment of execution, being effective for the duration of the transaction. In these cases the present tense should be used instead of a modal auxiliary verb.

And *and* or

The connectives *and* and *or*[32] may add more ambiguities. At first sight the difference between the two words might appear obvious – *A and B* means both of them and *A or B* presents a choice between them – but in some cases it is not that easy. For example, the sentence *Husbands and fathers have special rights* does not necessarily mean that a person must be both a husband and a father to enjoy special rights. Using the singular form can make the sentence clearer; assuming the intention is that it is sufficient to be either, it is better to write: *A person who is a husband or a father has special rights.*

Sometimes *and* has been construed as meaning *or*, usually to rescue faulty drafting as in *Re Capital Fire Insurance Association* ((1882) 21 Ch. D. 209, at p. 214). More frequently the difficulty is to determine whether *or* includes *and*, as when a will empowers trustees to apply trust income *for religious or educational purposes*. Almost certainly, the trustees can apply the income for purposes which are both religious and educational or partly in one way and partly in the other, and are not compelled to apply the whole of the income to a purpose which is religious but not educational or educational but not religious.

Difficulties such as these have led to an increasing use of the hybrid conjunction and disjunction *and/or*, but most authorities agree that *A or B or both* should be preferred (Mellinkoff 1963: 306–10). There is not always agreement as to what *and/or* means especially where it is used to link more than two nouns or adjectives. Even in the case of *A and/or B*, which probably means A or B or both of them, *A or B* is usually sufficient, and in case of doubt it is not unduly burdensome to write in full *A or B or both*. Frequently when a draftsman writes *A and/or B* closer analysis shows that he means *A with or without B* and does not in fact intend to refer to B alone. Unintended combinations are more likely when C or C and D are introduced.

When a positive statement is turned into a negative statement, it is usually, but not always, necessary to change *and* to *or*. This is something that foreigners are often unaware of. Take, for example, the statement *The company will pay a dividend and a bonus*. In negative form, depending upon the circumstances, it should probably read, *The company will not pay a dividend or a bonus*. To say *a dividend and a bonus* after *not* leaves open the logical possibility that one or the other, although not both, may be paid. In other cases *and* is appropriate, as when articles of association provide that where capital is paid up on shares in advance of calls the shareholder is not entitled to receive interest and to participate in profits. The words *both* and *either* can be used to increase clarity in such situations.

Also *every* and *each* must be used carefully*: every* refers to *all* members of a group while *each* refers to the individual members of the group, singly. Thus *A may buy /every/ /each/ painting exhibited in the house* may mean two things: (i) *A may buy no fewer than all paintings in the house* or (ii) *A may buy one or more of the paintings in the house.*

A frequent source of misunderstanding is the misconception among many German speakers that the word *beziehungsweise ('bzw')* automatically means *respectively* in English. Depending on how it is used it can mean four different things. It can actually mean respectively, as when one says *John and Mary were given apples and pears respectively,* in other words John received apples and Mary was given pears. On the other hand, it could mean *or* or it could mean *or* and *and.*[33] Finally, it can be used to simply narrow down what it is the speaker is trying to say and have the meaning of *that is to say, more specifically* or *more precisely.*[34]

Singular v. plural

As a general rule, it is preferable to draft in the singular rather than the plural. For example: *Each purchaser shall pay the purchase money in respect of the shares that he is purchasing* is better than *The respective purchasers shall pay the respective purchase moneys in respect of the shares that they are respectively purchasing.* To use the plural without *respective* or *respectively* as the case may require is to risk, among other things, the inadvertent creation of joint rights or obligations and problems of survivorship. Language of permission (may) compound difficulties. Thus: *The shareholders may notify the company* may mean any of the following: (i) *Any shareholder may...* (ii) *No fewer than all shareholders may...* and (iii) *The shareholders acting collectively may ...*

Expressions of time

Particularly in the case of expressions dealing with time, it is suggested that vague expressions – unless chosen intentionally – should be avoided, such as *forthwith, immediately, as soon as possible, within a reasonable time* or *within a substantial* or *short period of time.* It is better to specify a period in days or months within which the conduct should occur.

When referring to a point in time, it is often unclear whether the day in question is included or excluded. There are conflicting court decisions as to whether the prepositions denoting the beginning of a point of time *from, after, starting* and *on* and the prepositions stating the ending of a point in time *until, to, on, before, through* and *by* do exclude or include the given day. To achieve clarity, *inclusive* or *exclusive* should be added (Adams 2004: 135ff.; see also Asprey 2003: 179). The following are some alternative methods of ensuring certainty:

- From 12 March 2000 to 25 March 2000, both days included (or excluded).
- Until and including (or not including) 25 March 2000.
- On and from (or on and after) 12 March 2000.
- Commencing with (or on) 12 March 2000 and ending with (or on) 25 March 2000.

The preposition *within* denoting a span of time can have two meanings; such as in the sentence: *The buyer may exercise the option within ten days of the first anniversary of this contract.* This could mean the period after or before the first anniversary or both. Clarity would be achieved by saying *within seven days after the first anniversary* if a forward-running period is intended.

The use of common terms like *month* and *year* can be problematic since these terms are defined by statute and may have different meanings in English and German law.[35] If some terms are defined differently, the applicability of the statutory aid as a whole may be jeopardized.

The importance of word order

Inflectional simplicity, the lack of cases as well as only a natural but no grammatical gender,[36] often cause syntactic ambiguity. This can only be avoided by adhering to a rigid word order. The simplest rule is: keep the subject, verb and object close together. However, there are modifiers, limitations, conditions and so on which may cause syntactic problems in attempting to ascertain the exact meaning of a particular statement.

English grammar rules require the modifier[37] to be put next to what it modifies (antecedent rule). A modifier may precede or follow or occur between an enumeration leaving it open whether it refers to only one, several or all of the words. If the modifier follows a group of words, the rule of English grammar is that it refers only to the last word (rule of the last antecedent). Depending on the positioning of the adverb of time, the following sentence can have two different meanings:

> If this contract is terminated, the Agent shall be [*immediately*] instructed to cancel all outstanding work orders. (The Agent must be instructed immediately.)
>
> If this contract is terminated, the Agent shall be instructed to cancel all outstanding work orders [*immediately*]. (The Agent must cancel all outstanding work orders immediately.)

The word *only* is a notorious troublemaker in English contracts. In the following sentence the word *only* could go in any of seven places and produce five different meanings:

> Only she said that he shot her.
> She only said that he shot her.

She said only that he shot her.
She said that only he shot her.
She said that he only shot her.
She said that he shot only her.
She said that he shot her only.

Punctuation

What importance should be given to punctuation?[38] We Germans have strict rules, the English less so. Mellinkoff (1963: 366) even says: 'A characteristic lack of adequate punctuation (in the English language) is a major obstacle of precision in legal writing….' The old view is that the sense of a document should be gathered from the words and the context rather than from punctuation.[39] The well-known judge Sir Robert Megarry once said: 'Punctuation is a servant and not a master of substance and meaning.' Yet Sir Robert Caseman was hanged because of a comma (virgule) in the old English Treason Act of 1351 (Mellinkoff 1963: 167ff.)! An Australian court was called upon to analyse a worker's insurance policy describing the employer's business as *fuel carrying and repairing*. The question was: did the policy cover an employee who was injured when driving the employer's vehicle carrying bricks? The court interpreted the policy in the employee's favour by construing it to read as either *fuel, carrying, and repairing* or *fuel carrying, and repairing* (*Manufacturers' Manual Insurance Ltd* v. *Withers* (1998) 5ANZ Insurance Case 60–853).

Punctuation can remove ambiguities by using commas and distinguishing between *that* and *which*: *The inventory that was acquired during the relevant period* is a restrictive clause; *The inventory, which was acquired…* is an unrestricted clause. Omitting the comma in the first sentence probably converts the restrictive into a non-restrictive clause (Adams 2004: 153).

Interest in punctuation has been revived considerably in Britain in recent years where a book on punctuation has become a best-seller (Truss 2004) and the BBC has produced a number of programmes (quiz shows) testing the participants' knowledge of grammar.

Plain (= standard) English

The attractiveness of English as a contract language has increased with the trend towards plain (= standard = modern) English. Many English-speaking people have digested Fowler (1968) and Gowers (1986). Over the last 50 years the Campaign for Plain English has influenced written English and recommended the avoidance of verbosity, the passive voice, synonyms and abstract words.

Good drafting now seeks to avoid lawyerisms, unnecessary legal jargon and wordy phrases. Circumlocution can be avoided by substituting *as* for *having regard to the fact* and saying *where* or *if* instead of *in the event that*. Similarly, *binds* can be substituted for *is binding upon*, *before* can be substituted for *prior to*, *under* used instead of *under the provisions of* and *with reference to* can be replaced by *about* or *concerning*.[40]

Doubling, that is to say the use of several terms to describe a single concept, where a single term would be adequate for that purpose, should be avoided. Doubling is misleading, as it has the appearance of added certainty or suggests some additional meaning which does not exist. The following are examples of doubling: *agreed and declared, all or any, do and perform, goods and chattels, null and void, sell and assign, by and between* and *due and payable, each and every, from and after, have and hold, power and authority* and *true, correct and complete* (instead of *accurate*).[41]

Archaic words can be omitted or replaced by modern ones: *said* can be replaced with *the, that* or *those*, *same* can be replaced with *it, he, him* and so on and *aforesaid, hereunder, hereinbefore*,[42] and *such*[43] are mostly simply superfluous.[44]

It is no longer customary to write after the recitals leading into the operational part of a contract: *NOW, THEREFORE, in consideration of the premises and the mutual covenants set out herein and for other good and valuable consideration, the receipt and sufficiency of which are hereby acknowledged the parties hereby agree and acknowledge as follows:...* Instead simply: *It is agreed as follows:...* is sufficient.

Short sentences are preferable to long ones. These make it easier for the reader to comprehend the message contained in the document. The active voice should be used in preference to the passive voice. It is grammatically impossible to draft in the active voice without disclosing the legal subject of the sentence. Where a sentence is expressed in the passive voice the legal subject is disclosed only by implication unless a phrase beginning with the word *by* is incorporated. Usually the context indicates the legal subject, but a draftsman who uses the active voice does not need to rely on the context. Needless to say, expressions used in a document should have a consistent meaning throughout the document.

However, plain English, like many simplifications, can be dangerous. Thus advocates of plain English recommend replacing the prolixity *in connection with* by *under, with, about* or *concerning*. This also narrows the scope of an arbitration clause by excluding tortuous claims and issues affecting the underlying agreement (Russell et al. 2003: 59–61).

9.3.3 English canons of construction

An important peculiarity of a common law contract, which often is overlooked, is that the canons of construction/interpretation are different from those under civil law. Thus the same legal term, the same phrase in a contract may be given a different interpretation depending on whether the contract is construed under English or German law.

Plain meaning rule

For centuries English courts applied the 'plain meaning rule': the ordinary, literal, lexical, dictionary meaning of a word was decisive. To find out the lexical meaning of an ordinary English word[45] resort to an English dictionary like the American *Webster's* or the *Oxford English Dictionary* (= *OED*). The latter is the best starting point for a semantic search, as it gives in chronological order all uses and meanings a word has had from about the year 1000 to the present day. It thus recognizes that words may acquire a new meaning, that their meaning may change, become restricted and enlarged.[46]

Needless to say, common law lawyers apply the rules of English grammar when drafting a common law contract. They are often rigid in applying the antecedent rule and relate a modifier only to the nearest word it can possibly qualify.

Punctuation

Even today punctuation plays only a minor role in construing a contract.

Noscitur a sociis[47]

Nonetheless, a term is to be seen in its contextual setting. General words may be restricted by surrounding words.

Expressio unius

English law has rules on interpretation, some of which are known by Latin expressions, such as *expressio unius est exclusio alterius*.[48] Will excessively detailed definitions prove dangerous? Will the cautionary rider *unless the context requires otherwise* overcome this difficulty?[49]

Eiusdem generis

Where specific words, like *apple, pears, plums* belonging to a class (genus), are followed by general words, like *other goods*, the latter will be construed narrowly under the *eiusdem generis*[50] rule. In an attempt to avoid this effect, common law draftsmen insert words like *without affecting the generality of the foregoing* (what is the foregoing?), *without limiting the generality* and *including without limitation.*

Every word has a meaning

Under common law canons of construction every word must be given a meaning and nothing should be treated as superfluous (Adams 2004: 206). Therefore, the use of synonyms[51] may be dangerous, as synonyms may be given unforeseen meanings.

Contra proferentem

There is a common law rule of construction that ambiguous and unclear words should be construed against the party who chose them.[52] This rule exists in German law only where standard terms are involved.

Commercial or purposive interpretation

Under English canons of construction, the purpose of the contract and its commercial intention cannot be taken into account. This is significantly different from the position under German law where the purpose is of such importance that it can be given greater weight than the actual text of the contract.[53]

However, the commercial or purposive interpretation has now been introduced in England. In *Mannai Investments Co Ltd* v. *Eagle Star Life Assurance Co Ltd* [1997] AC 749 the House of Lords, by a majority of three (among them Lords Steyn and Hoffmann, both of whom come from South Africa[54]), overturned the rule that evidence about the factual circumstances in which a notice had been served should, generally speaking, be ignored. Instead the court held that the purpose of the wording should be considered (commercial interpretation).

The case concerned a 'break clause'[55] in a lease which permitted the tenant to terminate that lease on 13 January 1995. The tenant served a break notice on the landlord. Unfortunately for the tenant, that notice stated that: *Pursuant to Clause 7(13) of the lease we as tenant hereby give notice to you to determine the lease on 12 January 1995.*

The notice was clear and unambiguous. The semantic and syntactical analysis left no doubt. If applied rigidly and formalistically, the notice would have failed. However, knowledge of the background against which the notice was given clearly showed that the wrong date had been inserted. The House of Lords found that the break clause had only one purpose: to inform the landlord that the tenant wished to determine the lease in accordance with its terms. The House of Lords ruled in favour of the tenant and overruled precedents established over centuries.

Recitals

What meaning will a civil law court give to the recitals/preamble[56]/background/whereas[57] clauses which commonly set out the facts, background information, context (narrative or context recitals) and parties' intentions, purpose (purpose recitals), simultaneous transactions and lead into the main body, the operative part, of the contract? English courts regard recitals as subordinate to the body of the contract and place lesser weight on them in construing the contract as a whole. Where there is a contradiction between the recitals and the body of the contract (a contextual ambiguity), the meaning of the operative words will prevail (*Leggott* v. *Barrett* [1880] 15 Ch D 306 at p. 311; Butt and Castle 2001: 163). German courts regard the recitals as *Geschäftsgrundlage*, that is to say as the basis of the entire contract.

Rules of English grammar and punctuation

Apart from the rules of construction, what about the rules of grammar and punctuation? Are English contracts that are governed by a civil law to be construed according to the rules of English grammar? Does the modifier relate only to the nearest word it can possibly qualify under the antecedent rule? How can one resolve the ambiguities caused by *squinting* modifiers that may qualify what precedes them or what follows? How should German courts deal with English rules of punctuation? May a German judge pay as little attention to punctuation as English judges do?

Contract history

The above-mentioned decision of the House of Lords regarding the break clause does bring the canons of interpretation under common law closer to those of civil law. However, there are still marked differences when it comes to the details. The most striking is contract history. What was said during contractual negotiations and after execution of the contract may be used in German courts as evidence as to how certain words and phrases should be understood. Such parol evidence is still not admissible in English courts, although it is admissible in German courts. As is evident from this difference, the question of which country's canon of interpretation governs can be of vital importance.

Interplay of implied terms, frustration and good faith

The interpretation of contracts cannot be seen in isolation from other legal concepts and doctrines. It is surprising that common law applies the concept of implied terms so sparingly, and this despite the lack of codifications in the Continental sense and with only little statutory yielding law (*ius dispositivum*). The same applies to the doctrine of frustration which plays but a minor role compared with the civil law doctrines of *clausula rebus sic stantibus* (and the *Geschäftsgrundlage* in Germany).[58] Again, there is a reluctance to invoke good faith in common law (see Triebel et al. 1995: 65–7, 79–82).

There is thus an interplay between the importance of the wording of a contract on the one side and canons of interpretation and the application of the doctrines of implied terms, frustration and good faith on the other: where contracts are construed narrowly and judges are less willing to rewrite the contracts under the disguise of implied terms, frustration, good faith and other concepts, the exact wording of a contract becomes vitally important. No wonder that MAC clauses (material adverse change) are an invention of common law.[59]

9.3.4 Common law contracts before civil law judges and arbitrators

Judges and arbitrators know their native language best

What will a German judge or arbitrator do when construing an English legal term under common law? He might have recourse to Christine Rossini's *English as a Legal Language*[60] or another English legal dictionary.

If an English phrase is obscure or in dispute between the parties, the German judge or arbitrator may play it safe and request a translation under section 142 (3) of the German Code of Civil Procedure (*Zivilprozessordnung*) which states that:

> The Court may request a translation of a document written in a foreign language. The translation must be done by a translator authorized under the guidelines of the Land agency for the administration of justice.

Of course, there are many excellent translators. However, when it comes to a English legal term it is debatable whether a judge can rely on a linguist alone with regard to what is often a question of construction.

Foreign terms – law or fact?

A German judge is put into a difficult position when a contract which was written in English is governed by English law (or the law of another common law country).

Foreign law is in common law jurisdictions not a matter of law, but of fact. Thus an English judge when construing a German term of art will rely on the expert evidence of German lawyers, and often each party will provide opinions containing contradictory views.

In contrast, German law provides in section 293 of the German Code of Civil Procedure:

> The law which is in force in another state, customary law and by-laws require proof only to such extent as they are unknown to the court. In the establishment of these legal norms, the court is not limited to the evidence brought forward by the parties; it is empowered to make use of other sources of knowledge and to order whatever is necessary for the purpose of such utilization.

Thus, for a German judge English law is a question of law and not a question of fact. He is free to look up the meanings of English legal terms in law dictionaries. He need not rely on the evidence brought by the parties, but may resort to other sources and make the appropriate orders. In practice, the German judge will usually ask a university institute to prepare an opinion (Kegel and Schurig 2004: 501).

A judgment of first instance may be reversed in the second instance. But there is no appeal on questions of foreign law to the third instance, as an appeal may only be based upon a violation of German federal law or a violation of a legal provision which is also applicable in Germany outside the district of the appeal court. However, if a judge violates his procedural duty to ascertain the foreign law, this procedural issue may be subject to an appeal to a court of third instance (see section 545 (1) of the German Code of Civil Procedure).

9.4 English contracts under civil law

9.4.1 Different canons of construction/interpretation

More ambiguities will be created when an English contract is governed by civil law. One reason, which is often overlooked, is that the canons of construction/interpretation are different in common and civil law. Thus, the same legal term, the same phrase in a contract may be given a different interpretation depending on whether the contract is governed by English or German law. These differences of the methods of interpretation pose many questions and uncertainties as to how a contract written in English but governed by civil law is to be construed.

Does the plain meaning rule apply? Has an English word the meaning given in the English dictionaries and in the thick volumes of *Words and Phrases Judicially Defined?* Most probably so: for where English is used as a contract language, English words have to be given the meaning the words have in that language.

Are English contracts governed by civil law to be construed according to rules of English grammar? Where the meaning is not clear from the context, does the modifier relate only to the nearest word it can possibly qualify under the antecedent rule? Most probably so: for by using English also English grammar has been chosen. How should German courts deal with English rules of punctuation? May a German judge pay as little attention to punctuation as English judges do?

Do English legal rules of construction prevail, even if they lead to a different construction if German rules applied? What about *noscitur a sociis*? And what about *expressio unius* and the *eiusdem generis* rule? Is a German judge forced to give every word a meaning? Will a German judge construe a phrase against the party who had chosen it (*contra proferentem*), even if no standard terms are at stake?[61] If the contract is governed by German law, German rules of construction should also apply and not English ones.

Does purpose, which has played such an eminent role in the construction of statutes and contracts in Germany since the time of Jehring, have a wider impact than under common law?

Must German courts ignore the recitals where the operative part of the contract is beyond doubt? Or must it apply the doctrine of *Geschäftsgrundlage* which are often stated in the background provisions? This question should be decided in conformity with the choice of law.

Should contract history be ignored under the parol evidence rule? Certainly not, if German procedural law is applied. But what about the entire contract clause which does not allow adducing statements made outside the four corners of the contract?

9.4.2 Legal terms of art

Common law terms

Common law terms will ring a bell with a common law lawyer, but are unlikely to do so with a civil law lawyer. Likewise, civil law lawyers will recognize civil law concepts and terms which escape a common law lawyer. Often legal terms of one system of law have an equivalent in another system; however, the borders of their meaning are hardly ever the same. Rossini (1998: XXI) rightly warns: using English terms with a specific meaning under common law to describe a similar civil law term may produce a comparative law nightmare.

Thus, there are common law terms with no equivalent in civil law systems, like terms in land law (*fee simple*), *deed* and *consideration*. When used in a contract governed by civil law, these terms of art may denote the nearest equivalent in civil law terminology (*fee simple* for *dominium*, *deed* for *notarial document* might be meaningless and not to be understood at all (like *consideration*)).

More dangerous are common law legal terms with some counterpart in civil law terminology, however, often with a different reach, ambit and content in detail. It is to be recognized that exact transpositions of legal terms and concepts are impossible to achieve (McAuliffe 2006b). There are plenty of examples. The question always is: is the common law term to be understood as under common law or is it to be given the meaning under civil law?

- An outstanding example is the English legal term *dead freight*, which has a German counterpart, *Fautfracht*, which is regulated by sections 580ff. of the German Commercial Code (*Handelsgesetzbuch*). In a case decided by the German Federal Court of Justice[62] (BGH) a German shipper terminated a contract of affreightment (carriage of goods by sea) entered into with an English carrier. The parties agreed that the German shipper should pay *dead freight* of £50,000 (instead of the contractual freight of £100,000). German law governed the contract. A dispute arose as to whether *dead freight* should be given the meaning under section 580 of the German Commercial Code or whether the meaning of the English technical term should prevail. The German Federal Court of Justice gave the term its meaning under English law and ignored German law on the basis that an English technical term had been used (Triebel and Balthasar 2004: 2189–95)!
- A similar reasoning is found in an international arbitration case where the meaning of *will cause* in a memorandum of understanding (MoU) governed by Indonesian law was at stake. The question was whether these words were legally binding or not. The Arbitral Tribunal relied on English authority: although English law is not the governing law, the MoU is drafted in English. The English cases, which gave rise to much more careful debate, as to the nuances of pertinent expressions, are therefore instructive as a reference point for the purposes of establishing the intention of the parties as expressed in the MoU (*Yearbook of International Arbitration* 1978–, vol. 25, p. 202).

- *Force majeure* is a clause which causes great confusion under German law. Its effects are well settled under English law: it will excuse performance where events outside the control of a party make performance impossible. Such a clause makes sense under English law where – generally speaking – contractual liability is strict and not dependent on fault of a party (Triebel et al. 1995: 76). Under the fault regime of German law,[63] however, such a clause is meaningless and may be distorting: fault often requires more than just an event outside the control of a party; a *force majeure* clause may jeopardize the fault principle.
- This phrase appears often in contracts: *time is of the essence* which under English law entitles the other party not only to compensation but also to withdraw from the contract. The meaning of this is uncertain under German law.
- Similarly dangerous is the use of words which have been judicially defined under common law but are vague and difficult to translate into civil law.
- *Reasonable/best efforts/endeavours/good faith efforts*[64] are somewhat less than an absolute duty, but difficult to define under common law (Adams 2004: 88–94) and even more so under civil law.
- *Negligence* has various meanings. Negligence as a tort may overlap to some extent with pre-contractual breach (*culpa in contrahendo*) in German law. As reproachable conduct when breaching a contract it is often expressly described or implied as a duty to act diligently.[65] However, common law does not recognize the Continental distinction made between gross and slight negligence. Reckless, wanton or wilful negligence are difficult to classify in civil law.
- *Vicarious liability* – under German law, an employer will only be vicariously liable if he was at fault in selecting or in supervising an agent.
- *Without prejudice* may be a matter of evidence and of contract drafting: as a rule of evidence in common law it has no equivalent in civil law. The basic meaning is 'without loss of any rights'. A letter marked 'without prejudice' cannot later be used as evidence in court proceedings if the settlement negotiations fail. As a matter of contract drafting *without prejudice to* means without affecting another rule or sentence in the contract.[66]
- *Knowledge* and its various degrees are vague, if not ambiguous under common law. Thus, there is doubt whether *to the best of its knowledge*[67] requires a higher or lower degree than *to its knowledge*. Often civil law lawyers use *positive knowledge* meaning *actual knowledge* which is to

be contrasted with *imputed* and *constructive knowledge. Malice* under English law simply means that a person intentionally did something unlawful.[68]

- *Term* has at least three different meanings in English which can confuse foreigners: (i) term of a contract = condition or warranty; (ii) term of art = *terminus technicus,* and (iii) term = the duration, that is the period of time be it fixed or indefinite. Thus *term of notice* = *Kündigungsfrist.*
- An event of *default* is not tantamount to *Verzug,* but precedes a breach and covers instances before that point.

Civil law terms translated into English

A civil law lawyer drafting a contract in English may be tempted to translate terms of art from his native civil code into English which may be incomprehensible to a common law lawyer. The common law lawyer who is used to concrete terms will find the following to be utterly meaningless general terms and misty abstractions:

- *Declaration of intent* being a literal translation of the German *Willenserklärung* or the French *déclaration de volonté.*
- *Good faith* (*Treu und Glauben*) is a concept developed under German law from a *drop of social oil* into an obligation extending to every aspect of the performance of a contract; it has no equivalent in English common law (Zweigert and Kötz 1996: 147–9).
- *Notarization* to a common law lawyer merely means certification of a signature. It does not have the meaning given by the Latin *notariat* which requires that a document be read aloud verbatim, approved by the parties and signed by them and the notary public in the latter's presence. This function of notarization in respect of important contracts is fulfilled by the common law deed.

9.4.3 Use of common law precedents

Contracts governed by civil law are often written in a highly theoretical style and employ numerous abstract concepts. Common law lawyers often have great difficulty in understanding them. If an abstract civil law term is translated into English, it will often prove to be totally meaningless when read from the perspective of common law. The latter is all the more true since the meaning of the words used in the English translation will often have completely different connotations for the common law reader than those intended by the civil law writer. The general terms used in civil law reflect the degree of abstraction of the legal concepts and terms found in the Continental codifications. In view of this, civil law lawyers are more likely to dispense with detailed drafting and to rely on their code for a ready-made solution should a difficulty arise in connection with the contract.

Often in the course of a 'battle of forms' a dangerous compromise is reached by cobbling together of the forms of two parties from different jurisdictions. This is a fruitful source of dispute because under common law every word has to be given a meaning. In one case the mortgagee of a ship had taken out an insurance policy to protect himself against loss if the ship was damaged. Old English standard forms going back to the eighteenth century were cobbled together with conditions translated from Swedish. The Court of Appeal found it very difficult to determine the plain meaning and the commercial background of the two inconsistent texts.[69]

What happens more often is: a typical common law contract is taken out of the form books dealing with civil law and only minor amendments are added to the contract leaving its substance unchanged. Sometimes the many common law terms and concepts go unnoticed and cause no dispute regarding their meaning, but often they are a fruitful source of disputes leading to 'correcting' amendments or eventually even litigation.

Anglo-American contract practice has brought many different kinds of pre-contractual documents to Europe. We Europeans use their English names as loanwords, like: *heads of agreement, letter of intent, letter of comfort* and *term sheet*. Whether these pre-contractual documents are binding or not under common law is not settled, whether they bind the parties if civil law governs them is even less clear.

Contractual documents with English names are also used in Europe: *memorandum of agreement, memorandum of understanding* and *letter of agreement*. Where they are governed by a Continental law, there is also ambiguity as to whether they are binding. Common law lawyers distinguish clearly between two kinds of *attachments: exhibits* to a contract which are stand-alone documents, and *schedules* which are part of the contract and often contain long lists, such as representations and warranties.

Foreign concepts used in mergers and acquisitions (M&A) contracts governed by German law may be dangerous because they have a meaning under English law but not under German law. Jim Freund (1975; see also Triebel 1998) speaks of the *horsemen* under US M&A contracts which do not fit into the German legal system, yet they are constantly repeated in transactions governed by German law. The terms most frequently used to categorize different types of contractual obligations are *conditions, warranties, representations* and *covenants*.

Conditions[70] are obligations which are regarded as essential to the main purpose of a contract, whereas warranties refer to the less important terms that are collateral to the main purpose of the contract and usually mean a guarantee by one party that the thing sold is as represented or promised. The main difference between the two is the remedies available in the case of breach. If a term is a condition, the innocent party will be entitled to rescind the contract and to claim damages in addition. The seriousness of the breach will not be relevant. The breach of a warranty, on the other hand, will only entitle the innocent party to claim damages. By categorizing the terms of a contract as conditions or warranties, the parties define how important they are and the consequences of a breach.[71] As already discussed above, English courts will focus on a written contract when interpreting its provisions and not look at the circumstances surrounding it due to the parol evidence rule. Thus, the parties should be aware of the significance of their labelling a term in a certain way. To what extent German courts will take the above into account is unclear.

The word *representations* is frequently used to define terms concerning the disclosure of information. A representation is a presentation of fact made to induce the other party to enter into the contract; a false representation, a misrepresentation, entitles the other party to rescind the contract and to claim damages or both.[72] This is particularly important because there is no general duty to disclose information or act in good faith when entering into or fulfilling a contract under English contract law. The principle that prevails is *caveat emptor*, in other words *buyer beware*. Where a representation (statements of facts upon which a party relies) is made and proves to be false, it will be considered a misrepresentation and the remedies available will depend on whether it was fraudulent, negligent or innocent. The injured party may be entitled to damages or rescission.

Covenants are promises contained in a deed. Their main purposes are to avoid the need for consideration, but they will have no effect unless they also fulfil the formal requirements for deeds. In effect the use of the term *covenant* in a simple contract is merely a contractual obligation to do or not to do something.

9.4.4 Standard provisions/miscellaneous clauses/boilerplate language/household provisions and definitions

Household provisions as used in common law contract practice may have an unexpected impact on the construction of a contract. In addition to the choice of law and service of notice clauses, there are many others which may cause misunderstandings when read by civil law lawyers:

- An integrated contract (US)/entire agreement (UK)/four corner clause may exclude contract history even where it would be permitted under German law of evidence![73]
- Severability: the 'blue pencil rule' allows an English court to decide whether to sever an invalid provision from the rest of a contract and regard the remainder of the contract as valid. This test is also applied under German law. However, the typical clause under German law also imposes a duty on the parties to fill in gaps and omissions in a contract. Under common law such clauses could be void for uncertainty.
- Waiver clause: a failure to assert rights does not constitute a waiver – this may be similar to the common law doctrine of estoppel, but it is different from the German doctrine of *venire contra factum prorium*.
- It has become usual to put 'autonomous' definitions at the beginning of a contract and to put 'integrated' definitions in the body of the contract. Defined terms may be dangerous. Autonomous definitions are usually made by using the word *means*;[74] the definition can then be enlarged by adding the word *including* or restricted by adding the word *excluding*.

9.5 Some recommendations and warnings to civil law lawyers

9.5.1 Civil law terms in brackets

Several attempts have been made to protect a party who enters – without English advisors – into an English contract when English is not his/her native tongue. In earlier times when contracts were not that long (often with one party from a previous communist country) bilingual contracts were drawn up (with or without provisions determining the prevailing language). However, bilingual contracts are largely a thing of the past as modern, complex contracts encompass hundreds of pages.

Instead of bilingual contracts it has become usual to insert the civil law term in brackets to avoid the meaning of a common law legal term of art or the lexical meaning of an ordinary English word. So, for example, where in an M&A transaction the parameters of a variable purchase price are to be determined by a chartered accountant, his legal role will be difficult to describe in the English language: as arbitrator, expert or valuer. German legal terms in brackets (*Schiedsrichter* or *Schiedsgutachter*) would bring clarity.[75]

9.5.2 Inclusion of construction and language provisions

Since common law has strict canons of construction, simply putting the civil law terms in brackets and adding a choice of law clause may not be sufficient to protect the parties against surprises when it comes to the construction of a contentious provision in the contract. As shown above, a simple choice of law may not be sufficient to guarantee that a civil law judge or arbitrator will ignore these strict rules and apply the wider canons of the chosen civil law. It might well be wise to insert a clause that provides that the contract not only be governed, but also be construed, under the chosen law.

The language problem is actually even more difficult. To protect one party or both parties, it is important to recognize that there are different English languages and dialects: not only British and American English, but also new kinds of English, world English shaped as much by non-native as by native speakers (Baugh and Cable 2002: 404), even a Euro-speak[76] and UN-speak. Furthermore, there are many non-native speaking lawyers who use English as a world language or as the lingua franca (Hammel 2006). These different kinds of English may warrant a different approach when construing a contract written in a particular kind of English.

To avoid unpleasant surprises and disputes, civil law lawyers drafting a contract in English but based on civil law must ascertain the meaning of English legal terms, know the meanings of ordinary English words and consider the effects of English rules of grammar on the interpretation of a contract. This is rather cumbersome. They may wish to clarify that English is not the native tongue of both parties or of one party (which puts the other at an advantage!).[77] They may want to state in the contract that they have selected the English language as a language of convenience or as a concession to the other party. They can insert a provision, preferably as part of the choice of law clause, into the contract which could read as follows:

> This contract including any issues arising out of or in connection with it is governed by [...] law. This contract, its words and phrases are to be construed under [...] law paying regard to the use of English as language of convenience [concession]. Terms in brackets shall have their meaning under [...] law without recourse to English or any other law. English is not the native language of the parties and of their

advisors [one of the parties and its advisors]. The parties have agreed to English in the contract as a language of convenience [party x has agreed to English as contract language as a concession to party X].

Such a construction and language provision protects against a common law construction of the contract. However, it may create ambiguities other than those derived from common law construction: which meaning is to be given to a common law term or an English word if not the lexical English meaning? What other rules of grammar will determine uncertainties arising from a squinting modifier? However, such a construction and language clause may come nearer to the ultimate aim of every interpretation: the intention of the parties.

It is a difficult question whether other construction clauses, which are often employed by pedantic common law lawyers, should be recommended. Some of these clauses are useful, others harmless or even pointless, yet most of them are clumsy. Adams (2001: 115–21) sets out some of these:

- To avoid the many murky *hereofs, hereto: Any reference in this Agreement to a section, article, schedule, or exhibit is to a section, article, schedule, or exhibit in this Agreement.*
- To negate the stringent *enumeratio unius* rule: the words *include* and *includes* are to be read as if they were followed by a phrase *without limitation.*
- To clarify whether *or* is used in its inclusive or exclusive sense: unless the context clearly requires, *or* is not exclusive.
- To solve the many ambiguities of *shall*: the word *shall* means *has the duty to, must* means *is required to,* and *may* means *is permitted to.*

9.5.3 Warnings

It may not be very encouraging, but it is necessary to conclude with some warnings to civil law lawyers who are confronted with contracts drafted in English, even if these contracts are subject to their laws:

- Experience shows that young lawyers all over the world adopt the old-fashioned, archaic style and expressions used by previous generations readily and without thinking through their meaning and function. The unthinking use of common law precedents is all the more dangerous when civil law is to govern the contract. In international law firms there is a great temptation to use common law precedents without considering the governing law. In long contractual negotiations, the governing law is frequently left open until the very end with the result that there is then no time to check each clause for its compatibility with the governing law. Attempting to save effort by cobbling a contract together from forms from different jurisdictions is to say the least even more dubious.

- Many contracts are drafted in poor English which can only be understood by retranslating it into the writer's native tongue or not at all. Some mistakes may be harmless,[78] others are dangerous.[79] Many misunderstandings will be avoided if simple propositions are employed correctly: *notwithstanding,*[80] *subject to, without prejudice to, except, when, where, if, then.* It is astonishing what difficulties those small, but frequently used words cause to non-English speakers. The wrong use of these conjunctions often distorts the intended meaning.[81]
- Avoid vague terms which have frequently been the subject of common law litigation (*best endeavours* and *forthwith*) and which are even more uncertain against a civil law background.
- Avoid specific common law terms with no equivalent in civil law, such as *deed* and *consideration,* and be careful with the terms which have a meaning in both common as well as in civil law.
- Avoid semantic and syntactical contextual ambiguities, legalese and superfluous words and so on.

9.6 Conclusion

This essay is – in the first place – directed at civil law lawyers. They must realize the possible fallacies which even common law lawyers have to overcome and, on top of that, appreciate the additional pitfalls if the contract is governed by civil law.

Common law lawyers know best how to deal with pitfalls of their language. But once they meet civil law lawyers and subject their contract written in English to civil law, common law lawyers will be confronted with new and other pitfalls. Common law lawyers should understand the way civil law lawyers draft contracts under their system to understand what they want to express.

Notes

1. http://www.britishcouncil.org (last retrieval on 23.02.2008).
2. http://money.cnn.com/magazines/fortune/global500/2006/countries/A.html (last retrieval on 23.02.2008).

3. Over 10,000 French words were adopted into the English language during the Middle English period. Of these about 75 per cent have survived to the present day (Baugh and Cable 2002: 170, 178).
4. Mellinkoff (1963: 15) states: 'a vast section of the language of the law stems from French sources' and gives a list of legal terms of art derived from Norman French. This is, of course, not surprising since French was the language of the lawyers and the courts from the Norman Conquest until 1362 (Baugh and Cable 2002: 146, 170).
5. A civil law lawyer is surprised to find many Latin terms and maxims in common law which he does not find in civil law, even though it is based upon Roman law. Nonetheless, the Latin maxims used differ. The reason is that the civil law lawyer is familiar with classical legal Latin, whereas English law has adopted many medieval and new Latin expressions (Mellinkoff 1963: 71–82). For example:
   - *Res ipsa loquitur ≠ prima facie*
   - *Quid pro quo ≠ do ut des*
   - *Nemo dat quod non habet ≠ nemo plus iure transferre potest quam ipse habet.*
6. English developed from a synthetic to an analytical language (Baugh and Cable 2002: 166, 167).
7. Common law has various meanings: if contrasted with civil law, it covers the legal systems which are based on English law; if contrasted with equity, it means the set of rules developed by the Court of Chancery; if contrasted with legislation, it means judge-made law. In this essay common law is contrasted with civil law.

   Also on the Continent common law is gaining ever more dominance, especially under the threat of finance. Most countries with English as their primary language are governed by common law, first and foremost the US and England (exceptions are Scotland, South Africa, Zimbabwe, Sri Lanka and the state of Louisiana). A third of the world's population live in countries with a common law system.
8. It is self-evident that common law lawyers and judges, who are both bred in an English-speaking environment and trained in a common law system, will be more competent to draft, advise and decide on issues arising in connection with a contract that was written in English and is governed by English law than civil law jurists and judges.
9. For a civil law lawyer, the key to understanding common law is to understand land law. Other branches of common law developed much later (see Zweigert and Kötz 1996: 177ff.).
10. Such a construction would be impossible in a legal system – like the German one – which does not distinguish between a common law and an equitable system.
11. Wydick (2005: 19) defines a term of art as a short expression that (a) conveys a fairly well-agreed meaning, and (b) saves the many words that would otherwise be needed to convey that meaning.
12. This could well be due to the fact that judges are drawn from the ranks of senior barristers.
13. There is a reform of the German law of private limited companies (*Gesellschaft mit beschränkter Haftung*) pending where this Anglo-Saxon concept will be

introduced into German company law (see Triebel and Otte 2006: 1326; Otte 2006: 178–80, 192–3).

14. *Anspruch* (the right to request from the other party to do or omit to do something – see sect. 194 German Civil Code (*Bürgerliches Gesetzbuch*)). Common law has not – like Windscheid has done for German law – developed the concept of substantive law right and separated it from procedural remedies.
15. The word *precedent* itself is misleading, as it has at least two meanings: (a) a binding court decision; and (b) a model form (contract) (see also Mellinkoff 1963: 193, 194).
16. The best-known precedent book for contracts in England is Butterworth's *Encyclopaedia of Forms and Precedents* (1991) which comprises more than 90 volumes. The tyranny of the precedent books has a long history and goes back to before 1873 when the forms of action were abolished in England. West's Legal Forms and Warren's Forms of Agreement are commonly used in the USA. EDGAR, the electronic system used by listed companies to file their documents with the Securities and Exchange Commission (SEC), is frequently used today by lawyers experienced in this field.
17. This has been confirmed in many insurance contracts and charter parties (see Butt and Castle 2001: 56).
18. It can indeed be embarrassing for a lawyer if his client finds a clause in a contract between two companies entitling either party to rescind the contract if the other should die or become mentally ill.
19. The famous treatise of George Coode (1848).
20. Which is called the *case.*
21. Modern English contract writing, however, suggests a different order: putting circumstances, conditions, exceptions and limitations at the end (Wydick 2005: 44).
22. Under the Woolfe Reform the new Civil Procedure Rules of 1999 replaced legal jargon by more common words: *plaintiff* by *claimant, ex parte* by *applications without notice, discovery* by *disclosure, pleadings* by *statement of case, writ* by *claim form, subpoena* by *witness summons*, etc.
23. The word *execution* is ambiguous, as it has several meanings: (a) it is legal jargon for *signing* a contract; (b) it is a term for performing a contract, and (c) when carrying out a criminal sanction.
24. *Provisos* have an old history in English statute which usually stated *provisum est* meaning *it is provided that.*
25. Ambiguity comes in three forms: semantic (because words may have more than one meaning), syntactic (the uncertainty resulting from the arrangement of words in a sentence), and contextual (where different provisions of the same contract say contradictory things (see Child 1992: 315–42).
26. Adams (2004: 85ff.) distinguishes between two kinds of vagueness: where the meaning of the vague word is derived from an objective and a subjective assessment of the context.
27. Butt and Castle (2001: 107 fn. 33) where *forthwith* has been held to extend to 14 days, but also where a notice to be entered on Friday, but given on the following Monday was not *forthwith* (see also Asprey 2003: 176ff.).
28. There is a vast collection of cases in which *forthwith* was litigated. There is a general view that *immediately* is somewhat stricter (see Mellinkoff 1963: 311).

29. Under common law *substantial performance* may entitle a party to claim from the other the price subject to a claim for compensation.
30. Adams (2004: 20–49) distinguishes between the languages of obligation, performance, discretion, prohibition, policy, condition and representation (see also Asprey 2003: 193–204).
31. For the historical development of *shall* and *will* see Baugh and Cable (2002: 279ff.).
32. For a historical analysis see Mellinkoff (1963: 147–52).
33. *Du kannst mich anrufen bzw. schreiben* can mean *you can call or write* or probably both *call and write.*
34. *Ich komme aus England bzw. London.* In this case the *bzw.* means *I come from England or to be more exact London* and the use of *respectively* would be totally incorrect.
35. According to the Interpretation Act 1978 'month' is to be presumed to mean calendar month in Acts of Parliament; the Law of Property Act 1925 provides similarly for deeds and other written documents. At common law a 'month' was a lunar month (28 days).
36. Case marking has just about disappeared from the language and survives mainly in pronouns.
37. A modifier is a word, phrase or clause that changes the meaning of the word to which it is related.
38. For a historical analysis of punctuation see Mellinkoff (1963: 152–70).
39. So Sir William Grant MR in *Sandford* v. *Raikes* (1816) 1 Mer 646; Robinson (1980: 61) suggests inserting a construction clause in contracts: *In construing this document, full effect is to be given to the marks of punctuation* ... .
40. See Adams (2004: 208–10). Asprey (2003: 220–26) gives a full list of words and phrases to be avoided and suggests alternatives. See also Wydick (2005: 11).
41. For more examples see Adams (2004: 205).
42. Most *here* words may create a syntactical ambiguity, as it may be uncertain what *here* refers to in a contract of phrase.
43. *Such* is ambiguous, as it may mean 'of this kind' and also be a demonstrative, like *this, that, these, those.*
44. Daigneault (2005: 123–5) shows a table of archaic words to be replaced by simple and familiar words.
45. To find out the meaning of a term of art, be it a legal or technical one, special dictionaries must be used. For legal terms there are plenty of legal dictionaries available and also the books of *Words and Phrases Legally Defined.*
46. See Baugh and Cable (2002: 307–11). An illustration is *escrow,* a document signed and sealed, but not yet delivered; upon delivery it becomes a deed. Originally *escrow* was used as a security in conveyancing of land, but has now been extended to mean all kinds of security including retention money laid into a trust account.
47. *It is known from its associates.*
48. The rule is that 'express mention of one thing implies the exclusion of another'.
49. This rule in Continental methodology reminds one of the argumentum *e contrario* (*Umkehrschluss*).
50. Where general words follow the enumeration of particular classes of things, the general words will be construed as applying only to things of the same

general class as those enumerated. See *McBoyle* v. *United States* [1931], 283 U.S. 25, 51 S.Ct. 340, 75 L.Ed. 816.

51. The mixture of Old English, Norman French and Latin produced many synonyms which, though banned by the Plain English Campaign, are often found in English contracts, also in those drafted by non-common law lawyers (for a list of doublets and even triplets, see Mellinkoff 1963: 120–5, 345–66).
52. To negate this rule of construction, parties often agree on the following clause: *Each party has participated in negotiating and drafting this contract. Any ambiguity is to be construed as if the parties had drafted this contract jointly, as opposed to being construed against a party for drafting one or more provisions of this contract.*
53. Under German law, the purposive interpretation goes back to Rudolf von Jehring (1877).
54. The legal system in South Africa has elements of both Romano-Dutch law (civil law) and English law (common law). This may well have affected their Lordships' approach.
55. 'The Tenant may by serving not less than six months notice in writing on the landlord or its solicitors such notice to expire on the third anniversary of the term commencement date determine this Lease and upon expiry of such notice this Lease shall cease and determine and have no further effect ...'.
56. *Preamble* sounds strange to an Anglo-Saxon contract lawyer who would expect this term to denote the background to a statute or a treaty.
57. *Whereas* has more than one meaning: (a) *but on the contrary;* (b) *given the fact that.* It is in the latter sense that *whereas* is used in recitals.
58. The doctrine of frustration allows the contract to be automatically discharged when a frustrating event occurs so that the parties are no longer bound to perform the obligations under it. A frustrating event is an event which takes place after the contract has been formed.
59. A material adverse change clause gives a party the right to withdraw from an agreement/transaction before completion if certain detrimental events occur. It is standard market practice for takeover offers to be conditional upon there being no 'material adverse change'. This is designed to enable a bidder to terminate the offer in the event of a MAC in the business or prospects of the target company in the period after the takeover bid is announced.
60. Rossini (1998) explains common law terms and also contrasts them with civil law.
61. So-called *allgemeine Geschäftsbedingungen,* see sect. 310 German Civil Code (*Bürgerliches Gesetzbuch*).
62. BGH TransportR 1988, at p. 199.
63. Sect. 276 German Civil Code *(Bürgerliches Gesetzbuch*).
64. There is a downward graduation from an absolute obligation to best endeavours and reasonable endeavours. Butt and Castle (2001: 107) list judicial decisions of these expressions over a two-decade period (see also Daigneault 2005: 64ff.).
65. Anglo-Saxon lawyers will often insert a duty in contracts to act *with all due care and diligence,* which will not be necessary under the civil law concept of

fault, where the general principle of contractual liability depends on fault (intent or negligence) and is not absolute. An extension of the word *diligence* brought over from America is *due diligence,* an investigation into the affairs of the company by a buyer.

66. See below, note 81.
67. Sometimes the synonyms or near-synonyms are put together: *knowledge, information and belief.* However, it is questionable that the last two add anything to the first word.
68. Its meaning in everyday English is somewhat different – it means that a person did something with the intent to harm.
69. The Alexion Hope [1988] 1 Lloyd´s Rep 311, 320 (though applying English law); see also Butt and Castle (2001: 34).
70. The term *conditions* is ambiguous, as it has many meanings: (a) an operative fact, one on which the existence of some particular legal relation depends (so in Restatement (second) of Contracts § 224 (1989); (b) Coode distinguishes between *cases* and *conditions*; (c) conditions for closing as opposed to conditions for the effectiveness of a contract.
71. There is in fact a third group of terms called innominate terms or intermediate terms. These are terms which cannot be categorized as either conditions or warranties. The remedy for the breach of an innominate term will depend on the seriousness of its nature. If the breach is fundamental, that is to say the injured party has been deprived of substantially the whole of the benefit of the contract, he will be able to rescind the contract and claim damages. Otherwise he will be entitled to damages only.
72. So under the English Misrepresentation Act 1977.
73. A typical common law entire agreement clause contains three elements: (i) the entire agreement statement; (ii) previous agreements superseded; and (iii) no reliance on other representations (Daingneault 2005: 117).
74. It is ugly and wrong to write *shall mean* instead of the present tense, as neither the modal nor the future meaning of this verb is appropriate.
75. To make assurance doubly sure a reference to the provision in the civil code should be made, such as to sect. 317 German Civil Code (*Bürgerliches Gesetzbuch*) for a *Schiedsgutachter.*
76. 'Eurospeak' is a kind of international English, which developed rapidly since the UK joined the EU in 1973. According to McAuliffe (2006b): 'Eurospeak is, quite simply, a new language.' It has been severely attacked, as it contains an abundance of mistranslations and word creations derived from other European languages. Rossini (1998: xxii) speaks of 'ridiculous Eurospeak language evolved in Brussels…(whose) aberrations appear to have inflicted irreversible damage to the English language'.
77. A useful criterion is to start with the language and law facilities of the parties and their agents and advisors to a contract: whether all or only one side come from an English and common law background or none rather than impose the lexical meaning of a common law term to a non-English party (Triebel and Balthasar 2004: 2192ff.).
78. The following examples may be regarded as harmless:
    - The Director of x-company *from time to time* as contrasted with *for the time being:* the former case x-company may appoint a Director more than once, the latter means the Director at the relevant time.

- *To dismiss an employee for (important) reasons* simply does not make sense in English: *to dismiss him for cause* is the right expression, the employer may (be bound to) give grounds (= reasons which may be important) for doing so.
- Where a contract is just between two parties the preposition *between,* not the clumsy *by and between* and in no event *among* should be used. The latter is reserved where there are more than two parties.
- *Hereby* indicates the very act achieved by the contractual provision and *herewith* refers to an enclosure.
- If both parties sign a contract, it is an original, and there is no difference in other legal systems. However, counterpart is an original only signed by the other party.
- *To rescind* a contract means annulling the contract from the beginning, *cancelling* or *discharging* a contract only refers to the future.
- What sounds strange to a civil law lawyer is that a contract may be *discharged* both by *performance* and by *breach.*

79. The following examples may be regarded as dangerous: *exclusive* and *sole* in agency, distributorship and licence agreements: a principal who appoints an *exclusive* agent in a territory undertakes not to appoint another agent nor deliver itself into the territory; a *sole* agent is not protected against deliveries by the principal.
80. *Notwithstanding* is dangerous if used in phrases like *notwithstanding the foregoing* or *notwithstanding anything herein to the contrary,* as it may cause syntactical ambiguity.
81. *Notwithstanding* means the rule overrides another rule which is inconsistent with it (for a fuller analysis see Mellinkoff 1963: 85; Adams 2001: 161–3)*; subject to* has a contrary effect and means the rule is affected or an obligation negated by another rule. A second meaning refers to a rule of evidence: the without prejudice document or statement cannot be used as evidence, *if the negotiations fail or the proposal is not accepted. Except that* means that the rule has no effect on another rule, *where* and *when* introduces and restricts the rule to the stated circumstances (the *case* in the sense used by Coode), *if* introduces a condition*; then* may introduce the general rule (see Daigneault 2005: 75).

10
Isomorphism and Anisomorphism in the Translation of Legal Texts

Enrique Alcaraz Varó

10.1 Introduction. Pleasure, happiness and harmony. Isomorphism

As an introdution to the presentation and development of the central topic of this essay, which is 'Isomorphism and Anisomorphism in the Translation of Legal Texts', I would like, first of all, to find an appropriate framework for it, in order to make the former concepts as vivid and attractive as possible. Most of us will be prepared to accept that what is vivid and attractive immediately draws our attention and has therefore much greater chance of being quickly integrated into our cognitive domain.

For this purpose, I discuss three of the main goals of the human condition. These three goals have arisen both from observation and reflection on human conduct and from the reading of classical texts. I will express the three goals with three key words: pleasure, happiness and harmony. *Pleasure*, that is, the gratification of the senses or the mind, is probably one of the greatest motivating forces of human behaviour, including all kinds of activities, in particular intellectual work. In this sense, we might speak of *the enjoyment of pleasure*.

Happiness, on the other hand, is not an easy word to define, although the many synonyms that it has in most languages might help us grasp its meaning very readily. For a great number of people it could be defined as a sense of utter satisfaction, derived from the full integration of our souls into our environment. The problem with this sense of utter satisfaction is its brief duration: it is a very short-lasting fulfilment. It is such a transient and slippery feeling that some believe that we shall never reach it, and that we are only entitled to 'the pursuit of happiness'. This is what *The Declaration of Independence of the United States of America*, drafted during that brilliant period of modern history called *The Enlightenment*, says in its second paragraph. It mentions *the pursuit*, but it says nothing about its full *accomplishment*, possibly because it is a 'mission impossible'.

Harmony, understood as the pleasing arrangement of the parts of a whole, connotes 'balance', 'order', 'stability' and many other things, all of which lead to the idea of 'beauty'. Harmony is based on the underlying human belief that there is an aesthetic principle organizing life and nature. Jorge Wagensberg (2006: 156) has stated this principle very clearly when he affirms that 'when we do research, our minds are guided by something that could be called the *aesthetic criterion*'. Isomorphism, which is the idea of symmetry in the patterns of things in life, might be considered one of the properties or components of harmony.

Consequently, three of the main goals of the human condition, according to my judgement, might be the *enjoyment* of pleasure, the *pursuit* of happiness, and the *discovery* of the underlying aesthetic harmony in life and nature. The enjoyment of pleasure could be called the *hedonistic* or pleasure-seeking goal; the pursuit of happiness would be the *spiritual* goal, and the discovery of harmony, the *aesthetic* goal.

After this short consideration of three goals of the human condition, I would like to state at this point that the general objectives of this chapter are twofold: on the one hand, to discuss the concepts of isomorphism and anisomorphism in linguistics and culture, and on the other, to examine the application of these two concepts, especially the second one, to problems arising from the translation of legal texts.

10.2 Isomorphism and anisomorphism in language and translation

We have just said that isomorphism, understood as the symmetry in the patterns of things in nature or life, might be considered one of the properties or components of harmony. The concept of isomorphism originally belongs to modern algebra, which is the field where it originated (Lewandoswki 1982: 195–6). However, it soon spread out its influential power to other epistemological areas, both in science and the humanities. In the humanities we shall highlight its presence in traductology, formal linguistics and cultural linguistics. This traditional branch of linguistics has recently received an enthusiastic and diversified impulse in language studies (Guillén Nieto 2006: 106).

The concept of isomorphism was very productive and appreciated in structuralism and generativism. Structural linguistics assumed the discovery (procedures) of the neat and well-ordered patterns of language as one of its main research goals. European structural linguists, like Martinet (1968) or Lyons (1995), believed in the isomorphism of linguistic patterns; the former devoted more attention to isomorphism in questions of form, the latter to questions of meaning, in particular to semantic fields. The same could be said of anthropological linguists, like Sapir (1921), Malinowski (1935) or Whorf (1956), who approached the study of language as included in the cultural patterns of a community.

To a certain extent, traductology (Vázquez Ayora 1977) also had faith in a *sui generis* isomorphism; this may be noted if we read, for example, Eugene Nida's *Toward a Science of Translating* (1965). A few years later generativism, the paradigm that followed structuralism, also stood in for isomorphism. As a matter of fact, there was a great traductological project called EUROTRA, sponsored by the European Commission, based on the tenets of generativism, that believed that the surface structures of two sentences could find an isomorphic referent in their deep structure. Although the project did not succeed, the concepts of isomorphism and anisomorphism have found a place in traductology. As Gómez González-Jover (2006: 215) has clearly pointed out, we cannot close our eyes to the examination of the productive concept of anisomorphism between the linguistic systems of the source and the target language.

Does isomorphism really exist? It does, if we are prepared to accept the existence of anisomorphism. They go hand in hand, and one is understood as a function of the other. Anisomorphism exists at all levels. We have, for example, pairs of words in Spanish like *coloso/colosal, especie/especial, proceso/procesal*, etc., formed by a noun and an adjective, but the pair *derecho/*derechal* does not exist. The other way round also works: we have, for example, the adjective *benéfico* coming from the noun *beneficio*, or *ideológico* coming from *ideología*, but there is no formal originator of the word *jurídico*. In this case, we might conclude that there must be a semantic jump in order to construct a logical semantic pair, which would be formed by *derecho/jurídico*.

Rougly speaking, anisomorphism makes reference to gaps in the neat, beautiful patterns of nature, and our discovery of it is guided by the previously mentioned *aesthetic criterion*. We understand rules because there are exceptions, and we understand isomorphism because there is anisomorphism.

10.3 Linguistic anisomorphism in the translation of legal texts

Before the analysis in section 10.4 of the actual translation of anisomorphic terms, let us attempt to anticipate where some of the problems may lie. Accordingly, this section examines those problems under three subsections, 'English, two languages in one', 'Doublets in the English language' and 'Doublets in legal English'.

10.3.1 English, two languages in one

The translator of English texts into Spanish (or any other Romance language) should be aware all the time that English is not *one* language, but *two* languages that happily live together under the same label. One is a Latin-root language, and the other, a Germanic-root language. Both of them are specialized in different roles, but they actively cooperate with one another, especially from the point of view of neology, that is, the creation of new terms. Germanic-root words are more precise in the expression of everyday activities. Here are two examples illustrating this precision of nuances in the words *rain* and *shine* (Hidalgo and Alcaraz Varó 1985: 158, 185):

Rain

Shower: a fall of rain of *short duration.*
Cloudburst: a *sudden copious* rainfall.
Downpour: a *heavy* fall of rain.
Squall: a sudden fall of rain with *wind.*
Drizzle: *fine misty* rain.

Shine

Flash: to emit a *sudden* bright light.
Sparkle: send out *flashes* of light.
Glisten: to shine or sparkle brightly, especially of a *wet* surface.
Glitter: to shine brightly with *flashes* of light.
Glow: send out brightness or *warmth* without flame.
Gleam: to shine with a *soft and steady* brightness.
Glimmer: to shine *faintly* or unsteadily.
Glare: to shine in a *disagreeable* way.
Flicker: to shine in a *tremulous* way.

10.3.2 Doublets in the English language

We have said that words from a Latin source and from a Germanic source live happily together. For example, we have *shy* and *timid, put in* and *introduce, suitable and appropriate, enough and sufficient,* etc. A great deal of the English vocabulary could be arranged into doublets, where the first term is more common, and sometimes more informal than the second one. In other words, Latin-root words are often more formal than their Germanic counterparts. What has been said of common lexical units could be found in any area of knowledge. Here are some words proceeding from the healthcare field: *high blood pressure/hypertension, cough suppressant/antitussient, bruise/contusion*, etc.

10.3.3 Doublets in legal English

The number of examples in legal English is not small either. Here are some: *order/warrant, rob/steal*, and *permission/leave*:

> Order: The London firm took out *a freezing order* against the German contractors, blocking all their London assets.
> Warrant: A European arrest *warrant* has been issued against three international criminals.
>
> Rob: My mother was *robbed* of all her jewels.
> Steal: The secretary *stole* money from the cash register.
>
> Permission: The holder of the copyright gave them *permission* to reproduce some pages.
> Leave: They applied for *leave* to proceed out of the jurisdiction.

10.4 When the source language is legal Spanish. The case of *responsable, Administración* and *legal*

Bearing in mind what has been said about anisomorphism and about the nature of English (a language consisting of two languages arranged into doublets), this section examines the anisomorphism existing when translating Spanish legal terms into English. What is said in the next subsections of the Spanish technical words *responsable, Administración* and *legal* could probably be affirmed of their counterparts in most Romance languages.

10.4.1 The translation of the Spanish technical term *responsable* into English

When attempting to translate the Spanish word *responsable*, bilingual dictionaries offer at least four English terms: 'answerable', 'accountable', 'liable' and 'responsible'. Although they all share a great number of the same semantic features, each one of them carries specific connotation.

(a) The meanings of ***answerable*** *and* ***accountable***

'Answerable' and 'accountable' are probably the closest synonyms. I say 'probably', because when we try to systematize linguistic units, especially semantic units, we know we are treading across quicksand, since most words have dialectal, stylistic and idiosyncratic connotations. That is why many wise specialists say that linguistic use is not a 'yes/no question' but 'a more or less probable option'. According to the sources I have consulted, both 'answerable' and 'accountable' have got the same connotations; the first one is that you have to explain or give reasons for what or why something took place; the second is that you are burdened with the negative consequences of what happened. Both are classical and modern terms when we say, for example, that every man is *accountable* for his behaviour, and the meaning of the word *answerable* contained in the statement 'The King is not answerable to his subjects', pronounced in the seventeenth century, still keeps all its semantic freshness.

(b) The meaning of ***liable***

Probably most learned native speakers of English would be prepared to agree that 'liable', in a great number of contexts, is a legal term. If somebody has been negligent, that is, if they failed to fulfil the required duty of care, that person becomes liable to the injured one. You fail to fulfil the duty of care when you do not take reasonable care to avoid acts or omissions which you can reasonably foresee would be likely to injure persons who are so closely and directly affected by your act, that you ought reasonably to have that possible injury in contemplation. It is found in the expression *to find liable*. For example, in *Carmarthenshire CC* v. *Lewis* (1955), a driver died trying to avoid a schoolchild, and the school authority was *found liable* because it let a child out of school in circumstances where it was likely that he might cause an accident.

(c) The meaning of ***responsible****. Legal and moral senses*

If 'liable' is a typical legal term, I should underline that 'responsible' is a moral one, most of the time. In the expression 'You have not been responsible' it is implied that you have let down those who put their trust in you, for your supposedly good judgement and behaviour.

This differentiation between a moral sense and a legal sense is not uncommon in English. We can find doublets with these two different senses, that are not so clear in Spanish. For example, the Spanish *absolver* corresponds to two English words: 'absolve' (having a religious or moral meaning) and 'acquit' (with a clear legal sense), as when we say 'I absolve you of all your sins' and 'The defendant was acquitted of all the charges'. The same can be said of the Spanish *condenar*, corresponding to the English words 'condemn' (which has a religious or moral meaning or nuance), and 'convict' (with a clear legal sense), as when we say 'Citizens have condemned some dubious modern financial practices' and 'The defendant was convicted of manslaughter by the jury'. Likewise, something similar might be said of *inocente*. In English there are two words: 'innocent', as when we say 'His words were innocent', and 'not guilty', as in 'The jury found him not guilty'. Obviously this list of doublets is much longer.

10.4.2 The translation of the Spanish technical term *Administración* into English

The translation of the Spanish word *Administración* into English also presents hurdles that have to be surmounted. Here is a discussion of six of these problems.

(a) ***La Administración*** *in Spanish*

The word *Administración* has two meanings in political law: the first is a function, which is the well-ordered management, supervision and organization of the services designed for the enforcement of laws and regulations; the second is the body or group of administrative agencies or entities responsible for the actual enforcement of laws and regulations.

(b) 'Administration' in English

According to *Black's Law Dictionary* (Garner 2004), in the context of public law, 'Administration' is the practical management and direction of the executive department and its agencies. In this context, an 'Agency' is a governmental body with the authority to implement and administer. American administrative agencies are different from their Spanish counterparts. In Great Britain one possible translation might be 'The Crown' or 'Crown officers'.

(c) 'Administration' and Agency

On the other hand, in American English the word 'Administration' may be a synonym of 'Agency', as when we say the *Food and Drug Administration*.

(d) ***Administración, el Gobierno*** *and the Executive*

The Spanish word *el Gobierno* is equivalent most of the time to 'The Executive' in American English, and to 'The Cabinet' in British English.

(e) 'Government' and ***Estado***

The words 'Government' and *Gobierno* are not always equivalent. 'Government' most of the time corresponds to the Spanish *Estado*, as when we say government-owned (*de propiedad estatal*), or Government bonds (*bonos del Estado*). In English the term 'Government' includes the Legislature, the Executive and the Judiciary. I will illustrate this with two anecdotes. Some American states did not ratify the American Constitution until 1791, when the first ten amendments, the so-called Bill of Rights, were introduced setting 'a significant limitation to the powers of the government over the individual'. In this case 'government' is probably what we call *todo el poder del Estado*. The second anecdote comes from bilingual agreements between the USA and Spain during Franco's time. In Spanish it said *el Estado español*; the English translation was 'The Spanish Government'. Now those documents would probably talk about 'The Kingdom of Spain'.

(f) ***Estado de Derecho***

The word *estado* becomes more difficult to translate in the expression *estado de derecho*. It can be rendered into English in two ways according to the context. For example, in the expression *Algunos no respetan el estado de derecho* ('Some do not obey the rule of law'), *estado de derecho* is 'the rule of law', whereas in *España es un estado de derecho* ('Spain is a country that complies with the rule of law'), *estado de derecho* is 'a country complying with the rule of law'.

10.4.3 The translation of the Spanish word *legal* into English

Bilingual dictionaries usually give three words in English for the Spanish term *legal*:

(a) Statutory

It is applied to what is recognized or supported by an Act or statute from Parliament or Congress, not from common law. For example, 'statutory sick leave' makes reference to the permission to stay at home given to sick people by the corresponding Act.

(b) Legal

It is the general term derived from 'law'; in this sense it is the opposite of 'illegal', which is something violating a law or regulation. Sometimes it makes reference to rights, decisions, etc. from common law, unlike 'equitable' rights, decisions, etc., from 'equity' (see section 10.5).

(c) Lawful

It means the same as 'legal', but they have different connotations. 'Legal' may make more reference to formal aspects, whereas 'lawful' carries the connotation of 'rightful' – *de pleno derecho* – legitimate or ethical. To this effect, the current 'legal holder' of something may not be its 'lawful holder'.

Seen from the English side, the English word 'legal' is the adjective connected to 'law', a term that may have the following equivalences in Spanish:

(a) *Ley*, which is the precept from Parliament or Congress ordering or prohibiting something in connection with justice or the well-being of citizens.
(b) *Derecho*, namely, the set of principles, precepts and rules governing human relations.

Accordingly, the English term 'legal' can be translated into Spanish as:

(a) *Legal*, as in *El marco legal* (The legal framework). In this sense it could also be equivalent to 'statutory' in English.
(b) *Legal*, namely, allowed or authorized by law, as in *La detención no ha sido legal* (The arrest has not been legal).
(c) *Ajustado a Derecho*, as when we say *Una resolución ajustada a Derecho* (A legal decision).
(d) *Jurídico*, namely, connected with law in general, as when we say *El inglés jurídico* (Legal English).

10.5 Cultural anisomorphism in the translation of legal texts. Common law, statute law and equity

When we compare the Anglo-American legal system and its Continental counterpart, the number of cultural anisomorphisms that arise is incredible. Consider, for example, the peculiar terms *barrister* and *solicitor*, that coexist with *advocate* and *counsel* (*counsel for the defence, counsel for the prosecution*). To illustrate the point of cultural anisomorphism, I examine three genuine English legal concepts (*common law, statute law* and *equity*) that are clear representatives of the Anglo-American legal system.

When translators read sentences containing expressions like *Wallis* v. *Smith* (1882) 21 Ch D 243, *Lord Elphinstone* v. *Monkland* (1886) 11 App Cas 332,342 or *Congress* v. *Home Office* [1976] QB 629 they know they are reading precedents and therefore are dealing with common law. Common law is judge-made law and it consists of precedents that can be found in law reports:

In *Wallis* v. *Smith* (1882) 21 Ch D 243 the relevant clause provided that if the defendant were to commit a 'substantial breach' of the contract, he should pay £5000. It was held that the inclusion of 'substantial breach' meant that trifling breaches were excluded and the clause could therefore be construed as providing for liquidated damages.

In *Lord Elphinstone* v. *Monkland* (1886) 11 App Cas 332,342 Lord Watson said 'when a single lump sum is made payable by way of compensation on the occurrence of one or more or all of several events, some of which may occasion serious and others but trifling damages, the presumption is that be penal'.

In *Congress* v. *Home Office* [1976] QB 629 the Court of Appeal held unlawful demands of £6 by the Home Secretary as the price of refraining from revoking a valid and subsisting television licence. Lord Denning said the demands 'were an attempt to levy money for the use of the Crown without the authority of Parliament'.

When translators read sentences containing expressions like *Section 1(1) Section 111(1),* etc., they know they are dealing with the sections of an Act and therefore with statute law, consisting of sections. Acts are passed by Parliament, Congress or other legislatures:

Section 1(1) of the Wages Act 1986 provides: 'An employer shall not make any deduction from any wages of a worker ... unless (a) it is required or authorised ... by ... statutory provision or ... contract; or (b) the worker has ... signified in writing his agreement or consent ...'

Section 5(1) (a): 'A worker may present a complaint to an industrial tribunal – (a) that his employer has made a deduction from his wages in contravention of section 1(1) ...'

The council relied on Section 111(1) of the Local Government Act 1972. Equity is the third branch of Anglo-American justice. It is another peculiar feature of this system, when examined from the perspective of Continental law, as it is based on the sense of fairness of courts. In sum, it is the discretion that courts have to make decisions skipping the content of a legal rule, when they consider that its application would produce a greater damage or simply because it would be totally unfair.

To make things more complicated from a linguistic point of view, equity has created its own genuine vocabulary. The 'claimant' or 'plaintiff' in law (both common law and statute law) is called the 'petitioner', and the 'defendant' is known as the 'respondent'. The 'judgment' has become the 'decree'.

10.6 Conclusions

In closing, we might conclude that anisomorphism, both linguistic and cultural, embraces, at least, gaps, asymmetries and exceptions, whereas isomorphism makes reference to the 'recurrent beautifully well-defined patterns found in languages and in nature', that is, the aesthetic element we spoke about in our introduction when the *discovery of harmony* was brought up as one of the goals of the human condition. Consequently, we would like to suggest that the translator should be aware both of the *beautiful* isomorphisms and of the *perilous* anisomorphisms existing between the words and expressions of the two languages involved in the translation of legal pages. As a final remark, we would like to stress that anisomorphism cannot, at any rate, be reduced to a simple question of polysemy or of false friends; it is more complex than that.

11
Translation as a Dynamic Model in the Development of the Burundi Constitution(s)

Jean-Baptist Bigirimana

11.1 Introduction

In his panoramic considerations on 'Translation in Monolingual Societies', José Lambert devotes a few pages to translation and legislation (Lambert 2004: 78–81). One of his basic theses is that it is due to (the Western) tradition that the 'language and law' issue, or the language(s) and discourse(s) used in legal texts and in oral legal discourse, ignores the fact that legal discourse is to a large extent – simply – *translated* discourse: the making of legal discourse, at least in the European tradition, seems to owe a lot to translated discourse. In their own different traditions, experts in legal matters are not unaware at all of specific, i.e. microscopic translation 'problems', but mainly from the point of view of the exact correspondence ('equivalence') between the 'original' version of given legal texts and their output in another language, i.e. in the 'translated' version, which often happens not to be that simple. Lawyers, judges and researchers all realize that the correspondence or coincidence of legal texts in more than one language is never simple, since the concepts that are supposed to refer to the same phenomenon more than likely represent different positions in (at least) two different traditions; in the terminology shaped by translation studies (TS), they are not necessarily equivalent, and experts in TS tend to support the idea that their equivalence is never unproblematic: it is always asymmetric (Šarčević 1997). Many translators and translation trainers, together with legal experts, tend to summarize the difficulty as follows: how can one transfer particular words (terms, concepts) from one legal tradition into another? But according to particular trends in TS, there are much more basic issues at stake in legal translation; nothing is more ambiguous than the overall relationship between translated utterances (messages, written or oral) and their origins in other languages and related legal traditions. Whether their foreign origins and languages have been made explicit (as in the case of movies, literary works) or rather left implicit, invisible and hence seemingly unproblematic (as in many legal texts), they tend to affect the autonomy and the authority of (public) discourse, which may prove embarrassing in the case of legal discourse. The issue of translation as formulated within d*escriptive translation studies* (DTS) no longer (exclusively) focuses on the 'how-to' question. It includes more fundamental ideas about the relationships between different texts and traditions while also looking for more general and more specific traditions and relationships. The question 'Where does this word or concept or text come from?' may mean: 'Who exactly is telling me what (not) to do?' Hence the authority of the legislator can be called into question. Legal translations and the clearly 'foreign' origins in other languages of any legal texts can obviously become a treacherous issue: translation scholars have established that most translators can decide to go for 'invisible translations', which do not mention their foreign issues ('worüber man nicht spricht'; Levý 1969 calls them 'illusionist translations') rather than 'visible' (anti-illusionist) ones. For obvious reasons, i.e. due to their environment, legal translators tend to exclude the anti-illusionist option: laws are simply laws and we need not speak about their origins (Lambert 2004: 78–81). This is exactly where TS, and DTS in particular, claims to provide new insights, on the basis of theories and research models mainly developed by Gideon Toury (1980, 1995) and by a large group of researchers since the 1980s, as can be seen in the journal *Target*. Not only legal translation, but all translations are subject to such distinctions, and seen within internationalization and globalization frameworks, contemporary societies do have a strong tendency to opt for an illusionist strategy (Lambert 1989).

Most research on legal translation has focused so far on pragmatic issues, mainly on 'the difficulty of translating' and on the consequences of particular (bad, wrong or ambiguous) translations from the past and the more recent past. DTS insists on the necessity to study any translated interpretation of any given message on the basis of the assumption that it is inevitably conditioned by particular norms and priorities: instead of tackling practical (and normative) issues in view of future text production (the prospective and normative perspective), DTS inquires into the fundamental rules underlying intercultural (legal) communication. This implies that any translated legal text reflects some assumptions about law, about legislation, about legal style and discourse, about languages which deserve to be taken into consideration both from a large panoramic point of view and from a microscopic one. From this perspective, legal translation becomes part of legislation rather than being excluded from it. This seems to make sense from the moment it is actually relevant to assume that most legal traditions – and constitutions – have migrated from given languages into other languages. So, in principle they can hardly escape the basic thesis formulated thus far, i.e. that they are based on other legal 'norms' that have already been operational elsewhere and that hence cannot be universal or unproblematic. The exact origins of any legal tradition, their backgrounds and their transmission, and how exactly they have been transferred and reformulated, both in terms of language and discourse, become part of the legislation issue. This also implies that translating (or not translating) is part of the process and cannot be deemed unproblematic when it occurs or not.

In the *Handbook* article by Lambert (2004), it is asked explicitly whether only the Western legal traditions would happen to make use of translations with regard to the construction of legal systems, while leaving open the question where such constructions come from, which implies the use of so-called illusionist perspectives (e.g. 'This is how we put it, in our constitution, and French/other formulations are not our concern'). The question itself, once developed within a new discipline, is a strong argument in favour of the broadening of the perspectives and programmes about legal traditions beyond Europe. And it is on the basis of such questions in this chapter that the focus will be on situations such as those in Burundi – or perhaps in other African – legal traditions.

By definition, bilingual or multilingual legislation deserves to be envisaged as a challenge from the moment one wonders about the origins of any given legal formulation. In fact this begs the following questions: how can there be more than one legal text applying to my situation and which text does actually apply to my case? Moreover, if there is more than one, in more than one language, why would I submit to one particular text rather than to another, which I may actually prefer? In this regard, this chapter aims to analyse key issues of the Burundi constitution, which happens to be explicitly bilingual, and which has also been revised several times while mainly maintaining its bilingual tradition, which has been borrowed from another country, Belgium, where bilingualism has in fact developed in various stages (Busekist 1998). Whether the Burundi case is exceptional or rather common (in the African context) will not be discussed here, but the issue deserves to become programmatic. In recent years, Nelson Mandela and his country have invited Belgian experts to support them in the drafting of a multilingual constitution. It can be asked why European feedback was really needed (Deprez and du Plessis 2000). In the case of Burundi, Belgian feedback was probably less surprising, for simple colonial reasons. The question remains as to how given (new) constitutions in Africa deal with languages, with legal texts and with legal translation(s).

There is no doubt about the ubiquity of translation(s) in the history of West European legislation, or in the history of European constitutions. This may be remarkable in itself, since any constitution deserves to be envisaged as the Holy Book of any national legislation: what would the implications be if the Holy Books of many countries happened to be the result of importation? And why is this kind of importation not really taken seriously by the scholarship that analyses the entire issue of legislation? In the case of European legal traditions, the impact of the Roman empire on the development of civilization may be an answer, the Roman empire's impact being a substantial moment in the history of Europe. Is the role of the Roman legislation – or the role of the *Code Napoléon* – really that exceptional, or would the intercultural distribution of legal traditions (and their distribution in translated versions that are hardly ever acknowledged as translations) be one of the common practices in legal traditions as such?

Given the fact that 'law' and 'translation' have often been associated, in the past and probably also in the present, one of our questions ought to be: what kind of legislation is bilingual (or multilingual legislation, e.g. in the case of the European Union)? The translated status of law is made explicit in the case of bilingual or trilingual legislation and legal formulations are subject to comparison, which by definition proves a delicate matter for lawyers, judges, clients, etc. After all bilingual legislation is not at all unknown to lawyers, since it is one of the obvious features of countries such as Belgium and Canada, whereas multilingual legislation is unavoidable in Switzerland, in post-apartheid South Africa and, of course, within the EU. It seems that multilingual translation, after all, happens to be fundamentally different from the bilingual traditions listed so far because – as in the EU – they do not imply the side-by-side presentation (layout) that we are familiar with in bilingual countries: are multilingual legislations more invisible, more illusionist than bilingual ones?

The leap from Europe to South Africa, or vice versa, is less unexpected than we might imagine: perhaps one does not go without the other, because of colonial traditions as the story goes. It is not at all unknown that Nelson Mandela himself, being one of the symbols of decolonization, invited Belgian experts to help draft the new constitution. This happened at the end of the twentieth century. It is clearly not the only case of complex transfers of legal expertise from Europe to the African continent, as the case of Burundi will demonstrate. And the Burundi case cannot be disconnected from some of its neighbouring countries in (Southern) Africa. The striking observation to be made is that bilingualism has been part of constitutional history in Burundi as well as in Ruanda or in Congo-Zaïre. One can easily guess it has something to do with the Belgian influence on the legislation and constitutions of countries in the heart of Africa. It is not the least remarkable feature of the Burundi constitution that it has proved to be anything but stable through almost half a century of independence. On the other hand the use of bilingualism, hence of translation, has been a fundamental requirement, and this stems from the influence of the colonizing power: it seems to be 'a model', i.e. a pattern in legislation in a country that indeed has always been subject to linguistic distinctions and variation. How could constitutions ever be compatible with monolingualism and with monolingual constitutions, on a continent where the very idea of language – and writing – conflicts with the basic (Western?) views on language and languages? How can countries like Nigeria, Ivory Coast, the two Congos or the Kingdom of the Zulus distinguish between right and wrong when their populations make use of dozens and dozens of languages? In the case of Burundi, the multiplication into more than one language is only part of the general multiplication problem of legal texts, since the country has officially recognized five different constitutions in about half a century.

11.2 The linguistic and colonial landscape of Burundi

At first sight, neither Burundi nor its colonial history are that exceptional in an African context: the constitution itself has gradually developed from its colonial background, and it has been developed (first) in an imported language, i.e. in French, which explains why bilingualism was a structural condition from the beginning. Without any further investigation, one wonders whether other African countries would have behaved differently, i.e. without the use of any European lingua franca. Not unlike many other African countries, Burundi has attracted several colonial powers and traditions, and its neighbouring countries Congo-Zaïre and Ruanda, and perhaps other countries, have also helped shape its autonomy, especially in relation to its constitution. Two world wars have also had their impact. After the First World War German rule was replaced by a Belgian 'protectorate' in a twinned Ruanda-Burundi, which implied the link with European politics; and at least two neighbours, Ruanda and Congo, shared Belgian supervision until 1960, while Congo-Brazzaville, another big neighbour, happened to be under the umbrella of francophone culture – and power? – in Africa. There are no reasons for excluding the impact of other neighbours to the east, north-east and south of Burundi, but the very establishment of a Burundi nation in the 1960s as well as the first formulation of its legal autonomy – let us say its first constitution(s) – were supposed to be shaped from the beginning in the then fully dominant language of the colonizer. Sociolinguists have demonstrated that such interlinguistic situations are never static, and it is an obvious phenomenon that English, as the new lingua franca of globalization, has gained a given position in many of these countries, while French is still in a position of power. In terms of languages and cultural traditions, Burundi also happened to share some of its 'African' languages with its neighbouring countries: colonial bilingualism, i.e. the dependence on French, one of the European linguae francae on the African continent, was one of the cultural umbrellas that Burundi shared with Ruanda, Congo, etc.

The Burundi constitution itself provides us with interesting material about an exact sociolinguistic map of the country. First of all, French was imposed and gradually accepted as a new language, the colonial language by definition; the juxtaposition of Kirundi and French in almost all Burundi legal traditions is a sufficient indication of bilingual competences. To this very day, the use of French is quite common in Burundi courts. However, there are good arguments that make us recognize a much more complex linguistic situation. Bilingualism may be sufficiently complex for European societies, or for Canada; it is never a realistic representation of the linguistic dynamics of African societies. For example, Kirundi was not the only African language and French not the only European language involved. Moreover, it is not clear today what kind of impact the German language may have had on the population: there are not many facts supporting the idea of its survival after 1919, except maybe as a lingua franca among the more mobile groups involved in business in the areas north of Burundi. But Dutch (or 'Flemish', as it was often labelled) was the second language of the Belgian colonial power, and it did have an official status as we shall see: the first basis of the Burundi constitution was the Burundi counterpart of the (Belgian) bilingual *Moniteur,* in French and Dutch, from 1919 to 1961. There is at least one important shift in the political language policy after the Congo–Ruanda– Burundi independence: Dutch ceased to be one of the official languages, and French was recognized as the only official partner language in the Burundi constitution.

Hence we have good reasons for not submitting the Burundi traditions since, say, 1900 to the monolithic – and very Western European – view on language that the man in the street tends to accept almost blindly: sociolinguists have demonstrated time and again that we have to distinguish between official language policies and the everyday use of given languages. Anyway, while sticking to both French and Kirundi for quite some time, the legislative power clearly recognized the priority of two languages. An additional question – it is almost purely theoretical – is whether all citizens of Burundi are familiar with both languages, and/or whether both Kirundi and French may be 'acquired languages' for some subgroups in the population (in urban areas, for instance).

While there can be no doubt about the multilingual tradition of 'Burundi' for quite some time (centuries), there is considerable proof that Kirundi was the dominant common language. The sociolinguistic literature asserts broadly that there is no doubt: as a nation, the population in Burundi has one single national idiom (Ndimurukundo-Kururu 2004). Nowadays, Kirundi is the mother tongue of approximately 6 million Burundi-born nationals. French and other languages are in fact spoken by a minority of educated people, but French is quite dominant among the 'minority languages'. The basic features of the sociolinguistic situation in Burundi, as described by Ndimurukundo-Kururu (2004), Ntahombaye (1994), Frey (1993, 1996) and Queffelec (1992) among others, or through data available from the International Francophone Agency (AIF) show that only 3 per cent out of 6.1 million Burundians (as of 1997) can more or less use French. The dominant status of French in Burundi is rather de facto than *de jure*, at least openly since the 1993 constitution (and also since the 2005 constitutional text, see further). This is what Le Palec (1983: 33) and Calvet (1987: 116) observe about the subject, unlike Frey (1996: 244), who asserts that French has an official status which is quite different from its day-to-day use. Ntahomvukiye (1992) is of the opinion that

> Nous nous trouvons au Burundi (...) dans une société où, suite à la colonisation, la langue nationale a été supplantée par une langue étrangère dans tous les domaines où se joue le sort du présent et de l'avenir des gens. La langue nationale a été marginalisée, confinée dans des domaines jugés sans impact réel sur la société.[1]

The background of the Burundi sociolinguistic features is to be understood in terms of a French/Kirundi diglossia.[2]

11.3 The Belgian colonial legislation: a foreign model

Given the above sociolinguistic remarks, we can logically accept the hypothesis of a pre-colonial legal tradition: it was oral and formulated in Kirundi. Whether it was formulated in Kirundi only, cannot be ascertained at this stage: there are strong arguments in favour of multilingual legal – religious, social, political, etc. – traditions, but it is difficult to locate them well on the cultural maps.

There are similar difficulties as far as the survival of German is concerned: the German administration (1898–1919) has not left behind enough data to allow us to discover to what extent the German language and culture survived at all in the writings or the minds of Burundians. Conversely, the Belgians (1919–62) soon after their arrival set out decrees, orders, by-laws, etc., which have constituted the basis for the current written legal system in Burundi. A Belgian amendment dated 31 August 1925 linked, as far as the administrative and political level is concerned, the Ruanda-Urundi Territory to the former Belgian Congo (present RD Congo). The consequence is a mixture of oral (traditional) customs and written rules, but also of a kind of French–Dutch (Flemish) bilingualism, as the practice was prevalent in Metropolitan Belgium.

Of course the Belgian authorities started working out a legislation for the Burundi (and the Rwanda) administration. They published it in a journal entitled the *Bulletin Officiel du Ruanda-Urundi* from 1923, and then in the *Official Journal of Belgian Congo and Official Journal of Ruanda-Urundi* or *Bulletin Officiel du Rwanda-Urundi* (*BOR-U*). The journal was bilingual, as was the Belgian *Moniteur:* so there is no need to look any further for the exact model of the *Bulletin*. The Belgian Charte coloniale[3] institutes a sort of 'state bilingualism'. The latter provides *inter alia* that 'tous les décrets et lois couvrant les matières générales seront désormais écrits et publiés en français et en néerlandais, toutes les deux langues étant officielles'.[4] Both languages were obviously Belgian national languages.

11.4 From one bilingual *Bulletin* to the other: from *BOR-U* to *BOB*

Most countries, especially the European ones, have established and promoted their constitution as a real event, as a historical moment. Hence the revision of constitutions seems to be a paradox in itself. In the case of Burundi, such paradoxes have occurred several times. The remarkable thing is also that revision coincided with competition between various constitutional text models and with competition between – again – bilingual textual formulations.

Prior to 1962, Burundi did have quite a few legal rules, but no written constitution. During the colonial period, the legal apparatus made use of decrees and administrative by-laws without any reference to a given constitution. From 1923 on the Belgian legislators started a national *Bulletin*, which formed a kind of constitutional 'prehistory' because the journal was designed to circulate rules and other regulations during the colonial era. Since the first one in 1962 (immediately after Burundi had gained independence), several new constitutions (five so far) have been started at critical moments in the history of the new country. In July 1962, Burundi recovered its sovereignty and *BOR-U*, the official journal that was born with the Belgian protectorate, was replaced by *Bulletin Officiel du Burundi* (*BOB*), and by the *Bulletin Officiel du Rwanda* (*BOR*). As already mentioned, the shift from *BOR-U* to *BOB* (or *BOR* for Rwanda) involved a new language policy: Dutch was substituted by Kirundi, while French was maintained alongside Kirundi. In fact, French had already become the backbone of the quasi entire Burundi legal system (De Clerck 1968: 36; Lamy 1961: 33–6, 73–80). The 1961 provisional constitutional text was published in the *Bulletin* issue no. 2 bis of February 1962 of the former *BOR-U*, just a short time before it turned into *BOB*, which began along with independence and would be the channel for the 1962 'independence constitution' document.

It was a first and also a remarkable case that the legal–constitutional apparatus was available in French – at first – and then translated into Kirundi from that very moment. It is worth noting also that *BOB* shows the Kirundi text on the left, the French on the right, as if the former were the original, and the latter the translation. Article 21 of the 1962 constitution provides an equal status for French and Kirundi, but the habits of readers and intellectuals familiar with European (and Belgian) legal texts have their consequences: the layout is more influential than any statement, which implies that Kirundi is supposed to be the model for translation into French. At that very moment, legal experts from Burundi were exposed to a new situation, since Burundi never had a constitution, but their expertise was inevitably grounded in the Belgian bilingual tradition. From their cultural perspective, we can consider bilingual legal documents as a new genre in the legal and cultural landscape of the country: the genre had been imported, probably from Belgium and France (among other places?).

New genres are supposed to generate uncertainties and fluctuations, if not erratic behaviour. At the very beginning of Burundi independence, bilingualism was indicated and made visual as an official principle of the new nation-monarchy. And it has never been officially questioned since. But from the outset even the visual parallelism between Kirundi and French has not been unproblematic. One could take seriously the idea that this is a mere question of languages: even famous linguists among the translation theoreticians of the 1960s have been convinced that language 1 (whatever its name may have been) needed in principle more words or more space than language 2, but this kind of improvisation is no longer taken seriously among experts. There is no doubt about the fluctuating treatment of languages 1 and 2 in the Burundi constitution. But even within the left- or right-hand side of every page a minimum of improvisation can be observed: the Kirundi text, being the result of translation, happens to be shorter (and we feel entitled to assume that, at that moment, the translator did not insist on the necessity of a full translation); but the opposite is also relevant at many moments, where apparently the translator made more explicit the rules of his own country for the local population, in matters that neither the Belgian nor the French model had had any reason to work out. This implies that the translation, if not the constitution as a whole, finally becomes eclectic to the point that bilingualism is simply a theoretical rule, but does not form the basis of actual constitutional pragmatics. During the first 50 years of its existence, the Burundi constitution hence deserves to be envisaged as an eclectic textual construction in which translation occupies a central position.

Due to political instability, the first Burundian constitution (1962) was interrupted in October 1965, then officially suspended 'for ever' in July 1966, when Prince Ndizeye took over the 'Prince Regent' position in the absence of Mwami (King) Mwambutsa IV (opting for a 'Prince Regent' is not unknown among Belgian citizens who remember the days and years after the Second World War, but as a constitutional concept it is not well known at all, and the origins of such a concept have nothing to do with the country that had generated the constitution). The first military coup by Micombero in November 1966 and, simultaneously, the abolition of monarchy, neither restored the constitution nor drew up a new one until 1974. The third constitution was established in 1981 under Colonel Bagaza's regime: Bagaza's coup which took place on 1 November 1976, abrogated – yet again – the two-year constitution of the first Republic. The fourth constitution goes back to 1992, when international and internal pressure on Major Buyoya's military regime became too great – this started with a first coup in 1987. Since then, a pluralistic multi-party era has prevailed. Due to the quick change in regimes, it is hard to establish whether the first constitution remained active or familiar among experts from one period to the next (1962–2005).

11.5 Beyond bilingualism and binary traditions: looking for more 'models'

Our basic assumption is that the Belgian text formed the model for the Burundian text. There is little doubt about this issue, but the real question is rather when and how and why other models have been used, and to what extent the direct use of available models has interfered with the Belgian one, and to what extent translation happens to be (an unknown) part of the story. There is no real doubt about its administrative origins, in this case the so-called author, a Belgian expert, Professor René Massinon, has confessed his authorship to the author of this paper.[5] For any African francophone country, it is both a complex and an easy task to write a new constitution; it was easier to do so in the middle of the twentieth century than it would be nowadays. It was easy at that moment, for two main reasons: (a) the Belgian colonial power had already been functioning as a legislator for several decades, and it had a constitution; but (b) the country was a monarchy that has borrowed its constitution from the French *Code Napoléon* when France was already a Republic, let us say the legal mother Republic.

As our starting points have indicated, the very idea of translation is embarrassing to the extent that one 'language' (and version) appears to be 'prior' to the other one, and in case of 'interpretation', bilingualism and bilingual legislation do generate competition (Lambert 2004, forthcoming). In the Burundi case, one of the fascinating problems is the obvious use, not of one single 'model' or 'original', but of several possible ones. When looking for the origins of both the constitutional text and its translation, one is obliged to examine at least four sources: the Belgian, the French, then the Rwandese and the Congo constitutions, and it is not fully obvious that only contemporary – twentieth-century models – of the same period have been taken into consideration. Even nineteenth-century European models, such as the Belgian (or the French), had not yet fully disappeared from Africa in the second half of the twentieth century. Why exactly these constitutions (and countries) have been selected as models is in itself not difficult to guess: the reasons for this choice are either both historical and linguistic (as far as European backgrounds are concerned), or historical and geographical (as far as neighbouring countries in Africa are concerned). Historically speaking, Belgium had both the technical instruments (since Napoleon and since Belgian independence in the nineteenth century) and the power position needed for the establishment of a body of legal texts. As far as the form of the institutions and the political regime are concerned, Belgium is likely to have influenced and even shaped the first Burundi constitution. The opposite would have been rather surprising. But the French constitution from the time of Napoleon, which was the mother of many constitutions and regimes, also seems to have had some influence on the republican constitutions of Burundi. This is what can be established on the basis of the constitutional regime but also in terms of verbal formulation (see examples below). After all, Burundian jurists had studied in Belgium and France: they could hardly introduce concepts that had not already been circulating in their own (European) alma maters.

To this very day, Burundi does not have one particular constitution; this new country has simply generated five different constitutions in say half a century. Let us indicate with the aid of a scheme which events have influenced the dynamics of the nation building, and hence also the legislative principles. After a so-called multi-party era (1962), which refers to the willingness to recognize the so-called democratic model of societies, came the first military coup by Captain Micombero, coinciding with the advent of the Republic (the coup occurred in 1966, the constitution was distributed from 1974 on). Several coups and revolutions have since taken place: the second coup by Colonel Bagaza (1976), the third by Major Buyoya (1987), followed later by the second democratic and multi-party process (1992); then, during the last period of civil war (1993–2005), the constitution was abrogated by the second Buyoya coup in 1996. It is worth observing that at each of these events, the previous constitution was said to be abrogated and immediately replaced by a so-called transition text that was supposed to prepare a really (democratic) constitutional text. Table 11.1 represents the various key moments of the Burundi constitutional evolution.

Let us highlight that the legal text, including the constitution itself, is declared officially operational from the moment it is (has been) promulgated, and published in the official *Bulletin*, i.e. the *BOB*. In this regard, all changes and fluctuations in the constitutional formulations are simply part of the game, they become, say, the norm. Since the very first volume of the *Bulletin*, published on 9 March 1962 at Usumbura (now Bujumbura), the first 13 volumes have been produced in French and Kirundi (and never in French–Dutch), according to the constitution. In 2007, the *BOB* entered its forty-fifth year of publication and – officially – the end of its bilingual edition.

Since any constitutional texts and legal translation strategies cannot avoid depending on sociopolitical events, the Belgian model occupies an important place in the configuration as far as the Burundi case is concerned. And, as neighbouring countries with similar traditions, Congo and Rwanda have offered interesting alternative models to the Burundi translators-legislators. What is the link between sovereignty and the linguistic translation strategy in this case? It appears that (linguistic and other) technical devices are indicative of crucial political options within the country, among the languages and cultures involved, but also in

Table 11.1 Burundi constitutional evolution

The exact historical moment	*The event*	*Constitutional translation (if any)*	*Comment*
1 July 1962	Burundi independence		
1962 (Oct.): first constitution	Independence (July 1962)	French translated into Kirundi	The very first statutory constitution preceded by a provisional constitution (Nov. 1961;
1965–74			No constitution
1965	Prince Ndizeye enthroned		King Mwambutsa is no longer in power
1966	First Republic from a coup by Micombero and abolition of monarchy		Abolition of the monarchy is an important event; but the new military regime does not feel any need to establish any constitution
1974 (11 July): second constitution		French not translated	This incompatible with the constitution itself
1976 (1 Nov.)	Second Republic after a coup		
1976–81			No constitution
1981 (20 Nov.): third constitution		French translated into Kirundi	
1987 (4 Sept.)	Buyoya's coup		
1988	Ntega and Marangara		
1988–92	Debates on multi-party regime		
1992 (13 March): fourth constitution		French translated in to Kirundi	
1993 (21 Oct.)	Military coup and civil war		
1993 to	Civil war		
2000 (28 Aug.)	Arusha Peace Agreement		
2005 (18 March): fifth constitution		French translated into Kirundi	

terms of international post-colonial politics. Translation experts have established that any translation makes use of linguistico-technical solutions, called devices. The question always becomes what kind of principles may account for the selection and use of such devices. The fascinating thing is that, in the case of the Burundi constitution, translation options such as *loan, calque, adaptation, non-translation, new lexicon, new concepts,* etc. (i.e. the basic technical–rhetorical operations in translational operations: Lambert and Van Gorp 1985) are much more than mere technical devices, they reflect political, social, moral, religious and other value scales at work: the simple substitution of a single word for the previous one may look like an innocent – linguistic – operation, but there is a clear possibility of relying on political/social/ideological shifts linked with political shifts in the level of political power. Such shifts are at work within each individual new constitutional text, but also between them, during the 50–100 years of the written legal tradition of the constitution.

One or two examples will indicate how such translational solutions reveal the working schemes – and the underlying political and other priorities – among our translators, i.e. their underlying agenda:

- the concept of 'rule of law' was unknown until BuCo92 preamble and Buco92 Art. 54, and has been used since 1992; it has not been translated into the Kirundi version from 1992, which confirms the use of French models;
- *ubukuru nshingamateka*, which is supposed to render 'legislative power' (Buco62:119, 122) is a new concept in Burundi and may not sound 'Kirundi' to a Kirundi native speaker;
- *Raporo, Leta, Repubulika, Komine, iparaki* standing respectively for *report, state, Republic, commune (or district), public prosecutor's department* are some of the numerous loans used in a heterogeneous and unsystematic way; but in themselves, as such, they are imported concepts;
- one of the well-known key concepts is the Mwami (the king: BUco62:73), whose name became known through all the continent; but his 'ministers' (translated as *umushikirangoma*[6] a traditional public servant, a crown counsellor close to the king) as well as the judicial power (translated with the aid of a calque as *urwego rw'amasentare*, see Buco92: 164) cause great difficulties for the translators, who appear to shift from 'more domestic' into more international translation options.

In fact, many *loan* items are used (or not used): the translation option (strategy) that tried to avoid 'foreign' items as much as possible was much stronger at the beginning than after 1981. It may be enlightening to connect such options and hesitations with the 'zaïrization' promoted by Mobutu in Zaïre (or 'Congo', as it was called before and after a couple of decades of 'zaïrization'): the entire translation problem, in Burundi and elsewhere on the African continent, is supposed to illustrate the dynamics of the cultural autonomy movement, and it is not astonishing at all that the Burundi legal translations appear to be ambiguous and hesitant throughout the first 50 years of independence.

But the most striking phenomenon is the complex mixture of continuity and discontinuity in the relationships among the various constitutional texts under examination: the new legal Burundi is looking for its own language and discourse. This complex mixture is the leading principle, first of all, in the links between the five Burundi versions, then in the relationships with the two European models, the Belgian and the French. It would be easy to illustrate this general picture with the overall structure of the constitution(s). But let us – *hic et nunc* – reduce the document to the first chapters (Table 11.2).

Table 11.2 Content of the subdivisions of the constitutional text

Structure	*Burundi*					*Belgium*	*France*
	1962	*1974*	*1981*	*1992*	*2005*	*1831*	
Preamble	4§	4§	6§	11§	13§	–	
Title	I: Du Territoire et de ses divisions	I: L'Etat et sa souveraineté	I: De la République du Burundi	I: De L'Etat et la souveraineté du peuple	I: De L'Etat et la souveraineté du peuple	I: Du Territoire et de ses subdivisions	De la souveraineté
Subtitle					Sous-titre: des principles généraux		
Chapter	–	–	–	–	–		
Title	II: Des Burundi et leurs droits	II: Des libertés publiques et de la personne humaine	II: Des libertés publiques et des devoirs du citoyen	II: Des droits de l'homme, des devoirs de l'individu et du citoyen	II: De la charte des droits et des devoirs fondamentaux de l'individu et du citoyen	II: Des Belges et de leurs droits	II: Du Parlement
Title	III: Des pouvoirs	III: Du parti	III: Des partis	III: Du système des partis politiques	III: Du système des partis politiques	III: Des pouvoirs	III: Du Conseil économique

Strangely enough, continuity – let us call it textual stability – is in fact the first and most striking feature of these relationships. But within the microscopic features of the texts, the basic patterns seem also to be rather erratic, while indicating how each constitutional text may make use of several 'models' ('originals') at particular moments. And this is the key issue of our translation-focused analysis: without excluding more or less innocent (stylistic? linguistic?) changes in the legal text tradition, we can assume, on the basis of historical–descriptive research on translation, that the author(s) (should we call them 'translators' or 'authors' or 'legislators'?) of each of the constitutions adapt the previous texts from the moment the political and legal environment urges them to do so. As long as there is no necessity, they are satisfied with the tradition of their constitution; changes are supposed to have their *rationale*, whether on the level of language, grammar, or rather on the level of social, legal or political issues.

One of our key questions (and observations) is the complex organization of the revisions. Certain fragments (paragraphs) have survived well during the various revisions. But particular concepts (and text levels) have been subjected to fundamental revision from the second constitution on. As stable components, we can envisage everything linked with territory, citizens, etc.: they tend to be maintained from the beginning to the end. But the rights of the citizens, their relation with monarchy or Republic, with political parties (monopartism/multipartism) is heavily subjected to revision, first between versions 1 and 2 (the transition from monarchy to Republic), then between two subgroups of texts (versions 1 to 3 versus versions 4 and 5). Table 11.3 is just an introduction to crucial chapters in the history of Burundi as illustrated by translations.

In Burundi constitution (Buco) of 1962, nothing is said about political parties: this corresponds to the Belgian model in use (Belgian constitution of 1831 = Beco1831). But Buco1974[7] reads as follows:

> La République du Burundi adopte le principe du Parti Unique dénommé UPRONA. Article 19. Le parti décrit l'orientation politique

Table 11.3 Crucial chapters in the history of Burundi as illustrated by translations

Buco 1962	*Buco 1974*	*Buco 1981*	*Buco 1992*	*Buco 2005*	*Beco 1831*	*Frco 1958*
III: Des Pouvoirs	III: Du parti	III: Du parti	III: Du système des partis politiques	III: Du système des partis politiques	III: Des pouvoirs	III: Du Conseil économique

générale de la Nation et inspire l'action de l'Etat. Il contrôle l'action du Gouvernement et du pouvoir judiciaire. Article 20: Le parti reflète les aspirations profondes du peuple. Il l'éduque et l'encadre; il le guide pour la réalisation de ses aspirations.

It is not only new, but an important decision, to mention the very existence of political parties; the most spectacular shift is the substitution of the multi-party regime (1962–66) by the one-party one. And Buco1981 also sticks to the one-party Republic. There is no need to make clear that neither the French Revolution nor the Belgian one, in 1830, were familiar with one-party regimes. Which explains how and why the textual models imported from Europe are abandoned by the translators, who produce their constitutional texts along actual Burundi principles. Translation and legal text production go hand in hand, within every single individual text, but the systematic use of (European) models remains a leitmotiv from beginning to end. Such general trends are maintained through all basic political changes. In 1992 Buco1992[8] stressed: 'Le multipartisme est reconnu en République du Burundi.' While the fourth constitution just reintroduces multi-partism (Art. 1), it is worth noting that the 2005 text also insists on it, while making it more explicit in not less than ten articles. And Buco2005[9] starts as follows: 'Le multipartisme est reconnu en République du Burundi ... .'

It is clear that such shifts are not indebted to translation, but rather to writing or to editorial principles. And this is exactly our point: 'translation', as we would call it in everyday discourse, is often and systematically used, whereas in fact the users/citizens are simply convinced they are reading the national production of legal texts. It is exactly the mixture and combination of texts that allows the various constitutions to function and to change, i.e. to run the dynamics of the new country. What is assumed to have strongly inspired the first 'republican' constitution of Burundi (Buco1974), i.e. the constitution of France (Frco) of 1958, reads as follows:

> Les partis et groupements politiques concourent à l'expression du suffrage. Ils se forment et exercent leur activité librement. Ils doivent respecter les principes de la souveraineté nationale et de la démocratie. Ils contribuent à la mise en œuvre du principe énoncé au dernier alinéa de l'article 3[10] dans les conditions déterminées par la loi.

The main difference, simply, is the opposition between one-party and multi-party political systems. Whether this is the result of legal text

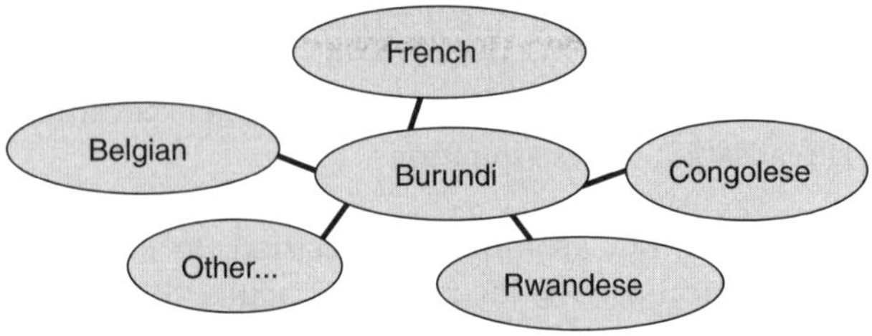

Figure 11.1 Possible models (matrix) of Burundi constitutional texts

production or the result of translation is not the issue at all, at least for the citizen. But the efficiency of this text production depends very heavily on the interwovenness of both and the invisibility of the patterns combined in one and the same single text, even in one and the same language, be it in two different languages displayed side by side.

It is impossible to provide, *hic et nunc,* a comprehensive survey of both the continuity and the continuity options through the various versions of the constitution, nor to indicate – except in very general terms – what kind of principles are underlying them. Anyway, besides the specific arguments that the authors of the various constitutions are supposed to have at any moment in their legislative task, it seems that they continue to make use of 'examples' from other countries: we keep calling them 'models' because of their systematic nature, because of their continuity. The textual environment of the translators' workshop happens to be limited to francophone texts and to those francophone legislative texts that belong to their immediate colonial background: not only the Belgian, but also the French constitution plays a role, whereas the neighbouring countries Rwanda and Congo-Zaïre provide interesting counter-examples of the options that the Burundi team like/dislike to take. The textual operation is both a positive and a negative 'decision process' (Levý 1969) in relation to the different models.

The final scheme should operate as interconnected circles as shown in Figure 11.1.

The key question in our global analysis of the Burundi constitution is where, when, how, etc. one out of the various constitutional models has been adopted, and whether the basic options have changed in a symptomatic way throughout the five different Burundi constitutions. The exact reasons why the textual matrix may have changed – on all text levels, within one particular chapter, within a given conceptual field, as well as between the different constitutions – cannot be explained before all possible levels have been examined in their interrelationships.

11.6 Concluding remarks

It is not the theoretical initial questions about legislation and translation as such, nor about language and law, but the set of interferences between the language(s) of law and translation that have actually taken place in a given (African) country during almost half a century. Besides examining who exactly decided that translations were needed, who was going to work them out, and how (in what kind of a language and/or discourse), we also would like to establish how an actual society – or legislator – i.e. the Burundi one, decided that a new constitution was really needed, how it was going to be different from the previous one, where the foreign ('original'?) models were going to come from, which ones were going to be forbidden or even taboo, and how the continuity of translation activities can be deduced, in this case from the text material and from the various versions that the Burundi population have been living with.

An additional interesting point, for our forum of scholars and scholarship, is that our keys for analysis are borrowed from one of the basic principles of DTS: if we really want to understand the dynamics of translation (and importation), the real object of study is the target pole, say the culture and community that decides that 'translation' – or whatever they call it, they often have excellent reasons for not mentioning the idea of translation at all – is the best option for legal efficiency. Maybe, after all, there could be a secret relationship between the non-mentioning of the translation idea as revealed by TS, and the silence that seems to surround the rich intercultural tradition of legal texts in general.

While analysing constitutional texts imported and translated into the Burundi world, one comes to find that the phenomenon is *replete* and made up with fluctuating and discontinuous components, gaps between the linguistic legislation provisions and practice throughout – at least – 40 years. Bilingual constitutions could not function without any importation, in this case, without translated discourse/legislation. The translation concept reveals a mixture of oral traditions transcribed and textualized on the one hand, and foreign written components on the other. The rather methodological description provided in this chapter is based on Lambert's functional approach to TS, that is an extension widening Toury's functional models, in particular with the aid of the 'norms' concept put to the fore in DTS, in the light of the findings of post-colonial studies. As far as legal texts are concerned in this case, from the beginning (1961) to the present, the basic options in the use of translation illustrate how the efficiency of translation as a legal and political strategy depends on given strategies, for example partly on its being implicit. Our further research will now focus on a detailed and comparative analysis of the corpus. One of the further questions will be to establish how particular and/or how representative the Burundi case is within the recent African traditions. How crucial is the translation component, as defined here, in the growth of legal organization in modern Africa/Burundi and in (re)shaping new (hybrid at this stage) identity?

Notes

1. 'In Burundi, we are within a society where, due to the colonization system the national language has been supplanted by a foreign language in all vital areas regarding people's present and future. The national idiom has been neglected and confined in domains that are irrelevant for society.'
2. In order to get a clear-cut look into the current French and Kirundi diglossia (for this concept, see Ferguson 1959 and Fishman 1980) within the legal and administrative sector, there is a need for a retrospective approach, going back to the colonial era with Germany and its German East Africa, as well as to the Belgian institutional power in Burundi (1916–62).
3. Colonial Chart (1908), a sort of official guidebook for colonial administrators and territories.
4. 'All decrees and laws covering general matters shall be written and published in French and Dutch, both languages being official' in *Document législatifs – Chambre*, R., no. 21, 26 ; Ann., I, S.E., pp. 333–4, 380–3, 392–401, 501–2, 690–5 ; II, 767–8. – *Sénat*, R., no. 68, 104, 128; *Ann.* pp. 171, 189 in Halewyck (1910: 109 my translation). See also Halewyck (1910: 113).
5. Enquiry by the author of this chapter: recorded documents are available with the author. René Massinon had been working as a legal counsellor for the Belgian colonial administration in Burundi before the latter became independent. He is a retired Professor of Law at the Free University of Brussels (ULB) and has published numerous articles, among them: 'La confrontation du droit écrit et de la coutume dans le cadre du régime politique, judiciaire et administratif au Burundi', *Paroles et Culture Bantoues, Annales du Musée Royal de l'Afrique Centrale de Turvuren*, Sciences Humaines.
6. *Ingoma* means 'kingdom' in this case.
7. Titre III, Art. 18 Du parti.
8. Titre III, Art. 53 Du système des partis politiques.
9. Titre III, Art. 75–85 Du système des partis politiques.
10. The third paragraph reads: 'La loi favorise l'égal accès des femmes et des hommes aux mandats électoraux et fonctions électives.'

References

T. Ackermann, *Art. 85 Abs. 1 EG und die Rule of Reason* (Cologne/Berlin/Bonn: Heymanns, 1997)

K. A. Adams, *Legal Usage in Drafting Corporate Agreements* (London: Greenwood Press, 2001)

K. A. Adams, *A Manual of Style for Contract Drafting* (American Bar Association, 2004)

E. Agostini, *Droit Comparé* (Paris: Presses Univ. de France, 1988)

J. E. Ainsworth, 'Categories and Culture: on the "Rectification of Names" in Comparative Law', *Cornell Law Review*, 82 (1996) 19–42

G. Ajani, 'By Chance and Prestige: Legal Transplants in Russia and Eastern Europe', *American Journal of Comparative Law*, 43 (1995) 93–117

E. Alcaraz Varó, *El Español Jurídico* (Barcelona: Ariel, 2002)

B. Anderson, *Imagined Communities: Reflections on the Origin and Spread of Nationalism* (London: NLB, 1983)

T. W. Arnold, *The Symbols of Government* (New Haven: Yale University Press, 1935)

A. Arnull, *The European Union and its Court of Justice* (Oxford: Oxford University Press, 1999)

M. M. Asprey, *Plain Language for Lawyers*, 3rd edn (Sydney: Federation Press, 2003)

P.S. Atiyah and R.S. Summers, *Form and Substance in Anglo-American Law: a Comparative Study of Legal Reasoning, Legal Theory, and Legal Institutions*, reprint (Oxford: Clarendon, 2002)

B. Aubin, 'Die Rechtsvergleichende Interpretation Autonom-Internen Rechts in der Deutschen Rechtsprechung', *Rabels Zeitschrift für Ausländisches und Internationales Privatrecht*, 34 (1970) 458–80

A. Augustinus, *On Christian Doctrine*, translated by D.W. Robertson, Jr (Upper Saddle River, NJ: Prentice Hall, 1997)

M. Baker (ed.), *Routledge Encyclopedia of Translation Studies* (London/New York: Routledge, 1997–2000)

J. Baleyte, *Dictionnaire Économique et Juridique*, 4th edn (Paris: Les Éditions de Navarre, 1995)

J. M. Balkin, 'Deconstruction', in D. Patterson (ed.), *A Companion to Philosophy of Law and Legal Theory* (Oxford: Wiley-Blackwell, 1996)

E. K. Banakas, 'The Method of Comparative Law and the Question of Legal Culture Today', *Tilburg Foreign Law Review*, 3/2 (1994) 113–53

A. Barak, *Purposive Interpretation in Law* (Princeton/Oxford: Princeton University Press, 2005)

R. Barents, 'Law and Language in the European Union', *EC Tax Review*, 1 (1997) 49–55

H. J. Bartels, *Methode und Gegenstand Intersystemarer Rechtsvergleichung* (Tübingen: Mohr, 1982)

F. Bartolini and R. Delconte (eds), *Il Codice Dell'Arbitrato* (Piacenza: La Tribuna, 2001)
A. Bastiansen, 'Augustine's Pauline Exegesis and Ambrosiaster,' in F. Van Fleteren and J. C. Schnaubelt (eds), *Augustine: Biblical Exegete* (New York: Peter Lang, 2001)
A. C. Baugh and T. Cable, *A History of the English Language*, 5th edn (London: Taylor and Francis, 2002)
J. Beauchesne, *Dictionnaire des Cooccurrences* (Montreal: Guérin, 2001)
L. Beaudoin, *Les Mots du Droit: Lexique Analogique Juridique*, 2nd edn (Cowansville, Quebec: Éditions Yvon Blais, 2004)
L. Beaudoin and M. Mailhot, *Expressions Juridiques en un Clin D'œil*, 3rd edn (Cowansville, Quebec : Les Éditions Yvon Blais, 2005)
Irène Bellier, 'The Commission as an Actor: an Anthropologist's View', in Helen Wallace and Alasdair R. Young (eds), *Participation and Policy-Making in the European Union* (Oxford: Clarendon Press, 1997), pp. 91–115
U. Belotti, 'The Language of Italian Arbitration Rules in English: Some Measurable Aspects', *Linguistica e Filologia*, 15 (2002) 113–41
U. Belotti, 'Generic Integrity in Italian Arbitration Rules', in V. Bhatia, C. Candlin and M. Gotti (eds), *Legal Discourse in Multilingual and Multicultural Contexts: Arbitration Texts in Europe* (Bern: Peter Lang, 2003), pp. 19–40
S. W. Bender, 'Consumer Protection for Latinos: Overcoming Language Fraud and English-Only in the Marketplace', *American University Law Review*, 5/4 (1996). Available at http://www.wcl.american.edu/journal/lawrev/45/bender.cfm (last retrieval 16.02.2008)
J. Bentham, *Defense of Usury* (New York: Theodore Foster, 1837)
L.O. Berglund, 'The Search for Social Significance', *Lebende Sprachen*, 4/35 (1990) 145–51
B. Bergmans, 'L'enseignement d'une terminologie juridique étrangère comme mode d'approche du droit comparé', *Revue internationale de droit comparé*, 1 (1987), 90–110
R. Bernhardt, 'Interpretation in International Law', in R. Bernhardt (ed.), *Encyclopedia of Public International Law*, vol. II (Amsterdam: North-Holland, 1995), pp. 1416–25
G. Bernini, 'Is There a Growing International Arbitration Culture?', in *ICCA* (1998), pp. 41–6
V. Bhatia, *Analysing Genre: Language Use in Professional Settings* (London: Longman, 1993)
V. Bhatia, C. Candlin and J. Engberg (eds), *Legal Discourse across Cultures and Systems* (Hong Kong: Hong Kong University Press, 2007)
V. Bhatia, C. Candlin, J. Engberg and A. Trosborg, A. (eds), *Multilingual and Multicultural Contexts of Legislation: an International Perspective* (Frankfurt am Main: Peter Lang, 2003a)
V. Bhatia, C. Candlin and M. Gotti (eds), *Legal Discourse in Multilingual and Multicultural Contexts: Arbitration Texts in Europe* (Bern: Peter Lang, 2003b)
V. Bhatia, C. Candlin and S. Wei, *Legal Discourse in Multilingual and Multicultural Contexts: a Preliminary Study* (Hong Kong: City University of Hong Kong, 2001)
V. Bhatia, J. Engberg, M. Gotti and D. Heller (eds), *Vagueness in Normative Texts* (Bern: Peter Lang, 2005)

S. Bissaron, *Guide du langage juridique – Les pièges à éviter* (Paris: Litec, 2002)
W. Blaau, 'The Rechtsstaat Idea Compared with the Rule of Law as a Paradigm for Protecting Rights', *South African Law Journal*, 107 (1990) 76–96
N. Blok, *Lord Mansfield en Lord Denning: 2 meesters van de Common Law* (Leiden: Universitaire Pers, 1965)
C. Borris, 'Common Law and Civil Law: Fundamental Differences and their Impact on Arbitration', *Arbitration*, 60/2 (1994) 78–85
C. Borris, 'The Reconciliation of Conflicts between Common Law and Civil Law Principles in the Arbitration Process', in S. N. Frommel and B. A. Rider (eds), *Conflicting Legal Cultures in Commercial Arbitration: Old Issues and New Trends* (The Hague: Kluwer Law International, 1999), pp. 1–18
O. Brand, *Das Internationale Zinsrecht Englands* (Tübingen: Mohr, 2002)
O. Brand, 'Grundfragen der Rechtsvergleichung', *Juristische Schulung* (2003) 1082–91
O. Brand, 'Conceptual Comparisons – towards a Coherent Approach to Comparative Legal Studies', *Brooklyn Journal of International Law*, 32/2 (2007a) 405–66
O. Brand, 'Art. 9', in J. Busche and P. T. Stoll (eds), *TRIPs: Internationales und europäisches Recht des geistigen Eigentums* (Cologne/Berlin/Munich: Carl Heymanns Verlag, 2007b)
P. Braselmann, 'Übernationales Recht und Mehrsprachigkeit. Linguistische Untersuchungen zur Sprachproblemen in EuGH-Urteilen', *Europarecht*, 1 (1992) 55–74
M. Brünjes and H. Janssen, 'Die italienische Autohypothek', *Juristische Schulung* (1995) 45–8
M. Burckhardt, *Auf dem Weg zu einer class action in Deutschland?* (Baden-Baden: Nomos, 2005)
P. Burke, 'Lost (and Found) in Translation: a Cultural History of Translators and Translating in Early Modern Europe', *European Review*, 15/1 (2004) 83–94
I. Burr and T. Mann, 'Die Charta der Grundrechte der Europäischen Union als Paradigma einer sprachenvergleichenden Auslegung im Europarecht', in I. Burr and G. Gréciano (eds), *Europa: Sprache und Recht* (Baden-Baden: Nomos-Verlagsgesellschaft, 2003), pp. 33–49
R. Burrows, *Words and Phrases Judicially Defined* (London: Butterworth, 1943–46)
A. von Busekist, *La Belgique. Politique des langues et la politique de l'Etat de 1780 à nos jours* (Paris/Brussels: De Boeck & Larcier, 1998)
D. Busse, *Recht als Text* (Tübingen: Niemeyer, 1992)
D. Busse, 'Interpreting Law: Text Understanding – Text Application – Working with Texts', in F. Olsen, R. A. Lorz and D. Stein (eds), *Language and Law – Theory and Society* (Düsseldorf: Düsseldorf University Press, 2008), pp. 239–66
P. Butt and R. Castle, *Modern Legal Drafting* (Cambridge: Cambridge University Press, 2001)
R. M. Buxbaum, 'Die Rechtsvergleichung zwischen nationalem Staat und internationaler Wirtschaft', *Rabels Zeitschrift für ausländisches und internationales Privatrecht*, 60 (1996) 201–30
H. L. Buxbaum, 'German Legal Culture and the Globalization of Competition Law', *Berkeley Journal of International Law*, 23 (2005) 101–23

T. Calvani, 'Some Thoughts on the Rule of Reason', *European Competition Law Review*, 22 (2001) 201–7
L.-J. Calvet, *La Guerre des langues et les politiques linguistiques* (Paris: Payot, 1987)
H. Capitant, *Vocabulaire juridique* (Paris: Presses Universitaires de France, 1930)
J.L. Casti, 'Complexity', in *Encyclopedia Britannica*, deluxe edn CD-ROM (2001)
G. Caussignac and D. Kettinger, 'Rédaction parallèlle au Canton de Berne – Koredaktion im Kanton Bern', *Législation d'aujourd'hui – Gesetzgebung heute*, 3 (1991) 77–87
M. Chaskalson, 'The Problem with Property: Thoughts on the Constitutional Protection of Property in the United States and the Commonwealth', *South African Journal for Human Rights*, 9 (1993) 388–411
S. Chatillon, 'Droit et Langue', *Revue internationale de droit comparé*, 54/3 (2002) 687–715
M.-J. Chen, *Inside Chinese Business* (Boston, Mass.: Harvard Business School, 2001)
B. Child, *Drafting Legal Documents*, 2nd edn (St. Paul: West Publishing Company, 1992)
N. Colneric, 'Recht und Sprache' in T. Lundmark and A. Wallow (eds), *Law and Language – Recht und Sprache* (Berlin/Hamburg/Münster: LIT, 2006), pp. 15–25
L.-J. Constantinesco, *Rechtsvergleichung*, vol. 2 (Cologne/Berlin/Bonn: Heymanns, 1972)
Contract Law of the People's Republic of China, adopted and promulgated by the Second Session of the Ninth National People's Congress, 15 March 1999. Available http://www.cclaw.net/download/contractlawPRC.asp (last retrieval on 12 May 2006)
G. Coode, *On Legislative Expressions; or, the Language of the Written Law* (Philadelphia: T. & J. W. Johnson, 1848)
G. Cornu, *Linguistique juridique*, 2nd edn (Paris: Montchrestien, 2000a)
G. Cornu, *Vocabulaire juridique*, 8th edn (Paris: PUF, 2000b)
F. Coulmas (ed.), *A Language Policy for the European Community: Prospects and Quandaries* (Berlin/New York: Mouton de Gruyter, 1991)
A. Covacs, 'La réalisation de la version française des lois fédérales du Canada', in J. Gémar (ed.), *Langage du droit et traduction. Essais de jurilinguistique/ The Language of the Law and Translation. Essays on Jurilinguistics* (Montreal: Linguatech et Conseil de la langue française, 1982), pp. 83–100
R.L. Creech, *Law and Language in the European Union: the Paradox of a Babel 'United in Diversity'* (Groningen: Europa Law Publishing, 2005)
P.-A. Crépeau, *Dictionnaire de droit privé et Lexiques bilingues*, 2nd edn (Cowansville: Les Éditions Yvon Blais Inc., 1991)
P.-A. Crépeau, 'La transposition linguistique', in G. Snow (ed.), *Français juridique et science du droit: textes présentés au deuxième colloque international du Centre international de la common law en français* (Brussels: Bruylant, 1995), pp. 51–61
K. Cunningham, 'Translating for a Larger Union – Can We Cope with More Than 11 Languages?', *Terminologie et Traduction*, 2 (2001) 22–3
Vivian Curran, 'Comparative Law and Language', in M. Reimann and R. Zimmermann (eds), *Oxford Handbook of Comparative Law* (OUP, 2006), pp. 695–707
E. W. Daigneault, *Drafting International Agreements in Legal English* (Vienna: Kluwer Law International, 2005)

M. Damaška, 'A Continental Lawyer in an American Law School: Trials and Tribulations of Adjustment', *University of Pennsylvania Law Review*, 116/8 (1968) 1363–78

R. David, *Traité élémentaire de droit civil comparé* (Paris: Librairie Générale de Droit et de Jurisprudence, 1950)

R. David, *English Law and French Law* (London: Stevens, 1980)

L. De Clerck, 'La place de la coutume dans le droit actuel du Burundi', *Revue administrative et juridique du Burundi*, 2/1 (1968)

P. De Cruz, *Comparative Law in a Changing World*, 2nd edn (London/Sydney: Cavendish, 1999)

Gerard-René deGroot, 'Legal Translation', in J. Smits (ed.), *Elgar Encyclopedia of Comparative Law* (EE Publishing, 2006), pp. 423–33

J. Delisle, H. Lee Jahnke and M.C. Cormier (eds), *Terminologie de la traduction. Translation Terminology. Terminología de la Traducción. Terminologie der Übersetzung* (Amsterdam/Philadelphia: John Benjamins Publishing Company, 1999)

K. Deprez and T. du Plessis, *Multilingualism and Government. Belgium, Luxembourg, Switzerland, Former Yugoslavia, South Africa* (Hatfield: Van Schalk, 2000)

Y. Dezalay and B. G. Garth, *Dealing in Virtue: International Commercial Arbitration and the Construction of a Transnational Legal Order* (Chicago: University of Chicago Press, 1996)

E. Didier, *Langues et langages du droit: étude comparative des modes d'expression de la common law et du droit civil, en français et en anglais* (Montreal: Wilson and Lafleur, 1990)

E. Didier, 'La common law en français. Étude juridique et linguistique de la Common law en français en Canada', *Revue internationale de droit comparé*, 43 (1991) 7–56

L. A. DiMatteo, 'The Counterpoise of Contracts: the Reasonable Person Standard and the Subjectivity of Judgment', *South Carolina Law Review*, 48 (1997) 293–355

C. Dollerup, 'The Vanishing Original', *Hermes, Journal of Linguistics*, 32/2004 (2004), 185–99

I. Dore, *The UNCITRAL Framework for Arbitration in Contemporary Arbitration* (London/Dordrecht/Boston: Graham & Trotman/Martinus Nijhoff, 1993)

C. R. Drahozal, 'Commercial Norms, Commercial Codes, and International Commercial Arbitration', *Vanderbilt Journal of Transnational Law*, 33 (2000) 79–146

U. Drobnig, 'Methods of Sociological Research in Comparative Law', *Rabels Zeitschrift für ausländisches und internationales Privatrecht*, 35 (1971) 496–504

U. Drobnig and P. Dopffel, 'Die Nutzung der Rechtsvergleichung durch den deutschen Gesetzgeber', *Rabels Zeitschrift für ausländisches und internationales Privatrecht*, 46 (1982) 253–307

U. Drobnig and S. van Erp, *The Use of Comparative Law by Courts* (The Hague: Kluwer, 1999)

J. Dubois, *Dictionnaire de linguistique et des sciences du langage* (Paris: Larousse, 1999)

Duden, Das große Fremdwörterbuch: Herkunft und Bedeutung der Fremdwörter, 3rd edn (Mannheim/Leipzig/Vienna/Zurich: Dudenverlag, 2003)

Duden – Das Synonymwörterbuch: ein Wörterbuch sinnverwandter Wörter, 3rd edn (Mannheim/Leipzig/Vienna/Zurich: Dudenverlag, 2004)

D.A. Edward, 'How the Court of Justice Works', *European Law Review*, 6 (1995) 539–58

C. Elliott, *French Legal System and Legal Language: an Introduction to French* (London/New York: Longman, 1998)

Encyclopaedia of Forms and Precedents, ed. by Lord Millet (London: LexisNexis Butterworths, 1991)

T. Endicott, *Vagueness in Law* (Oxford: Oxford University Press, 2000)

J. Engberg, 'Statutory Texts as Instances of Language(s): Consequences and Limitations on Interpretation', *Brooklyn Journal of International Law*, 29 (2004) 1135–66

W.N. Eskridge, 'Public Values in Statutory Interpretation', *University of Pennsylvania Law Review*, 137 (1989) 1007–93

W. N. Eskridge, 'The New Textualism', *UCLA Law Review*, 37 (1990) 621–91

J. L. Esquirol, 'Continuing Fictions of Latin American Law', *Florida Law Review*, 55 (2003) 41–114

G.R. Evans, 'Augustine on Exegis against the Heretics,' in F. Van Fleteren and J. C. Schnaubelt (eds), *Augustine: Biblical Exegete* (New York: Peter Lang, 2001)

I. Even-Zohar, 'FORUM. The Making of Culture Repertoire and the Role of Transfer', *Target*, 9/2 (1997) 373–81

I. Even-Zohar, 'FORUM. Some Replies to Lambert and Pym', *Target*, 10/2 (1998) 363–9

W. Ewald, 'Posner's Economic Approach to Comparative Law', *Texas International Law Journal*, 33 (1998) 381–6

C. W. Fassberg, 'Language and Style in a Mixed Legal System', *Tulane Law Review*, 78 (2003) 151–74

N. Fennelly, 'Legal Interpretation at the European Court of Justice', *Fordham International Law Journal*, 20 (1997) 656–79

K. Fenning, 'The Origin of the Patent and Copyright Clause of the Constitution', *Journal of the Patent Office Society Law*, 11 (1929) 438–45

M. Fenster, 'The Symbols of Government: Thurman Arnold and Post-Realist Legal Theory', *Buffalo Law Review* (2003) 1053–118

C. A. Ferguson, 'Diglossia', *Words*, 15 (1959) 325–40

A. von Feuerbach, 'Blick auf die deutsche Rechtswissenschaft', in A. von Feuerbach, *Kleine Schriften*, reprint of the German edition 1833 (Osnabrück: Zeller, 1966)

J. Fidrmuc and V. Ginsburgh, *Languages in the EU: the Quest for Equality and its Cost* (London: Centre for Economic Policy Research, 2004)

J. A. Fishman, 'Bilingualism with and without Diglossia, Diglossia with and without Bilingualism', *Journal of Social Issues*, 23/2 (1980) 29–38

J. A. Fishman, 'Ethnolinguistic Democracy: Varieties, Degrees and Limits', *Language International*, 5/1 (1993) 11–17

J. A. Fishman (ed.), *Handbook of Language and Ethnicity* (New York: Oxford University Press, 1999)

R. Fjeld, Interpretation of Indefinite Adjectives in Legislative Language', in F. Mayer (ed.), *Languages for Special Purposes: Perspectives for the New Millennium* (Tübingen: Narr, 2001), pp. 643–50

G.P. Fletcher, 'Fair and Reasonable: a Linguistic Glimpse into the American Legal Mind', in R. Sacco and L. Castellani (eds), *Les multiples langues du droit européen uniforme* (Turin: L'Harmattan Italia, 1999), pp. 57–70

J. A. Fodor, *Concepts: Where Cognitive Science Went Wrong* (Oxford: Oxford University Press, 1998)

H. W. Fowler, *Modern English Usage*, 3rd edn (Oxford: Oxford University Press, 1968)

A. P. Frank, N. Greiner, T. Hermans, H. Kittel, W. Koller, J. Lambert and F. Paul (eds), *An International Encyclopedia of Translation Studies*, vol. 1 (Berlin/New York: de Gruyter, 2004)

G. Frankenberg, 'Critical Comparisons: Re-Thinking Comparative Law', *Harvard International Law Journal*, 26 (1985) 411–55

J. Freund, *The Anatomy of a Merger* (New York: Law Journal Press, 1975)

C. Frey, 'Trois langues et plusieurs normes pour une minorité grandissante de francophones au Burundi', in D. de Robillard and M. Beniamino (eds), *Le français dans l'espace francophone* (Paris: Champion, 1993), pp. 243–59

C. Frey, *Le français au Burundi, lexicographie et culture* (Vanves: AUPELF-EDICEFS, 1996)

L. M. Friedman, 'Thoughts on Comparative Legal Culture', in J. H. Merryman and D. S. Clark (eds), *Essays in Honor of John Henry Merryman on his Seventieth Birthday* (Berlin: Duncker & Humboldt, 1990), pp. 49–57

H.-G. Gadamer, *Wahrheit und Methode*, 4th edn (Tübingen: Mohr, 1975)

S. Garland, 'Hispanic Court Cases: the Verdict is All in the Translation', *Christian Science Monitor* (7 Dec. 1981)

B. A. Garner (ed.), *A Dictionary of Modern Legal Usage*, 2nd edn (Oxford: Oxford University Press, 1987)

B. A. Garner (ed.), *Black's Law Dictionary*, 8th edn, 1st reprint (St. Paul, Minn.: Thomson West, 2004)

G. Garzone, 'Arbitration Rules across Legal Cultures: an Intercultural Approach', in V. Bhatia, C. Candlin and M. Gotti (eds), *Legal Discourse in Multilingual and Multicultural Contexts: Arbitration Texts in Europe* (Bern: Peter Lang, 2003), pp. 177–220

J.-C. Gémar, *Langage du droit. Essais de jurilinguistique* (Quebec: Conseil de la langue française, 1982)

J.-C. Gémar, *Traduire ou l'art d'interpréter. Langue, droit et société: éléments de jurilinguistique*. Vol. 2: *Application. Traduire le texte juridique* (Sainte-Foy, Quebec: Les Presses de l'Université du Québec, 1995)

J.-C. Gémar, 'Traduire le langage du droit: langue, droit et traduction', in A. P. Frank, N. Greiner, T. Hermans, H. Kittel, W. Koller, J. Lambert and F. Paul (eds), *An International Encyclopedia of Translation Studies*, Vol. 1 (Berlin/New York: de Gruyter, 2004), pp. 737–47

J.-C. Gémar and N. Kasirer, *Jurilinguistique: entre langues et droits – Jurilinguistics: between Law and Language* (Montreal, Les Éditions Thémis; Brussels, Les Éditions juridiques Bruylant, 2005)

J.-C. Gémar and H.-T. Vo, *Difficultés du langage du droit au Canada*, 2nd edn (Cowansville: Les Éditions Yvon Blais Inc., 1997)

A. Gidi, 'Class Actions in Brazil – a Model for Civil Law Countries', *American Journal of Comparative Law*, 51/2 (2003) 311–408

S. G. Gilles, 'On Determining Negligence: Hand Formula Balancing, the Reasonable Person Standard, and the Jury', *Vanderbilt Law Review*, 54 (2001) 813–61

H. Gillomen, 'Wucher und Wirtschaft im Mittelalter', *Historische Zeitschrift*, 250/2 (1990) 265–301

A. Gómez González-Jover, 'Meaning and Anisomorphism in Modern Lexicography', *Terminology*, 12/2 (2006) 216–34
M. Gotti, *Investigating Specialized Discourse* (Bern: Peter Lang, 2005)
M. Gotti and M. Dossena (eds), *Modality in Specialized Texts* (Bern: Peter Lang, 2001)
M. Gotti and S. Šarčević (eds), *Insights into Specialized Translation* (Bern: Peter Lang, 2006)
E. Gowers, *The Complete Plain Words* (London: David R. Godine Publisher, 1986)
J. P. Gridel, *Le signes et le droit* (Paris: Lib. gén. de droit et de jurisprudence, 1979)
G.R. de Groot, 'Rechtsvergleichung als Kerntätigkeit bei der Übersetzung juristischer Terminologie', in U. Haß-Zumkehr (ed.), *Sprache und Recht* (Berlin/New York: Walter de Gruyter, 2002), pp. 222–39
B. Großfeld, 'Probleme der Rechtsvergleichung im Verhältnis Vereinigte Staaten von Amerika–Deutschland', *Rabels Zeitschrift für ausländisches und internationales Privatrecht*, 39 (1975) 5–28
B. Großfeld, 'Vom Beitrag der Rechtsvergleichung zum deutschen Recht', *Archiv für die civilistische Praxis*, 184 (1984) 289–321
B. Großfeld, 'Language and the Law', *Journal of Air Law and Commerce*, 50 (1985) 793–803
B. Großfeld, 'Sinn und Methode der Rechtsvergleichung', in K. P. Berger (ed.), *Festschrift für Otto Sandrock* (Heidelberg: Recht und Wirtschaft, 2000), pp. 329–40
B. Großfeld, 'Comparatists and Languages', in P. Legrand and R. Munday (eds), *Traditions and Transitions* (Cambridge: Cambridge University Press, 2003), pp. 154–94
B. Großfeld and O. Brand, 'Das Recht in Goethes *Iphigenie auf Tauris*', *Juristenzeitung*, 54/17 (1999) 809–14
B. Großfeld and M. Hülper, 'Analphabetismus im Zivilrecht', *JuristenZeitung*, 54/9 (1999) 430–3
B. Großfeld and Y. Wang, 'Das Europäische Recht aus der Sicht Chinas', *Zeitschrift für vergleichende Rechtswissenschaft*, 94 (1995) 292–309
R. Grutman, 'Multilingualism and Translation', in M. Baker (ed.) *The Routledge Encyclopedia of Translation Studies* (London and New York: Routledge, 1997), pp. 157–60
M. Gustafsson, *Some Syntactic Properties of English Law Language* (Turku: University of Turku, Department of English, 1975)
E.-A. Gutt, 'A Theoretical Account of Translation – without the Translation Theory', *Target*, 2/2 (1990) 135–64
H. C. Gutteridge, 'The Comparative Aspects of Legal Terminology', *Tulane Law Review* (1938) 401–11
H. Haarmann, 'Language Politics and the New European Identity', in F. Coulmas (ed.), *A Language Policy for the European Community: Prospects and Quandaries* (Berlin/New York: Mouton de Gruyter, 1991)
M. Halewyck, *La charte coloniale. Commentaire de la loi du 18 octobre 1908 sur le Gouvernement du Congo belge* (Brussels: Imprimerie du Roi, 1910)
U. R. Haltern, *Verfassungsgerichtsbarkeit, Demokratie und Misstrauen: das Bundesverfassungsgericht in einer Verfassungstheorie zwischen Populismus und Progressivismus* (Berlin: Duncker & Humblot, 1998)

A. Hammel, 'The Role of Plain English in Legal Translation', paper delivered at the Language and Law Conference, Düsseldorf, 17–19 May 2006

C. Harlow, 'Voices of Difference in a Plural Community', in P. Beaumont, C. Lyons and N. Walker (eds), *Convergence and Divergence in European Public Law* (Oxford: Hart, 2002), pp. 199–224

D.J. Harris, *Cases and Materials on International Law*, 6th edn (London: Sweet & Maxwell, 2004)

H. Helm, 'Das Verbraucherleitbild des Europäischen Gerichtshofs und des Bundesgerichtshofs im Vergleich', in E. Keller, C. Plassman and A. von Falck (eds), *Festschrift für Winfried Tilmann* (Cologne/Berlin/Munich: Carl Heymanns Verlag, 2003)

H. Henry, 'Kulturfremdes Recht erkennen', *Zeitschrift für Rechtsvergleichung*, 38 (1997) 45–55

T. Hermans (ed.), *The Manipulation of Literature: Studies in Literary Translation* (London: Croom Helm, 1985)

T. Hermans, 'Models of Translation', in M. Baker (ed.), *The Routledge Encyclopedia of Translation Studies* (London and New York: Routledge, 1997) pp. 154–7

T. Hermans, *Translation in Systems. Descriptive and System-Oriented Approaches in Translation Studies* (Manchester: St. Jerome, 1999)

B. Heß, 'Die Anerkennung eines Class Action Settlement in Deutschland', *JuristenZeitung*, 55/8 (2000) 373–82

V. Heutger, 'Law and Language in the European Union', *Global Jurist Topics*, 3/1 (2003)

P. Hidalgo and E. Alcaraz Varó, *La literatura inglesa en los textos* (Alcoy, Alicante: Marfil, 1985)

J. Hiller, 'Language, Law, Sports and Culture: the Transferability of Words, Lifestyles, and Attitudes through Law', *Valparaiso University Law Review*, 12 (1978)

R. Hiltunen, *Chapters on Legal English: Aspects Past and Present of the Language of the Law* (Helsinki: Suomalainen Tiedeakatemia, 1990)

E. J. Hobsbawm, *Nations and Nationalism since 1790: Programme, Myth, Reality* (Cambridge/New York: Cambridge University Press, 1990)

E. J. Hobsbawm, 'Language, Culture and National Identity', *Social Research*, 63/4 (1996) 1065–80.

E. J. Hobsbawm and T. Ranger (eds), *The Invention of Tradition* (Cambridge/New York: Cambridge University Press, 1996)

C. Hodges, *Multi-Party Actions* (Oxford: Oxford University Press, 2001)

W. S. Holdsworth, 'Lord Mansfield', *Law Quarterly Review*, 53 (1937)

M. Horiba, 'Reader Control in Reading: Effects of Language Competence, Text Type, and Task', *Discourse Processes*, 29/3 (2000) 223–67

D. L. Hovland, 'Error in Interpretation: Why Plain Error is Not Plain', *Law and Inequality Journal*, 11 (1993)

U. Hübner and V. Constantinesco, *Einführung in das französische Recht*, 4th edn (Munich: Beck, 2001)

J. Husa, 'Farewell to Functionalism or Methodological Tolerance?', *Rabels Zeitschrift für ausländisches und internationales Privatrecht*, 67/3 (2003) 419–47

J. Husa, 'Methodology of Comparative Law Today', *Revue international de droit comparé*, 58/4 (2006) 1095–117

M. Hyland, 'Comparative Law' in D. M. Patterson (ed.), *A Companion to Philosophy of Law and Legal Theory* (Oxford: Wiley-Blackwell, 1999), pp. 184–200

ICCA (International Council for Commercial Arbitration), *International Dispute Resolution: Towards an International Arbitration Culture.* Albert Jan van den Berg (gen. ed.) (Dordrecht: Kluwer Law International, 1998)
K. Ipsen, *Völkerrecht*, 4th edn (Munich: Beck, 1999)
F. G. Jacobs, 'Approaches to Interpretation in a Plurilingual Legal System', in M. Hoskins and W. Robinson (eds), *A True European: Essays for Judge David Edward* (Oxford/Portland, Ore.: Hart Publishing, 2003), pp. 297–305
M. S. Jacobs, 'Toward a Process Based Approach to Failure to Warn Law', *North Carolina Law Review*, 71/1 (1992), 121–99
S. Jarvin, 'Leading Arbitration Seats: a (Mostly European) Comparative View', in S. Frommel and B. Rider (eds), *Conflicting Legal Cultures in Commercial Arbitration: Old Issues and New Trends* (The Hague: Kluwer Law International, 1999), pp. 39–61
E. Jayme, 'Das "Sprachrisiko" im deutschen internationalen Privatrecht unter besonderer Berücksichtigung der Rechtsprobleme türkischer Arbeitnehmer in der Bundesrepublik Deutschland', *Annales de la Faculté de Droit d'Istanbul*, 44 (1981)
E. Jayme, 'Droit et langue', in E. Jayme, *Rechtsvergleichung* (Heidelberg: C. F. Müller, 2000)
R. von Jhering, *Der Kampf ums Recht* (Vienna: Manz, 1872)
R. von Jhering, *Der Zweck im Recht*, vol. 2 (Leipzig: Breitkopf & Härtel, 1877)
Z. Jianhua and Y. Guanghua, 'China's Uniform Contract Law: Progress and Problems', *UCLA Pacific Basin Law Journal*, 17 (1999)
J. Jonas, 'Ein zeitgenössischer Rezeptionsprozess am Beispiel des türkischen Zivilrechts', *Juristische Schulung* (1987) 266–70
J. L. Jowell (ed.), *Lord Denning: the Judge and the Law* (London: Sweet & Maxwell, 1986)
O. Kahn-Freund, 'Comparative Law as an Academic Subject', *Law Quarterly Review*, 82 (1966) 40–61
W. J. Kamba, 'Comparative Law: a Theoretical Framework', *International and Comparative Law Quarterly*, 23/3 (1974) 485–519
S. L. Karamanian, 'Overstating the Americanization of International Arbitration: Lessons from ICSID', *Ohio State Journal on Dispute Resolution*, 5/19 (2003) 5–35
P. Kaseva, 'The Initiator of Translations', unpublished MA thesis (University of Helsinki, 2000)
N. Kasirer, 'Pothier from A to Z', in B. Moore (ed.), *Mélanges Jean Pineau* (Montreal, Éditions Th.mis, 2003), pp. 296–395
G. Kegel and K. Schurig, *Internationales Privatrecht*, 9th edn (Munich: Beck, 2004)
D. Keleman and E. C. Sibbitt, 'The Americanization of Japanese Law', *University of Pennsylvania Journal of International Economic Law*, 23 (2002) 269–324
R. Kiener and R. Lanz, 'Die Amerikanisierung des Schweizerischen Rechts und ihre Grenzen', *Zeitschrift für Schweizerisches Recht*, 119 (2000) 155–74
U. Kischel, 'Delegation of Legislative Power to Agencies: a Comparative Analysis of United States and German Law', *Administrative Law Review*, 46 (1994) 213–56
U. Kischel, *Die Begründung: zur Erläuterung staatlicher Entscheidungen gegenüber dem Bürger* (Tübingen: Mohr Siebeck, 2003)
U. Kischel, 'Vorsicht, Rechtsvergleichung!', *Zeitschrift für vergleichende Rechtswissenschaft*, 104 (2005) 10–30

U. Kischel, 'Darf der Gesetzgeber das Bundesverfassungsgericht ignorieren', *Archiv des öffentlichen Rechts*, 131/2 (2006) 219–54

I. Kitamura, 'Brèves réflexions sur la méthode de comparaison franco-japonaise', *Revue internationale de droit comparé*, 47/4 (1995) 861–9

D. Klein, 'The Islamic and the Jewish Law of Usury', *Denver Journal of International Law and Politics*, 23(1995) 535–54

H. Koch, 'Legal Aspects of a Language Policy for the European Communities: Language Risks, Equal Opportunities, and Legislating a Language', in F. Coulmas (ed.), *A Language Policy for the European Community: Prospects and Quandaries* (Berlin/New York: Mouton de Gruyter, 1991)

J. Kohler, 'Über die Methode der Rechtsvergleichung', *Zeitschrift für das Privat- und öffentliche Recht der Gegenwart*, 28 (1901) 273–84

J. Kohler, *Vom Lebenspfad* (Mannheim: Bensheimer, 1902)

U. Königer, *Die Bestimmung der gesetzlichen Zinshöhe nach dem deutschen internationalen Privatrecht* (Berlin: Duncker & Humblot, 1997)

T. Koopmans, 'Comparative Law and the Courts', *International and Comparative Law Quarterly*, 45/3 (1996) 545–56

H. Kötz, 'Der Bundesgerichtshof und die Rechtsvergleichung', in C.-W. Canaris et al. (eds), *50 Jahre Bundesgerichtshof: Festgabe aus der Wissenschaft* (Munich: Kurt Beck Verlag, 2000), pp. 825–43

H. Kötz, 'Alte und neue Aufgaben der Rechtsvergleichung', *Juristenzeitung* (2002) 257–64

A. Kuper, *Culture: the Anthropologists' Account* (Cambridge: Cambridge University Press, 1999)

D. Kutzner, *Lord Denning* (Berlin/Hamburg/Münster: LIT, 2001)

A. Labelle, 'La corédaction des lois fédérales au Canada. Vingt ans après: quelques réflexions', in *Proceedings of the Conference on Legal Translation, History, Theory/ies and Practice* (Geneva and Bern: ESTI-ASTTI, 2000)

P. Lalive, 'On Communication in International Arbitration', *The American Review of International Arbitration*, 3/1–4 (1992) 79–82

J. Lambert, 'La Traduction, les langues et la communication de masse: les ambiguïtés du discours international', *Target*, 1/2 (1989) 215–37

J. Lambert, 'Auf der Suche nach literarischen und übersetzerischen Weltkarten', in A. P. Frank, K.-J. Maass, F. Paul and H. Turk (eds), *Übersetzen, verstehen, Brücken bauen. Geisteswissenschaftliches und literarisches Übersetzen im internationalen Kulturaustausch* (Berlin: Erich Schmidt, 1993), pp. 85–105

J. Lambert, 'Literature, Translation and (De)Colonization', in T. Hyun and J. Lambert (eds), *Translation and Modernization* (ICLA, 1995), pp. 98–117

J. Lambert, 'FORUM. "Communication Societies": Comments on Even-Zohar's "Making of Culture Repertoire"' *Target*, 10/1 (1998) 353–6

J. Lambert, 'La Traduction dans les sociétés monolingues', in A. Frank, N. Greiner, T. Hermans, H. Kittel, W. Koller, J. Lambert and F. Paul (eds), *An International Encyclopedia of Translation Studies*, vol. 1 (Berlin/New York: de Gruyter, 2004), pp. 69–85

J. Lambert, 'Globalization and Translation', in A. Frank, N. Greiner, T. Hermans, H. Kittel, W. Koller, J. Lambert and F. Paul (eds), *An International Encyclopedia of Translation Studies*, vol. 2 (Berlin/New York: de Gryuter, forthcoming)

J. Lambert and H. Van Gorp, 'On Describing Translations', in T. Hermans (ed.), *The Manipulation of Literature. Studies in Literary Translation* (London/Sydney: Croom Helm, 1985), pp. 42–53

E. Lamy, 'Le problème de la codification de la coutume au Rwanda et au Burundi', *Revue juridique de droit écrit et de coutumier au Rwanda et au Burundi*, no. 2 (March–April 1961) 33–6; no. 3 (June 1961) 73–80

M. Langer, 'From Legal Transplants to Legal Translations: the Globalization of Plea Bargaining and the Americanization Thesis in Criminal Procedure', *Harvard International Law Journal*, 45/1 (2004) 1–65

S. Lazareff, 'International Arbitration: towards a Common Procedural Approach', in S. Frommel and B. Rider (eds), *Conflicting Legal Cultures in Commercial Arbitration: Old Issues and New Trends* (The Hague: Kluwer Law International, 1999), pp. 31–8

P. Legrand, 'How to Compare Now', *Legal Studies*, 16/2 (1996) 232–42

P. Legrand, 'The Impossibility of "Legal Transplants"', *Maastricht Journal of European and Comparative Law*, 4 (1997)

P. Legrand, *Le Droit Comparé* (Paris: Presses Universitaires de France, 1999)

A. Lenhoff, 'America's Legal Inventions Adopted in Other Countries', *Buffalo Law Review*, 1 (1951)

A. Lenhoff, 'America's Cultural Contribution to Europe in the Realm of Law', *Buffalo Law Review*, 16/7 (1964)

A. Le Palec, *Brazzaville: Note sur la situation linguistique de deux quartiers*. Actes de la Ve Table Ronde des Centres de Linguistique Appliquée d'Afrique Noire. Bulletin de I'AELIA, 1983

L. Lessig, 'Fidelity as Translation', *Texas Law Review*, 71 (1993) 1165–268

S. Levinson, 'Translation: Who Needs It?', *Fordham Law Review*, 65 (1997) 1457–68

J. Levý, *Die literarische Übersetzung. Theorie einer Kunstgattung* (Frankfurt am Main: Athenäum, 1969)

T. Lewandowski, *Diccionario de lingüística* (Madrid: Cátedra, 1982)

K. Lipstein, 'The Reception of Western Law in India', *International Social Science Bulletin*, 9 (1957) 85–95

M. Lohaus, *Recht und Sprache in Österreich und Deutschland: Gemeinsamkeiten und Verschiedenheiten als Folge geschichtlicher Entwicklungen; Untersuchung zur juristischen Fachterminologie in Österreich und Deutschland* (Gießen: Köhler, 2000)

K. M. Lord, 'Note: Bootstrapping an Environmental Policy from an Economic Covenant: the Teleological Approach of the European Court of Justice', *Cornell International Law Journal*, 29 (1996) 571–606

M. Loubser, 'Linguistic Factors into the Mix: the South African Experience of Language and the Law', *Tulane Law Review*, 78 (2003) 105–50

J. Lyons, *Linguistic Semantics* (Cambridge: Cambridge University Press, 1995)

K. McAuliffe, 'Law in Translation: the Production of a Multilingual Jurisprudence by the Court of Justice of the European Communities', unpublished Ph.D. thesis (The Queen's University of Belfast, 2006a)

K. McAuliffe, 'Translation at the Court of Justice of the European Community', paper delivered at the Language and Law Conference, Düsseldorf, 17–19 May 2006 (2006b)

J. McClung Nading, 'Property under Siege: the Legality of Land Reform in Zimbabwe', *Emory International Law Review*, 16 (2002)

P. J. McConnaughay, 'Rethinking the Role of Law and Contracts in East–West Commercial Relationships', *Virginia Journal of International Law*, 41/2 (2001) 420–40

R. A. MacDonald, 'Legal Bilingualism', *McGill Law Journal/Revue de droit de McGill*, 42 (1997) 119–68

I. McLeod, 'Literal and Purposive Techniques of Legislative Interpretation: Some European Community and English Common Law Perspectives', *Brooklyn Journal of International Law*, 29 (2004) 1109–34

I. McLeod, *Legal Method* (Basingstoke: Palgrave Macmillan, 2005)

A. W. McReynolds, 'What International Experience can Tell U.S. Courts about Same-Sex Marriage', *UCLA Law Review*, 53/4 (2006) 1073–105

B. Malinowski, *Coral Gardens and their Magic*, vol. 2 (London: Allen Unwin, 1935)

G. F. Mancini and D. T. Keeling, 'Language, Culture and Politics in the Life of the European Court of Justice', *Columbia Journal of European Law*, 1 (1995) 397–413

H.–P. Mansel, 'Rechtsvergelichung und europäische Rechtseinheit', *Juristenzeitung* (1991) 529–34

P. Manzini, 'The European Rule of Reason – Crossing the Sea of Doubt', *European Competition Law Review*, 23/8 (2002) 392–9

L. M. Marasinghe, 'Some Problems Associated with a Language Switch-Over in the Third World', *Verfassung und Recht in Übersee*, 10 (1977)

B. Markesinis, *Foreign Law and Comparative Methodology* (Oxford/Portland: Hart, 1997)

B. Markesinis, *Comparative Law in the Courtroom and Classroom 77 and 125* (Oxford/Portland: Hart, 2003)

A. Martinet, *La linguistique synchronique: études et recherches* (Paris: PUF, 1968)

H. P. Marutschke, *Einführung in das japanische Recht* (Munich: Beck, 1999)

U. Mattei, 'Why the Wind Changed: Intellectual Leadership in Western Law', *American Journal of Comparative Law*, 42/1 (1994) 195–218

R. Meertens, *Guide anglais–français de la traduction* (Paris: Chiron Éditeur, 2002)

I. A. Mel'cuk, *Dictionnaire explicatif et combinatoire du français contemporain* (Montreal: Presses de l'Université de Montréal, 1984)

D. Mellinkoff, *The Language of the Law* (Boston: Little, Brown & Co, 1963)

J. Meyer (ed.), *Kommentar zur Charta der Grundrechte der Europäischen Union* (Baden-Baden: Nomos-Verlagsgesellschaft, 2003)

Ralf Michaels, 'The Functional Method of Comparative Law', in M. Reimann and R. Zimmermann (eds), *Oxford Handbook of Comparative Law* (OUP, 2006), pp. 340–73

J. M. Miller, 'A Typology of Legal Transplants: Using Sociology, Legal History and the Argentine Example to Explain the Transplant Process', *American Journal of Comparative Law*, 51 (2003) 839–86

G. L. Murphy, *The Big Book of Concepts* (Cambridge, Mass.: MIT Press, 2002)

K. Nadelmann and A. von Mehren, 'Equivalences in Treaties in the Conflicts Field', *The American Journal of Comparative Law*, 15 (1967) 195–203

N. Nadorff, 'Book Review', *University of Miami Inter-American Law Review*, 32 (2001)

B. Ndimurukundo-Kururu, 'Problématique de la législation linguistique au Burundi', 2004, Available http://www.francophonie-durable.org/documents/colloque-ouaga-a1-ndimurukundo.pdf (last retrieval on 15.01.2008)

P. von Nessen, 'The Americanization of Australian Corporate Law', *Syracuse Journal of International Law and Commerce*, 26 (1999) 239–66
H. Neumayer, 'Grundriss der Rechtsvergleichung', in R. David and G. Grasmann (eds), *Einführung in die großen Rechtssysteme der Gegenwart*, 2nd edn (Munich: Kurt Beck Verlag, 1988), pp. 1–78
E. A. Nida, *Toward a Science of Translating* (Leiden: Brill, 1965)
E. A. Nida and C. R. Taber, *The Theory and Practice of Translation* (Leiden: Brill, 1969)
C. Nord, *Translating as a Purposeful Activity: Functionalist Approaches Explained* (Manchester: St Jerome, 1997)
P. Ntahombaye, 'Politique et aménagement linguistiques au Burundi', in P. Martel and J. Maurais (eds), *Langues et sociétés en contact* (Tübingen: Max Niemeyer, 1994), pp. 517–28
H. Ntahomvukiye, 'La question linguistique au Burundi: les préalables d'une entreprise terminologique dans une situation de "langue dominée"', *Terminologie Nouvelle*, 7 (1992)
F. Olsen, 'The Drama of Comparative Law', *Utah Law Review* (1997) 275–80
W. Ong, *Orality and Literacy: the Technologizing of the Word* (London: Methuen, 1982)
E. W. Orts, 'The Rule of Law in China', *Vanderbilt Journal of Transnational Law*, 34 (2001) 43–116
E. Örücü, *The Enigma of Comparative Law: Variations on a Theme for the Twenty-First Century* (Leiden/Boston: Martinus Nijhoff Publishers, 2004)
S. Otte, *Das Kapitalschutzsystem der englischen private limited company im Vergleich zur deutschen GmbH* (Hamburg: Kovac-Verlag, 2006)
Oxford English Dictionary, 2nd edn (Oxford: Oxford University Press, 1963)
V.V. Palmer, 'Introduction to the Mixed Jurisdiction', in V.V. Palmer (ed.), *Mixed Jurisdictions Worldwide: the Third Legal Family* (Cambridge/New York: Cambridge University Press, 2001), pp. 3–80
R. Pathak, 'When and Where do National Courts Reflect an International Culture When Deciding Issues Relating to International Arbitration?', in *ICCA* (1998) 173–86
P. Pattison and D. Herron, 'The Mountains Are High and the Emperor is Far Away: Sanctity of Contract in China', *American Business Law Journal*, 40/1 (2003) 460–510
J. Paulsson, 'Arbitration Unbound: Award Detached from the Law of its Country of Origin', *International and Comparative Law Quarterly*, 30 (1981) 358–87
J. Pelikan, *The Mystery of Continuity: Time and History, Memory and Eternity in the Thought of Saint Augustine* (Charlottesville: University of Virginia Press, 1986)
S. Q. Peng, 'Guanxi: Management and Legal Approaches to Establish and Enhance Interpersonal Trust', *Journal of Psychology in Chinese Societies*, 2/1 (2001) 51–76
R. Peritz, *Competition Policy in America, 1888–1992* (Oxford: Oxford University Press, 1996)
A. Peters and H. Schwenke, 'Comparative Law beyond Post-Modernism', *International and Comparative Law Quarterly*, 49 (2000) 800–34
R. Phillipson, *English-Only Europe? Challenging Language Policy* (London and New York: Routledge, 2003)
A. Popovič, *Dictionary for the Analysis of Literary Translation* (Edmonton: Department of Comparative Literature, the University of Alberta, 1976)

E. Posner, 'Symbols, Signals and Social Norms in Politics and the Law', *Journal of Legal Studies*, 27 (1998) 765–98

R. Pound, 'Some Thoughts about Comparative Law', in H. Dölle (ed.), *Festschrift for Ernst Rabel* (Tübingen: Mohr, 1954), pp. 7–16

A. Pym, *Method in Translation History* (Manchester: St. Jerome, 1998a)

A. Pym, 'FORUM. Note on a Repertoire for Seeing Culture', *Target*, 10/2 (1998b) 357–61

A. Pym, 'Against Praise of Hybridity', *Across Languages and Cultures*, 2/2 (2001) 195–206

A. Quéffelec, 'Le plurilinguisme en Afrique. Exposé introductif du colloque international de Bujumbura sur les plurilinguismes, organisé par l'Université du Burundi en Décembre 1990', *Dire*, 4 (1992) 5–18

E. Rabel, 'Deutsches und amerikanisches Recht', *Rabels Zeitschrift für ausländisches und internationales Privatrecht*, 16 (1951) 340–59

D. Reimer, 'Die materiellen Bestimmungen der Berner Übereinkunft', *GRUR Int.*, (1967)

J. Reitz, 'How to Do Comparative Law', *American Journal of Comparative Law*, 46/4 (1998) 617–36

O. Remien, 'Über den Stil des europäischen Privatrechts', *Rabels Zeitschrift für ausländisches und internationales Privatrecht*, 60 (1996) 1–39

J. Rivero and J. Waline, *Droit administratif*, 18th edn (Paris: Dalloz, 2000)

S. Robinson, *Drafting* (London: Butterworths Law, 1980)

H. Roland and L. Boyer, *Dictionnaire des expressions juridiques* (Lyon: Éditions l'Hermès, 1983)

F. Roman, 'Class Actions in Canada: the Path to Reform', *Advocates' Society Journal*, 7 (1988)

K. S. Rosenn, 'The Jeito: Brazil's Institutional Bypass of the Formal Legal System and its Developmental Implications', *American Journal of Comparative Law*, 19 (1971) 516–49

K. S. Rosenn, 'Brazil's Legal Culture: the Jeito Revisited', *Florida International Law Journal*, 1/1 (1984) 1–43

S. Rosenne, 'The Meaning of "Authentic Text" in Modern Treaty Law', in R. Bernhardt, W. K. Geck, G. Jaenicke and H. Steinberger (eds), *Völkerrecht als Rechtsordnung Internationale Gerichtsbarkeit Menschenrechte: Festschrift für Hermann Mosler* (Berlin/Heidelberg: Springer-Verlag, 1983), pp. 759–84

C. Rossini, *English as a Legal Language*, 2nd edn (The Hague: Brill, 1998)

R. Rotondo, 'Die Zerstörung von Montecassino' (2004). Available at http://www.30giorni.it/te/articolo.asp?id=3493 (last retrieval on 10.02.2008)

D. Rowe, 'Debates over Group Litigation in Comparative Perspective', *Duke Journal of Comparative and International Law*, 11 (2001) 157–63

F. Russell, D. Sutton and J. Gill, *On Arbitration*, 22nd edn (London: Sweet & Maxwell, 2003)

R. Sacco, 'Legal Formants: a Dynamic Approach to Comparative Law', *American Journal of Comparative Law*, 39 (1991) 1–34 (Part 1), 343–401 (Part 2)

R. Sacco, 'La traduzione giuridica', in U. Scarpelli and P. Di Lucia (eds), *Il linguaggio del diritto* (Milan: Edizioni Universitarie di Lettere, Economia e Diritto, 1994), pp. 475–90

R. Sacco, 'Mute Law', *American Journal of Comparative Law*, 43/3 (1995) 455–67

R. Sacco, *Einführung in die Rechtsvergleichung* (Baden-Baden: Nomos, 2001)

S. Saleh, 'La perception de l'arbitrage au Machrek et dans les pays du Golfe', *Revue de l'Arbitrage*, 4 (1992)
S. Salmasi, 'English as a *Lingua Franca* at the European Union: the Undertakings of Pride?', *Recherches Anglaises et Nord-Américaines*, 36 (2003) 113–20
E. Sapir, *Language* (New York: Harcourt, 1921)
S. Šarčević, 'Translation of Culture-Bound Terms in Laws', *Multilingua: Journal of Cross-Cultural and Interlanguage Communication*, 4/3 (1985) 127–33
S. Šarčević, *New Approach to Legal Translation* (The Hague/London/Boston: Kluwer Law International, 1997)
S. Šarčević, 'Creativity in Legal Translation: How Much Is Too Much?', in A. Chesterman, N. G. San Salvador and Y. Gambier (eds), *Translation in Context. Selected Contributions from the EST Congress, Granada 1998* (Amsterdam/Philadelphia: John Benjamins Publishing Company, 1998), pp. 281–92
S. Šarčević, *New Approach to Legal Translation*, 2nd edn (The Hague/London/Boston: Kluwer Law International, 2000)
C. Schäffner, 'Parallel Texts in Translation', in L. Bowker (ed.), *Unity or Diversity? Current Trends in Translation Studies* (Manchester: Saint Jerome Publishing, 1998), pp. 83–90
C. Schäffner and B. Adab, 'Translation as Intercultural Communication – Contact as Conflict', in M. Snell-Hornby, Z. Jettmarová and K. Kaindl (eds), *Translation as Intercultural Communication. Selected Papers from the EST Congress, Prague 1995* (Amsterdam: Benjamins, 1997), pp. 325–37
C. Schäffner and B. Adab, 'The Idea of the Hybrid Text in Translation: Contact as Conflict', *Across Languages and Cultures*, 2/2 (2001) 167–80
P. Schlechtriem, 'Das 'Sprachrisiko' – ein neues Problem?', in H. Ehmann (ed.), *Festgabe für Hermann Weitnauer* (Berlin: Duncker & Humblot, 1980)
A. F. Schnitzer, *Vergleichende Rechtslehre*, vol. I (Basel: Verlag für Recht und Gesellschaft, 1961)
T. Schroeder, 'A Recipe for Concept Similarity', *Mind & Language*, 22 (2007) 68–91
M. Schweitzer, 'Art. 314 EGV', in E. Grabitz (ed.), *Das Recht der Europäischen Union, Kommentar*, vol. 2 (Munich: Beck, 1999)
H. Seckelmann, *Zinsrecht* (Baden-Baden: Nomos, 1992)
S. D. Seligman, R.A. Kapp and E. J. Trenn, *Chinese Business Etiquette* (New York/Boston: Warner, 1999)
H. von Senger, *Einführung in das chinesische Recht* (Munich: Beck, 1994)
H. von Senger, 'Von der Vergleichung des Rechts zur Vergleichung der Gesellschaftsführung – Deutsche Hauptmahlzeit und chinesische Nachspeise – Lässt sich im 21. Jahrhundert angesichts einer auch kulturell verstandenen Globalisierung das europäische Konzept der Rechtsvergleichung', *Zeitschrift für Rechtsvergleichung*, 47/2 (2006) 43–62
E. Seymour, 'Euro-English: the New Pidgin?', *Terminologie et traduction*, 3 (2002) 22–32
M. B. Shulman, 'No Hablo Ingles: Court Interpretation as a Major Obstacle to Fairness for Non-English Speaking Defendants', *Vanderbilt Law Review*, 46 (1993)
M. Shuttleworth and M. Cowie, *Dictionary of Translation Studies* (Manchester: St. Jerome Publishing, 1997)
D. Simon, 'A Third View of the Black Box, Cognitive Coherence in Legal Decision Making', *University of Chicago Law Review*, 71 (2004) 511–86

I. Simonnæs, 'Zur Frage der rechtskulturellen Unübersetzbarkeit anhand eines Vergleichs zwischen Norwegen und Deutschland', in L. Eriksen and K. Luttermann (eds), *Juristische Fachsprache, Kongressberichte des 12th European Symposium on Language for Special Purposes* (Münster: LIT, 1999), pp. 133–56

G. Smith, 'Nuisance Law: the Morphogenesis of an Historical Revisionist Theory of Contemporary Economic Jurisprudence', *Nebraska Law Review*, 74 (1995) 658–741

M. Snell-Hornby, *Translation Studies. An Integrated Approach* (Amsterdam: Benjamins, 1988)

L.M. Solan, *The Language of Judges* (Chicago: The University of Chicago Press, 1993)

L. M. Solan, 'The New Textualists' New Text', *Loyola of Los Angeles Law Review*, 38 (2005) 2027–61

L. M. Solan and P. M. Tiersma, 'Speaking of Crime: the Language of Criminal Justice', *Journal of Criminal Law and Criminology*, 96 (2005) 367–84

A. Souaiaia, 'On the Sources of Islamic Law and Practices', *Journal of Law and Religion*, 20 (2005) 123–49

G. Steiner, *After Babel* (Oxford: Oxford University Press, 1977)

A. Stephan, 'Emergenz', in H.J. Sandkühler (ed.), *Enzyklopädie Philosophie*, vol. 1 (Hamburg: Meiner, 1999), pp. 303–5

F. Sturm, 'Geschichte, Methode und Ziel der Rechtsvergleichung', *Juristische Rundschau* (1975)

L. A. Sullivan and W. Fikentscher, 'On the Growth of the Antitrust Idea', *Berkeley Journal of International Law*, 16/2 (1998) 197–223

R. Sullivan, 'The Challenges of Interpreting Multilingual, Multijural Legislation', *Brooklyn Journal of International Law*, 29 (2004) 985–1066

M. Suzuki, 'The Protectionist Bar against Foreign Lawyers in Japan, China and Korea: Domestic Control in the Face of Internationalization', *Columbian Journal of Asian Law*, 16/2 (2003)

M. Tabory, *Multilingualism in International Law and Institutions* (Alphen ann den Rijn: Sijthoff and Noordhoff, 1980)

Y. Taniguchi, 'Is There a Growing International Arbitration Culture? An Observation from Asia', in *ICCA* (1998) 31–40

W. Tetley, 'Nationalism in a Mixed Jurisdiction and the Importance of Language (South Africa, Israel, and Quebec/Canada)', in *Tulane Law Review*, 78 (2003) 175–218

G. Teubner, 'Legal Irritants: Good Faith in British Law or How Unifying Law Ends up in New Divergences', *Modern Law Review*, 61 (1998) 11–32

B. H. Thompson, 'Chief Justice William H. Rehnquist: Prizing People, Place, and History', *Standard Law Review*, 58 (2006) 1695–704

P. M. Tiersma, *Legal Language* (Chicago: The University of Chicago Press, 1999)

G. Toscani, 'Translation and Law – the Multilingual Context of the European Union Institutions', *International Journal of Legal Information*, 30/2 (2002) 288–307

G. Toury, *In Search of a Theory of Translation* (Tel Aviv: The Porter Institute for Poetics and Semiotics, 1980)

G. Toury, *Descriptive Translation Studies and Beyond* (Amsterdam: Benjamins, 1995)

A. Trosborg, 'Translating Hybrid Political Texts', in A. Trosborg (ed.), *Text Typology and Translation* (Amsterdam: Benjamins, 1997), pp. 145–58

V. Triebel, 'Anglo-amerikanischer Einfluss auf Unternehmenskaufverträge in Deutschland – eine Gefahr für die Rechtsklarheit', *Recht der Internationalen Wirtschaft* (1998) 1–7

V. Triebel and S. Balthasar, 'Auslegung englischer Vertragstexte unter deutschem Vertragsstatut – Fallstricke des Art. 32 I Nr. 1 EGBGB', *Neue Juristische Wochenschrift* (2004) 2189–96

V. Triebel and S. Otte, 'Reform des GmbH-Rechts – MoMiG – ein vernünftiger Schritt zur Stärkung der GmbH im Wettbewerb', *Zeitschrift für Wirtschaftsrecht*, (2006) 1321–7

V. Triebel, K. von Hase and P. Melerski, *Die Limited in Deutschland* (Frankfurt am Main: Recht und Wirtschaft, 2006)

V. Triebel, S. Hodgson, W. Kellenter and G. Müller, *Englisches Handels- und Wirtschaftsrecht*, 2nd edn (Frankfurt am Main: Recht und Wirtschaft, 1995)

L. Truss, Eats, *Shoots & Leaves: the Zero Tolerance Approach to Punctuation* (New York: Gotham Books, 2004)

F. Tung, 'Passports, Private Choice, and Private Interests: Regulatory Competition and Cooperation in Corporate, Securities, and Bankruptcy Law', *Chicago Journal of International Law*, 3 (2002)

J. A. Usher, 'Languages and the European Union', in M. Anderson and E. Bort (eds), *The Frontiers of Europe* (London and Washington: Pinter, 1998), pp. 222–34

G. Van Calster, 'The EU's Tower of Babel – the Interpretation by the European Court of Justice of Equally Authentic Texts Drafted in more than one Official Language', *Yearbook of European Law*, 17 (1998) 363–92

J. Van Doren, 'Is Jurisprudence Politics by other Means? The Case of Learned Hand', *New England Law Review*, 33 (1998) 1–38

F. Van Fleteren, 'Principles of Augustine's Hermeneutic: an Overview,' in F. Van Fleteren and J.C. Schnaubelt (eds), *Augustine: Biblical Exegete* (New York: Peter Lang, 2001)

G. Vázquez Ayora, *Introducción a la traductología* (Washington: Georgetown University Press, 1977)

L. Venuti, *The Translator's Invisibility. A History of Translation* (London/New York: Routledge, 1995)

J. P. Vinay and J. Darbelnet, *Stylistique comparée du français et de l'anglais. Méthode de traduction* (Chomedey, Quebec: Éditions Beauchemin, 1977)

J. Vincent and R. Guillien, *Lexique des termes juridiques*, 10th edn (Paris: Dalloz, 1995)

J. Wagensberg, *A más cómo, menos por qué* (Barcelona: Tusquets Editores, 2006)

E. Wagner, 'Translation of Multilingual Instruments in the EU', 2000, available at http://ec.europa.eu/translation/reading/articles/pdf/2000_tp_wagner.pdf (last retrieval on 11.02.2008)

E. Wagner, 'Producing Multilingual Legislation in Switzerland', *Clarity. Journal of the International Association Promoting Plain Legal Language*, 53 (2005) 18–20

E. Wagner, S. Bech and J. M. Martínez, *Translating for the European Union Institution* (Manchester, UK and Northampton, Mass.: St. Jerome Publishing, 2002)

A. Wallow, 'Herausforderung zu begrifflichen Reflexion: Recht und Sprache aus der Sicht des Rechtsvergleichers', in T. Lundmark and A Wallow (eds), *Law and Language – Recht und Sprache* (Berlin/Hamburg/Münster: LIT, 2006), pp. 3–15

C. Warren, *The Making of the Constitution* (Boston: Little, Brown and Company, 1928)

A. Watson, *Legal Transplants: an Approach to Comparative Law*, 2nd edn (Athens: University of Georgia Press, 1993)

A. Watson, 'Aspects of Reception of Law', *American Journal of Comparative Law*, 44/2 (1995) 335–51

A. Watson, *Law out of Context* (Athens: University of Georgia Press, 2000)

S. Weatherill, 'The Evolution of European Consumer Law and Policy: From Well-Informed Consumer to Confident Consumer?', in H.W. Micklitz (ed.), *Rechtseinheit oder Rechtsvielfalt in Europa?* (Baden-Baden: Nomos, 1996)

A. Weber, 'Art. 314 EG' in H. von der Groeben and J. Schwarze (eds), *Kommentar zum Vertrag über die Europäische Union und zur Gründung der Europäischen Gemeinschaft*, vol. 4, 6th edn (Baden-Baden: Nomos-Verlagsgesellschaft, 2004)

Webster's Third New International Dictionary (Springfield, Mass.: Merriam Webster, 2002)

M. Weston, 'Translating at the European Court of Human Rights', *Terminologie et traduction*, 3 (1995) 121–34

E. de Wet, 'Can the Social State Principle in Germany Guide State Action in the Field of Social and Economic Rights?', *South African Journal of Human Rights*, 11 (1995) 30–50

B.L. Whorf, *Language, Thought, and Reality* (Cambridge, Mass.: MIT Press, 1956)

F. Wieacker, *Privatrechtsgeschichte der Neuzeit*, 2nd edn (Göttingen: Vandenhoeck & Rupprecht, 1967)

W. Wiegand, 'The Reception of American Law in Europe', *American Journal of Comparative Law*, 39/2 (1991) 229–48

W. Wiegand, 'Americanization of Law: Reception or Convergence?', in L. M. Friedman and H. N. Schreiber (eds), *Legal Culture and the Legal Profession* (Boulder, Colo. and Oxford: Westview Press, 1996), pp. 137–53

A. Wierzbicka, *Semantics, Culture and Cognition: Universal Human Concepts in Culture-Specific Configurations* (New York: Oxford University Press, 1992)

S. L. Winter, *A Clearing in the Forest: Law, Life, and Mind* (Chicago: University of Chicago Press, 2001)

Words and Phrases. Permanent edition (St. Paul: West Publishing Company, 1940–73)

R. C. Wydick, *Plain English for Lawyers*, 5th edn (Durham, NC: Carolina Academic Press, 2005)

Yearbook of International Arbitration, vol. 25 (The Hague: Kluwer Law International, 1976–)

Z. Yuhong, 'Drafting Policy on Bilingual Legislation – Comments on the Hong Kong Securities and Futures Bill', *LC Paper*, no. CB(2), (2000). 1136/00–01 (01)

R. Zimmermann, 'Die UNIDROIT-Grundregeln der internationalen Handelsverträge in vergleichender Perspektive', *Zeitschrift für europäisches Privatrecht* (2005) 264–90

K. Zweigert and H. Kötz, *Einführung in die Rechtsvergleichung*, 3rd edn (Tübingen: Mohr Siebeck, 1996)

K. Zweigert and H. Kötz, *Introduction to Comparative Law*, 3rd edn (Oxford: Oxford University Press, 1998)

Index